INTO THE BLACK

Paul Brannigan and Ian Winwood are two of the UK's foremost music writers. The editor of TeamRock.com, Brannigan is the author of the *Sunday Times* bestseller *This Is a Call: The Life and Times of Dave Grohl*, while Winwood has written for *Rolling Stone*, the *Guardian*, *Mojo*, *Kerrang!*, *NME* and the BBC.

The first volume of their Metallica biography, *Birth School Metallica Death* was published to huge acclaim in 2013, and was a *Sunday Times*, *NME* and *Independent* Music Book of the Year.

'A chronicle of rare authority with exclusive access . . . The superstar years will doubtless make even more entertaining reading.' *Daily Telegraph*

'Big, and impressive, and, like its subject, irresistible.' *Sunday Times*

'This first part of the band's story is so definitive that, when it comes to the topic of the band's early days, nothing else matters.' *Kerrang!*

'The Metallica story has been told many times before, but seldom as entertainingly or as smartly as this . . . Winwood and Brannigan's vivid prose makes this well-worn saga seem somehow fresh and fascinating again. The second volume promises to be an absolute belter.' *Metal Hammer*

'A well-researched look at everything from frontman James Hetfield's initial crippling shyness to Lars Ulrich's bolshie arrogance and all points in between . . . what emerges is a refreshingly honest look at the ups and downs of life in the juggernaut of a heavy metal band.' Doug Johnstone, *Big Issue*

'The scrupulously researched story of the band's early days with deep detail gleaned from over two decades of first-hand exposure to the guys and new interviews with key supporting figures.' *Q*

'Brannigan and Winwood have done a fine job of chronicling the golden age – in studio, on stage and among the crowd – taking us up to 1991 and the eve of the Black Album's release. Even for those who know the story inside out, it's a pacy and punchy read, going from chapter to chapter at roughly the same speed as the riff from "Battery" and with plenty of nuggets along the way.' *RTE 10*

'Though by no means authorized, it's hard to imagine the tale of San Francisco metal behemoths Metallica being told any more authoritatively than it is here . . . Given that the authors rarely flinch from the group's shortcomings, the second volume should make for similarly gripping reading.' *Mojo*

'Brannigan and Winwood have worked closely with the band over the years, and it shows, both in the access they've gained, the anecdotes they witnessed first-hand and the warmth they afford their subjects. No stone is left unturned as the band's insane life is meticulously researched . . . Volume 2 will pick up the baton next year to complete the picture. On this evidence, it'll be worth the wait.' *Classic Rock*

INTO

✝

THE

✝

BLACK

✝

THE INSIDE STORY OF METALLICA
1991–2014

PAUL BRANNIGAN & IAN WINWOOD

FABER & FABER

First published in Great Britain in 2015
by Faber & Faber Limited
Bloomsbury House
74–77 Great Russell Street
London WC1B 3DA

Typeset by Palindrome
Printed and bound in the UK by CPI Group (UK) Ltd, Croydon, CRO 4YY

A CIP record for this book
is available from the British Library

ISBN 978–0–571–29576–0

2 4 6 8 10 9 7 5 3 1

CONTENTS

INTRODUCTION

You would be hard-pressed to find a better example of a self-fulfilling prophecy than Metallica's tour of European festivals in the summer of 2014. With James Hetfield, Lars Ulrich, Kirk Hammett and Robert Trujillo having appeared in this setting on no fewer than thirteen of the past fourteen summers, the notion that these are 'special occasions' is obvious nonsense. Realising this, the band devised a gimmick that they no doubt believed to be a Unique Selling Point. Anyone buying a ticket for the concerts was given the opportunity to compile their own bespoke set list by voting for the songs they wanted Metallica to play.

The results made for depressing reading. On each of the sixteen European Metallica By Request dates, fans nominated 'Master of Puppets' as being the track they would most like to hear. Below this the choices were similarly uniform and familiar. 'One', 'Battery', 'Enter Sandman' and 'Fade to Black' were titles that attained top five status in towns and cities from Stevenage to Warsaw.

That each selection represents the highest standards of modern metal is not in doubt. It's just that, really, the songs are no longer actually all that modern. Not just that, but Metallica play these tracks all the time anyway.

That fans would vote for a set list that is the same as it would have been without the poll is perverse.

If you were hoping to see Metallica in Europe in the summer of 2014 and to hear, say, 'Bleeding Me', 'No Leaf Clover' or 'All Nightmare Long', hard lines.

In once more pushing such big-hitters to the fore, lesser

heard but equally fine compositions are again punted into the long grass. At least as far as the fields and stadiums of Europe are concerned, it is a case of Metallica having boxed themselves in to such a degree that their audience no longer cares to think outside of it.

The self-fulfilling prophecy. The band as brand.

✝

To find the answer as to why this might be, one must follow the money. Asked by *Rolling Stone*'s David Fricke if these days Metallica toured simply to pay the bills, Kirk Hammett responded with a straight answer.

'That's every year,' he said. 'The cycles of taking two years off don't exist any more. We were able to do that because we had record royalties coming in consistently. Now you put out an album, and you have a windfall maybe once or twice but not the way it used to be – a cheque every three months. [So instead] we have to go out and play shows, and we're totally fine with that.'

James Hetfield put this in even starker terms.

'We're doing what we can to keep things alive here,' he said.

Despite a scarcity of new music, in recent times Metallica have kept themselves busy. In 2012 and 2013 the band conceived and executed their own bespoke festival, the Orion Music + More event, a jamboree comprising many different styles of music as well as numerous exhibitions and installations. Staged first in Atlantic City and then in Detroit – two of America's less salubrious cities, to be sure – each year the event was a critical smash and a commercial failure.

Orion Music + More, Hetfield explained, was 'a disaster financially and it's not able to happen again because of that'.

Despite having sold 110 million albums over the course of a thirty-three-year career, it is possible that since 2010 Metallica have lost more money than they have made.

Fans in all but a handful of cities in the US might well wonder just what has happened to a band about whom they might still be obsessed. The quartet do not perform at as many festivals in the US as is the case in Europe because there aren't the number of festivals at which they can appear. The solution to this problem is obvious – they could head out on tour. The reason Metallica have done not done this (or at least have not done this for five years now) is because they are afraid to.

'I'm not sure what's going on in the States as far as rock and metal goes,' was Hetfield's take on this wretched state of affairs. 'Concert-wise . . . there's not really any willingness to get a big show out there and make it worthwhile to actually get out and play. You see other bands gathering up six different bands just to go out and play. It's pretty tough in North America.'

Here James Hetfield is missing the point. The group to which he has dedicated more than half of his life were never the same as 'other bands'.

That *was* the point.

But is it still?

In 2014, does the bell now toll for Metallica?

†

The period covered by *Into the Black* is the most fascinating of the band's career. With the exception of 'The Black Album', the years 1991 to 2014 may not always have been the quartet's finest hours in terms of music – although much of their output during this time is far better than it is credited with being – but when it comes to derring-do, grand gestures, collective insanity, creative chutzpah and the talent and will required to conquer a planet, it is a tale that stands equal to any rock soap opera of the past 40 years.

The authors of this book were on hand to witness many of the events described within. It has been more than two decades now since we first interviewed Metallica, and in the intervening years we have found our often disbelieving eyes in their company on at least forty occasions (not to mention innumerable telephone interviews). Much of this book is written from the point of view of these first-hand accounts, as well as from hours of taped interview footage.

Despite evidence to the contrary, it remains the opinion of this book's authors that it would be unwise to write Metallica off entirely. Over the years the group's dynamic might have changed – how could it not? – just as its appetite for new music has been distracted by folly. But more than any other band of their size, Metallica are still capable of wild and courageous ideas, and of provoking genuine surprise. And who knows, if the evidence of the music on 'Lords of Summer', the sole new track aired on the By Request trek, can be trusted, it might even be that James Hetfield, Lars Ulrich, Kirk Hammett and Robert Trujillo are once more able to locate the musical greatness that once flowed so naturally from their fingertips.

But at such a late hour, such an outcome is not certain. Until it is, the question remains: is there life in the old gods yet?

1 – DON'T TREAD ON ME

A queue of rock fans gathered on West Hollywood's fabled Sunset Strip is hardly an occurrence likely to make the evening news. But as a crowd convened on the evening of Sunday August 11, 1991, observers with a keen eye for detail would have noticed something different from the norm. Those waiting in a more or less orderly line on this notable thoroughfare were different from the usual faces familiar to 'The Strip'. For although this was still a rag-bag collection of young rock fans, these were people – mostly male – who looked as if they'd just come from a shift at a blue-collar workplace rather than a day spent in the company of stylists whose techniques suggested artisans who were losing their eyesight.

The hour was just a cigarette-break shy of midnight. For the first time in this new decade, Metallica were about to unveil a new studio album, a self-titled collection that had already come to be known as 'The Black Album'. As if this alone were not a cause for excitement, the band's decision to make their fifth album available to fans living in or near Hollywood gave the introduction of what was just one of literally hundreds of CDs released that year the feeling of a Special Occasion.

At one minute past midnight, fans were let loose on the shop floor of the West Hollywood branch of Tower Records, a one-storey building that looks more like a prefab shack than an emporium of the recorded arts. In 1991 'Tower on Sunset' was North America's most iconic record shop. As is the case with so many other record shops all over the world, today it is closed for business.

The idea of allowing patrons to purchase an album from midnight on its day of release was not new, although it was still relatively unusual. In 1987 U2 had introduced their blockbusting fifth album, *The Joshua Tree*, at the branch of Tower Records in South Kensington, London. The difference here, however, was that while fans of the Irish band comported themselves in a manner befitting those whose tastes ran to thoughtful and considered Celtic rock, Metallica's crowd behaved like a performers in a drunken am-dram production of *Animal House*.

Come the witching hour the scene within resembled a zoo in which the animals had been freed from their enclosures.

A film crew was on hand to capture the chaos. Hands lunged towards boxes of CDs and cassette tapes as sales registers beeped like a symphony of smoke alarms. The album was also being pumped at a volume sufficient to dent skulls through speakers positioned throughout the air-conditioned store. For those not gathered on Sunset Boulevard, local rock radio station K-ROQ broadcast news of the good-natured stramash.

For Metallica themselves – and for Lars Ulrich in particular – the symbolic chutzpah of this event would not have gone unnoticed. In August 1991 it had been almost nine years since the group had packed up their possessions and left Los Angeles for permanent exile in San Francisco. During their short LA existence the group had performed for small crowds in the city in which they had formed, their basketball boots finding little traction on LA's unforgiving thoroughfares. Metallica might have made their debut live appearance in West Hollywood (a two-set stand that comprised only the band's third and fourth concerts) supporting Barnsley's entirely unreconstructed Saxon, but in the time that had elapsed since this 1982 performance at the Whisky a Go Go – a club situated just yards from Tower Records –the quartet had not once returned to 'The Strip' as a live act. In these earliest of days Los Angeles had dismissed Metallica with the gravest insult in its arsenal – it ignored them.

'It was very lonely being Metallica in LA in 1982, that I can tell you,' was how Ulrich recalled those times.

But if his band had lost the battle with the city of Los Angeles, Lars Ulrich, James Hetfield, Kirk Hammett and Jason Newsted were about to win the war.

✝

Clutching a copy of 'The Black Album' in his hand, inside Tower Records a young fan breaks with convention. Rather than looking into the camera pointed at his face and screaming the word 'Metallica!' with as much force as his lungs will allow, instead he offers a thought that neatly encapsulates one of the core beliefs of millions of the band's fans.

'Finally,' he says, 'someone in metal is saying something right.'

With their fifth album, Metallica were also trying something new. 'The Black Album' saw the quartet reverse their juggernaut from out of the over-developed cul-de-sac in which they had parked themselves (and, seemingly, bricked themselves into) with 1988's constipated . . . *And Justice for All* set. This they did with a root-and-branch re-imagining of their songs, their style and their sound.

That this was so was established even before the album was released. As the one member of Metallica who can be said to have had 'a vision' – actually, 'the vision' – of what his band's next collection should sound like, Lars Ulrich also understood, as if by instinct, which song from the album should be its calling card. Almost a quarter of a century after the fact, it is unimaginable that the group would have chosen any song other than 'Enter Sandman' with which to kick open the doors of the Nineties. But the truth is that this was not something apparent to everyone in and around the Metallica camp. Towards the end of 'The Black Album's torturous nine-month recording sessions, Ulrich and Hetfield accompanied producer Bob Rock to a bar in Vancouver and were treated to the following opinion.

'You've got an incredible album,' said the Canadian. 'You've got, as far as I'm concerned, five or six songs that are going to be classics, both with your fans but also on the radio. But the first song [from] this album that should come out is "Holier Than Thou".'

Wrong. Dead wrong. By opting to introduce 'Enter Sandman' – a single which stage-dived its way to the top five in the UK singles chart – to fans and listeners of modern rock radio (as well as, emphatically, Music Television) Metallica treated the world to the most sumptuous and seductive introduction to a hit single since . . . actually, there is no *since*. With a growing sense of menace that builds the stage on which the signature riff penned by Kirk Hammett can shift air on an industrial scale, within days of becoming public 'Enter Sandman' had established itself as the first Metallica song to become known by people who previously had never before heard the group's name (and in many ways remains so to this day). With James Hetfield's masterful ear for fitting lyrics precisely into the available space, the words 'exit light' and 'enter night' evoke a man who sounds as if he is in control of such things. The effect is a minimalist chorus of maximum force. In little over five minutes, here Metallica had learned valuable new lessons in ways of harnessing a power that in the past had sometimes overwhelmed them.

On a musical level 'The Black Album' is unfailingly sophisticated. In each of the collection's twelve songs Metallica fight and win a battle against every instinct they had indulged on . . . *And Justice for All*. In place of tempo changes and the kind of endless curiosity normally reserved for police officers armed with a search warrant, the authors put their shoulders to creating aero-dynamism and the kind of spacious throb that comes packed with atmospheric pressure.

The word for all this was 'groove', which Lars Ulrich used in interviews at the time at least as much as he used his other favourite word, 'fuck'. Examples of this litter the album, from the cripplingly heavy 'Sad But True' to the monumental 'The God That Failed'. Even the almost uniformly mid-paced nature of 'The Black Album' served the band well by creating the impression that this was but one piece of music, a template of varying moods separated only by one or two seconds of silence every five or six minutes.

While this was the first Metallica album to sound entirely effortless, the truth is that it was anything but. Bob Rock's jibe during the recording process, that 'their friends in Anthrax and Megadeth' would tease them if they heard too much melody on the album, might have been deliciously barbed, but the producer's efforts in translating his charges' industrial strengths into an organic and magnificent whole were not without reward. True, 'The Black Album' was a release that cost a million dollars to record, but the results make this (at the time staggering) amount sound like a bargain. And while Metallica's fans and contemporaries might have questioned (at tireless length) the group's decision to employ 'pop metal' producer Bob Rock in the first place, the band themselves were free of doubt. As Hetfield explained, it was all about the sound. Even when working with bands whose music stood diametrically opposed to his own (such as was the case with Bon Jovi and Mötley Crüe), Rock's work thundered and shone.

'The sound of the albums was great,' he said. As for everything else, he explained, 'The songs were crap and the bands were fucking gay.'

✝

Lars Ulrich was in Budapest when he learned that 'The Black Album' had walloped its way to the top of the US *Billboard* album chart at the first time of asking, and where it would remain for the next month. Ulrich and his band mates were on tour as special guests to AC/DC on the Monsters of Rock caravan when he learned of his group's first no. 1 album anywhere in the world. In his room a fax arrived from the band's management company, Q Prime, in New York City. It stated, simply, that Metallica were atop the *Billboard* Hot 200. Ulrich considered the piece of paper he now held in his hand and wondered what it was that was delaying the attendant fireworks and marching band.

'You think one day some fucker's gonna tell you, "You have a no. 1 record in America", and the whole world will ejaculate,' he says. 'I stood there in my hotel room with this fax [which read] "You're number one" and it was, like, "Well, okay." It was just another fucking fax from the office.'

Alongside its success in the US, 'The Black Album' also debuted at the summit of the charts of no fewer than seven other countries – the UK and Australia among them – and was top five in a further five nations. By the end of the decade, Metallica was the eighth-best-selling album of the Nineties in the US, having spent more than four and a half years on the *Billboard* listings.

Not everyone could be said to be overly chuffed with what Metallica had achieved, though. Rock's joke about irate peers crying foul had a predictably prophetic ring. As has been seen, this was a group that was not only viewed as having responsibilities to their own artistic instincts (the only thing that mattered) but also a duty of care as standard bearers for a now rapidly stagnating thrash metal scene, as well as God knows what else. The response from old friends rapidly disappearing in Metallica's rear-view mirror may not have been universally dismissive, but much of it did carry with it what must have been for its targets an infuriating subtext of class treason.

Having gathered his thoughts for at least ninety seconds, Dave Mustaine offered his view that 'The Black Album' featured just one interesting song, this being 'The Unforgiven'. From the genre's noisiest outpost, Slayer drummer Dave Lombardo put down his drumsticks in order that he might throw his copy of

Metallica's latest album down the stairs – literally.

'I can definitely understand people going, "Oh, 'Enter Sandman', 'Nothing Else Matters' – what happened?",' Lars Ulrich later reflected. '[But] if we had've made . . . *And Justice for All* [Part] II, that would have been the sell-out . . . We had a fear of being stuck. With some of our peers we saw that there was a Status Quo element that we saw was not for us.'

Metallica's capacity to disassociate themselves from hotbeds that were now leaving them cold remains unmatched. When it came to thrash metal, the notion that the genre had run its course was confirmed by the very fact that so many of its practitioners had so quickly come to adopt the reactionary and conformist mindset that their genre had challenged just a few years earlier. More than this, though, was the question of why on earth Metallica would wish to associate themselves with a community in creative decline? All of this *stuff* was in the past; while the future was one of open water and endless space.

Released in an extraordinary period for American rock – a six-week span that saw the release of Nirvana's *Nevermind,* Pearl Jam's *Ten*, Red Hot Chili Peppers' *Blood Sugar Sex Magik* and Guns N' Roses *Use Your Illusion* parts 1 and 2 – with 'The Black Album' Metallica went from being the world's most commercially significant cult band to being a mainstream concern.

But by coming to dine above the salt, the band learned quickly just how much things had changed. Despite having spent eight years talking to members of the press, in 1991 Ulrich discovered that these efforts counted for nothing. The truth was, there remained hundreds of journalists and publications that knew nothing of metal's now all-conquering heroes.

It seems surreal to recall these times but, in the days before the Internet, entertainment reporters were reliant on two or three sheets of paper supplied by a band's record label to provide them with a potted history of the group to whom they were about to speak. In the case of Metallica, it seems that some writers failed even to manage this. With a phone cradled to his ear, it was with equal measures of bewilderment and amusement that Ulrich noticed that many publications believed 'The Black Album' to be a debut.

Meanwhile, though, a better class of opinion-former was beginning to take note. Metallica being at no. 1 in the US meant attention from that country's pre-eminent music publication, *Rolling Stone*. While it would be wrong to say that the magazine founded by Jann Wenner in 1967 did not write about metal bands – Mötley Crüe, for one, had in the past graced the front page – given the choice, they would rather not. It is, though, to the magazine's credit that when it came to Metallica its editorial team recognised something different from the norm. That this was true had been signalled by a four-star review of 'The Black Album' that treated the collection with the respect it deserved, while avoiding exit-strategy caveats concerning the genre it represented.

Not content with this, *Rolling Stone* also placed Metallica on their cover on not one but two occasions during the album's two-year cycle. The first story came in the weeks following the CD's release, the point at which many in the wider musical world were still rubbing their eyes and attempting to make some kind of sense of the hairy, unsmiling men staring out at them.

'I know there were a lot of bands that went, "Oh yeah, Metallica – they sell a lot of records but they can't play or write songs," ' reported a gleeful Ulrich. 'I was just reading an interview with [The Cult front man] Ian Astbury where he said that going to a Metallica concert was one big wanking session with all these guys jerking each other off – and where's the femininity? Well, excuse me! So this is a big "Fuck you", not especially to Ian Astbury, but for all those people who felt that way for years and years, who came up and smiled to our faces, but as soon as they walked away they were laughing at us.'

Elsewhere, while Jason Newsted confessed, 'I never thought we'd have a no. 1 album playing the kind of music we do,' James Hetfield expounded on the notion that his band no longer felt compelled to defend their territory like wolves. Now, he explained, they were merely Dobermann Pinschers. 'We're just a little more confident,' was his opinion. 'We're not afraid to hear a suggestion and adapt it to our thing. '

'Before we didn't want to hear it,' he added. 'Now we'll hear it [and] then we'll say, "Fuck you!" '

For *Rolling Stone*, Hetfield was now a Person of Interest, and it was to the front man alone that Metallica's second *Rolling Stone* cover feature was dedicated. In a marriage of words and pictures that did everything right, the magazine showed just why it had maintained its position as market leader for more than a generation. The front cover was a master class. Shot by the Texan-born portrait photographer Mark Seliger, the image that screamed forth from magazine racks the world over saw a topless James Hetfield standing on flat and barren earth, his legs astride and teeth bared. He holds a black Gibson Explorer guitar next to a headline that reads, 'The leader of the free world speaks.'

With such a brazen statement, *Rolling Stone* recognised Hetfield as being a man of substance, if not always wisdom. Just as millions of metal fans suddenly found themselves drawn to Metallica's lyrics in a way that had never before been the case for any band of their kind, so too *Rolling Stone* recognised deep waters when they saw them. But while many fans of the band listened to the lyrics on 'The Black Album' and heard the voice of God, this was the God of the Old Testament. Sounding like a man who carries a gun, on songs such 'Wherever I May Roam' ('carved upon my stone, my body lies but still I roam'), 'Of Wolf and Man' ('I hunt therefore I am, harvest the land, taking of the fallen lamb') and 'The God That Failed' ('broken is the promise, betrayal, the healing hand held back by the deepened nail, follow the God that failed'), Hetfield gives the impression of a man who has taken the most fundamental of American principles and subtly adjusted it to his own ends: Give him liberty, or he'll give you death.

This motto was propelled recklessly to its logical conclusion on the most misguided – and, actually, most misunderstood – track on 'The Black Album', the hawkish 'Don't Tread On Me'. The point the song makes is simple, and not without some kind of logic – the most reliable way of maintaining peace is to make sure that one is always primed for war. This hard-headed outlook, however, is not the song's real problem. The problem is one of jingoism. The lifting of Leonard Bernstein's melody from the *West Side Story* song 'America' signals trouble only a few seconds after the song has started. But whereas *West Side Story* lyricist Stephen Sondheim pirouettes around the original melody with phrases such as 'automobile in America, chromium steel in America, wire-spoke wheel in America . . .' James Hetfield has only gracelessness to offer; not so much wire-spoked wheel as a tin ear. 'Love it or leave it,' he says of the country of his birth, as if these were the only two options available. He also speaks of liberty 'shining with brightness', which, to be fair, is a lot more impressive than a beacon of hope that shone with darkness. But just as the cliché and nonsense running wild through the song's verses threaten to torpedo 'Don't Tread On Me', the song reaches its conclusion in a chillingly convincing manner. As the music swells beneath him, Hetfield warns, 'touch me again with the words that you will hear evermore' before adding in a manner befitting a man with whom even the hardiest of fools would hesitate to tangle, 'Don't tread on me!'

On the evidence of this, one might assume that the safest way of speaking to Hetfield might be from behind bullet-proof glass. Appearances, though, often deceive, and the occasion of the *Rolling Stone* cover feature was the first time he had been subjected to the type of questions asked by a magazine that interviewed not just rock stars but also presidential candidates.

The journalist in question was David Fricke, then as now America's best and most authoritative rock reporter. In an interview that is by turn therapy session and politically minded interrogation, the Metallica front man unveiled himself and shed his public armour.

On the subject of his then burgeoning reputation as a heavy drinker, the front man revealed, 'I used up all my hangovers. It was basically [me] waking up, not feeling very good and not wanting to do a show. I started to feel a sense of responsibility, at least to myself, let alone anybody else, to play better.'

At another point in the interview Fricke questioned Hetfield on comments he had made to the *New Musical Express* about how rap music was an 'extra black' phenomenon, and how the genre's lyrics took the form of '[the rapper saying] me, me, me, and my name is in this song'.

To this line of enquiry Hetfield responded, 'They say a lot of "I'm this, I'm this, I'm doin' this, you got to do this with me." It's just not my cup of tea. Some of the stuff, like [rapper Ice T's utterly hopeless metal band] Body Count, our fans like it because there's aggression there. I love that part of it. But the [Body Count song] "Cop Killer" thing, kill whitey – I mean, what the fuck? I don't dig it.' (Despite there being no real evidence of a racialist strain in the front man's DNA, using the word 'they' at the start of the quote above is ill-judged.)

Next Hetfield – by this point a skilled and dedicated hunter – gave this thoughts on conservation, albeit with a less than forensic eye for scientific detail.

'There are too many people on the fucking planet,' he said. 'I love nature. I love the wilderness, and there is not much more of it left. It makes me hate people. Animals, they don't lie to each other. There is an innocence within them. And they're getting fucked.'

Not least by James Hetfield armed with a hunting rifle.

But as *Rolling Stone* readers the world over wondered quite how one animal might go about lying to another, Hetfield was gone, once more on his way on a journey ever skyward.

✝

To argue that at this point in their career Metallica were not 'playing the game' is disingenuous. But while 'Enter Sandman' may have supplied the booster rockets that propelled 'The Black Album' into the midnight sky, the track itself was served most effectively not by rock radio but by television.

It seems strange to think back, but at the beginning of the Nineties Music Televison actually used to play music videos. In fact the channel did nothing but play music videos. For the most part the playlist – as it existed outside 'specialist' programmes such *Yo! MTV Raps!*, the independently minded *120 Minutes* and the self-explanatory *Headbangers Ball* – appeared as if they were compiled to cater for people who liked their music some way off in the background, presumably with their television playing very quietly and in a different room. But while in 1991 MTV gorged itself and force-fed its viewers innumerable airings of Bryan Adams's blockbusting and fully nauseating '(Everything I Do) I Do It For You', sometimes, if only very occasionally, the channel would throw on the air something that made rational people question their otherwise wisely held believe that MTV was a corrosive influence.

The phrase 'necessary evil' springs to mind. For while in 1984 Dead Kennedys front man Jello Biafra insisted that 'MTV [should] get off the air', by 1991 few bands could get off the ground without the channel's assistance. Metallica, of course, were the exception. But in making their point by waiting eight years to film their first video clip (for . . . *And Justice for All's* 'One'), by the Nineties the quartet were ready to come in from the cold.

In 'Enter Sandman' MTV found its perfect foil. With lyrics that lent themselves to visual interpretation, the group had found the ideal vessel with which to launch themselves on the air. Hetfield's twisted lullaby about a child who knows that Mr Sandman is coming to bring him not a dream but a nightmare is ripe with unusually precise imagery. Not all of this imagery is good ('heavy thoughts tonight, and they aren't of Snow White' is certainly not one of the front man's better couplets) but much of it is, and in a grandly cinematic sense.

Directed by Wayne Isham, the video for 'Enter Sandman' is a piece of likeable nonsense that allowed Metallica to look suitably 'metal' without appearing uncommonly stupid. Fast-cut and lavishly coloured, the clip features a variety of different nightmares. Here snakes writhe around on a child's bed, a young man is chased by a Heavy Goods Vehicle and (most terrifying of all) Lars Ulrich gurns manically every time the camera is trained on his bare-chested body. MTV loved what they saw, and aired the clip throughout the day and night for weeks on end.

'Enter Sandman' was the perfect recruiting sergeant for innumerable fans now flocking to the band's flame. These newcomers, however, what not always made welcome by others that had been at the quartet's side for years and who were beginning to bristle at just how easy it now was to discover music that previously had been hidden from the ears of the mainstream. 'Enter Sandman' was Exhibit A in the case for the prosecution, a song and music video that stood jarringly at odds with everything the band had been 'about' up until the summer of 1991.

Metallica *had* changed, this we know. The only question that mattered, however, was whether this change was creatively sincere. The old showbiz gag about how sincerity is the key to any performer's success, and that once you can fake that you've got it made, is just that, a gag. The truth could not be more different. Insincerity – fraudulence, in other words – is always the first thing to be spotted by any member of an audience paying even half a mind to what it is they're being sold.

The implication that, with the success of 'Enter Sandman', Metallica had forever turned their backs on their more creatively challenging instincts is wholly unfair. What's more, they were about to prove it.

The second single unleashed from 'The Black Album' was 'The Unforgiven', one of the finest compositions to which the group have put their name. A tale of strangulated potential and emotional cruelty, the song tells the story of a 'new blood [who] joins this earth' and 'quickly he's subdued' where through 'constant pained disgrace' the young boy 'learns their rules'. (Note, by the way, that it is not merely *the* rules to which the song's subject is forced to adhere, but *their* rules, those laid down by *the others*.) This is a nightmare that can only end, as it does, in the narrator's death, the point at which even his tormentors recognise 'a tired man' who 'no longer cares', a tragic figure, who 'prepares to die regretfully'.

This compellingly miserablist anti-fantasy is drawn from the same well of despair as are songs such as Morrissey's 'Yes, I Am Blind' and Nirvana's 'Heart-shaped Box'. There is no hope here, no chance of redemption, no means of escape aside from death itself. Were 'The Unforgiven' merely a flight of imaginary fancy, an exercise in creating a vision of personal dystopia, then the words printed on the lyric sheet of 'The Black Album' would be impressive enough. But this is James Hetfield's own personal nightmare, his own Room 101, and in committing this sparse and gruelling lyric to paper he has exposed his gravest vulnerabilities to anyone who cares to listen.

Clearly, then, a song that is less a twisted take on the Brothers Grimm and more a sleepless demon of a kind that stalked the movements of Josef K would not be at all well served by A. N. Other heavy metal video, even one as expertly realised as 'Enter Sandman'. But the clip filmed to accompany 'The Unforgiven' is so far from the norm as to exist in its own world entirely.

Matt Mahurin is not an average music video director. Born in Santa Cruz, California, on January 31, 1959, Mahurin first came to prominence as both a photographer and illustrator. In the former field, his pictures have graced the cover of *Time* magazine on numerous occasions, including an infamous shot of O. J. Simpson in which the removal of colour saturation darkened the erstwhile American football player's skin and led to the charge that the magazine was unnecessarily focusing on Simpson's race. As a photographic essayist Mahurin has heard his shutter click in locations ranging from the Clemens Unit prison in Texas to abortion clinics across the US, as well as collections harvested from visits to (among other places) Haiti and Belfast. A number of Mahurin's prints form part of the permanent collection within the beautiful confines of the Metropolitan Museum of Art on Manhattan's Upper East Side. His work as a video director began towards the end of the Eighties with credits that included Tracy Chapman's 'Fast Car' and REM's 'Orange Crush'.

Metallica first approached Mahurin in 1989 with the request that he direct the video clip for 'One'. This request was politely declined, as the band stipulated that they wanted the video to feature snippets of the film *Johnny Got His Gun* – on which the lyrics to the parent song are based – and Mahurin 'didn't like using other people's work in [his] own work'. Three years later, though, the band was back, asking the same question but in a different context and with a different song.

'They had a vision that stretched beyond a video in its obvious form of a three-, four- or five-minute video,' says Mahurin today, speaking from his home in Long Island. 'They saw this as an opportunity to do something epic. Their songs are pretty epic anyway, I think, but also lyrically a lot of them have this kind of fable that you can sort of unfold and get connected to. And what was cool about it was that they were treating the video as you would a short film. Normally videos are put out to serve the band and to show the musicians to the world, or if it's an older artist to keep their career going and keep people connected to them. But what was great about this is that it pretty much turns those ideas on their head. Instead of having a band performing to the song with some other images crammed in, instead it's the images themselves that take precedence. On "Unforgiven" you don't know which came first, the song or the film. In that sense it's more like traditional film-making, where the song becomes the soundtrack to the movie.

'But in my work as a photographer and an illustrator,' he continues, 'I've prided myself on pushing myself and challenging conventions. I can't see the point in doing something that's been done before. I want to at least try and create something that people have never seen before.'

With 'The Unforgiven', he certainly managed that. Twenty-one years after the fact, the director is unable to recall the video's precise budget but does remember it being 'hundreds of thousands of dollars . . . a bloody fortune, and I work pretty simply as well.' Pockets bulging with cash, Mahurin was able to build a set in New York's Navy Yards and to hire extra hands to help realise in full 'this movie, this thing about phobia, that I had in my head'. In preparation for the shoot Metallica were shown illustrative story boards, all of which they approved. According to the film-maker's recollections, 'The band were happy to let me do my thing . . . they seemed to trust my instincts.'

'Metallica were a really smart band to work with,' he says. 'You know, I'm not going to go into the studio and tell them how to mix a song or play a guitar solo, and similarly they left me alone as a film-maker. They just showed up when they were needed.'

Metallica were on the set for 'The Unforgiven' for just one day, and flew in to New York by private jet. By this point the tour in support of 'The Black Album' was well under way and the band's diary did not contain a great deal of latitude. But the entire shoot took four days, an amount of time virtually unheard of in the field of promotional videos.

This, though, is as it should be as 'The Unforgiven' is unlike any other music video, of the time or since. As was the case with 'One', Metallica cut more than one version of the film (in this case, two). One version features footage of the band performing live, albeit in images that appear only infrequently. This more conventional working has much to recommend it: it is poignantly shot, its narrative thread is non-linear and unusual, and the overall feel of the images on screen chimes harmoniously with the song it is there to serve.

But it is the second, less often seen, version of 'The Unforgiven' that is truly extraordinary. One of the oddest and most beautifully realised pieces of short-film making – here the term 'music video' is an ill-fitting description – the piece begins with a segment of music not from the start of the song, but rather a refrain from its middle. Clocking in at almost twice the length of the track itself, the film then opts to do something that no other piece of its kind had dared to do, or even thought to do: it makes its point without any music at all. After barely a minute of on-screen footage, Metallica's music disappears, and does not reappear for almost five whole minutes.

With Mahurin assuming the role of cinematographer as well as director, the film is shot in flint-hard black and white. But it is more than the monochromatic tones that suggest that this is a film set in a world entirely devoid of colour. The viewer is presented with the image of a boy standing bare-chested, who, while not quite being emaciated, does not appear to be overly well fed either. Then comes a shot from the boy's point of view, showing a frame that is crowded with the hard faces of older men. By this point the only sounds the viewer hears are, by turn, the ticking of a pocket watch and the sound of birdsong from some distant place, presumably, where things live in freedom.

The film's geographical setting is immaterial, but more than this the exact nature of the child's dwelling is unclear. At certain points water cascades from a hole in a stone wall, so might be this be an aqueduct? The one piece of furniture to which the child in the film appears to have access is a wooden chair, on to which he clambers in order to investigate the source of the water. Could it be that he's trying to escape? More alarmingly, why is there a strange image of a human face hanging from an uneven rock wall, and why does the child have to pass through it as if it were a cat-flap in order to find any kind of genuine shelter? And who is feeding the boy? Who, and where, are his parents?

This final question appears to be a pressing one, as the first noises the viewer hears from the infant's mouth are not words but rather the kind of noises that might be made by a wild animal. It is as if the child is being kept secluded in order that he might learn – what? – the language of God? But, no, that's not it either, because seconds after this the protagonist is seen in the company of a young girl in a white dress. As the pair play – the young boy smitten in a manner that he is years away from comprehending – the viewer can discern words spoken in English. In the girl's company, the boy seems happy. But she, and it, are not to last.

By the time Kirk Hammett's lead guitar comes scything into range (in what is one of the great guitar solos of the twentieth century) things on-screen have taken a turn for the worse. The child is now gone, and in his place stands the sinew-ripped torso of an elderly man. As Hammett teases histrionic notes from his guitar, the old man dances in a way that suggests that he has gone mad. As the song glides to its graceful conclusion, on-screen the wizened figure rummages among the detritus of a life that was never his. In a moment of awful cruelty, the viewer is shown a keyhole; moments later the character on-screen happens upon a key. But it is much, much too late to discover what lies on the other side of the door.

As the eleven-minute, thirty-three-second clip fades to black, literal-minded viewers may have asked themselves what it all meant? But this is to miss the point. With the song's lyric as a guide, Matt Mahurin's masterful short film is a study not so much of loss but of things that were never uncovered – let alone loved or savoured – in the first place. Alongside this, viewers might marvel at, or be unnerved by, the length of time and the resonant clarity with which the film-maker's images stayed with them.

'Actually, not long after I'd made the video I was on a train from New York to Washington DC,' remembers Mahurin. 'In a really wild coincidence, sat on the two seats in front of where I was sitting were two college kids. I could hear them talking and much to my amazement they were talking about the 'Unforgiven' video. They were discussing the meaning of the old man and of the kid that was in the video. Obviously they had no idea that I'd directed the thing. Just as obviously, I couldn't help myself so I joined in their conversation, and so the three of us discussed various aspects of the piece and what they might mean and stuff like that.'

In a just and fair world, the 'theatrical' version of 'The Unforgiven' would be at least as widely discussed (and as widely revered) as is the video for 'One'. A key reason why it is not might be that, unlike 'One', the piece did not arrive out of an otherwise empty blue sky, but was instead just another component in a frenzy of activity upon which Metallica were embarked. But this union between band and director remains one of the most inspired collaborations of the group's career. And if nothing else it contradicts the notion that with 'The Black Album' they had permanently steered the wheels of their juggernaut closer to the centre of the road.

✝

Elsewhere Metallica went about their business in a much more quotidian manner. With their music now spreading like an airborne disease, and with their faces appearing on MTV as often as Madonna's, it is feasible to argue that in 1991 this was a band that didn't actually need to head out on tour at all. As the first metal act in history – metal, as opposed to 'hard rock' – to bludgeon their way on to the high table of the multi-platinum set, why now tour at all? And if you are going to tour, surely take it a little easier than in years past.

Not a bit of it. Metallica's Wherever I May Roam tour – which in time metamorphosed into the Nowhere Else to Roam tour – endured for twenty-three months and comprised no fewer than 301 concerts, most of which lasted for more than three hours. Until their efforts were superseded twenty years later by 30 Seconds to Mars, Metallica's excursion looked like being a globe-crawl the duration of which would never be beaten. Today in Q Prime's New York office there hangs a frame inside which are printed every single date and venue of the 301 concerts Metallica performed in the name of their unnamed fifth album. The thing looks like the Washington DC Vietnam War Memorial.

But all journeys begin with a single step, and on the Wherever I May Roam tour Metallica made theirs in the direction of the Phoenix Theater in the modest Californian 'city' of Petaluma, where the band undertook a two-night stand. As was the case with their startling lack of preparation for a stadium tour with Van Halen in support of . . . *And Justice for All* (in this case, a single performance at the Troubadour club in Los Angeles), the quartet felt that this was the only tune-up they required. After this, it was 'All aboard!' the private jet for a transatlantic flight over to the Old World.

With just four dates ticked off the docket, Metallica's fifth appearance on the Wherever I May Roam tour saw the group appear onstage at Donington Park, then as now their spiritual home. Despite pulling scenery-chewing faces for the benefit of audiences that number well into the millions, Lars Ulrich confesses that this inhospitable and remote racetrack hard by the East Midlands Airport is now the only venue capable of flooding his central nervous system with pre-show nerves.

In 1991 the drummer certainly had plenty of cause for butter-flies, even stage-fright. As in 1987 (the last time Metallica had appeared at Donington Park) his band's live engine was covered in rust. Their last appearance at the racetrack had been one of the worst performances ever seen on the Monsters of Rock stage, an appearance so wretched that Iron Maiden bassist Steve Harris could be seen at the side of the stage *wincing*. Four years on and Metallica had once again crawled one place up the bill; this time AC/DC were the only band to appear onstage after the San Franciscans, with (in reverse order) Mötley Crüe, ambitious Seattle rockers Queensrÿche and fast-emerging Georgian retro-stars the Black Crowes as the day's first attraction. Some members of the rock fraternity felt that Metallica's third appearance at Castle Donington should have been as headliners. But the band's decision not to lobby for top spot was a wise one. The San Franciscans were received by the vast crowd as if they were the last act of the day, while the responsibility of closing the show went to AC/DC. For their part Metallica were left with the simple task of delivering a thirteen-song set in the 'Special Guest' slot that was strong enough to remind people that the band was back. This they managed to do.

By 1991 rock music in general was 'smashing through the boundaries' of more than just taste and trends. On September 28 the Monsters of Rock caravan – its bill strengthened by the addition of emerging Texan act Pantera – arrived in Russia for an appearance at the Tushino airfield in north-west Moscow. Previously the headquarters of the Russian air force, and the launch site for the Workers' Day flyover above Red Square each

May, on this gloomy autumn day the field was occupied by no fewer than a million people (with unofficial estimates placing this figure at a million and a half) amassed for a free concert in worship of 'Western' rock. As far as signs went that the socialist ideals of Lenin's November revolution were dead, the view from Tushino airfield was hard to beat.

The presence of AC/DC atop the bill afforded the rolling sea of faces the opportunity to see a band whose status was by any measure legendary. But for an audience seeking an outlet for their anger and alienation, Metallica were the only game in town. The San Franciscans had not come all this way to disappoint. Footage from the occasion shows a band that at times appears impossibly intense. This was fitting, as the occasion was not without its own measure of turmoil; in the crowd Russian military officers proved themselves to be truncheon-happy to a degree that appalled Jason Newsted.

But at least the quartet onstage were fully equipped to provide their own lesson in violence. As its title had always suggested, closing song 'Battery' seemed more than sufficient both to energise a million people as well as to beat into surrender anyone who might choose to question the authority of the music being played. Moments later, backstage Lars Ulrich posed for a photograph with a snare-drum skin splattered with his own blood, with the words 'bleeding for Moscow' written above. And once again the notion that the 'Old Metallica' was now dead simply did not tally with the shock waves the group had volleyed into the turbid Moscow sky.

The quartet's transition from arena-botherers to ball-park figures was further cemented on October 12 when the group returned to the Oakland Coliseum – at the time trading under the catchy name of the Networks Associates Coliseum – for the Day on the Green festival, this time as headliners. But if the top-of-the-bill bow in the Bay Area's most troubled city served notice on their intentions to become 'The Biggest Band in the World', the quartet's most significant hop-with-the-jet-set would wait until the following spring.

†

The occasion was both serious and celebratory. Staged on April 20, 1992, the Freddie Mercury Tribute Concert was a diamond-studded event in honour of the Queen front man, who had died of AIDS at his London home just five months earlier. Appearing onstage before 72,000 people that night were Elizabeth Taylor, Liza Minnelli, Elton John, Robert Plant, George Michael, David Bowie, Annie Lennox, Lisa Stansfield, and bands such as Guns N' Roses, Def Leppard and – seeming almost comically out of place – Metallica. This discomfiture was rather charmingly encapsulated backstage by a bewildered Lars Ulrich who had seconds earlier been glad-handed by an unnamed and insincere 'well-wisher'. Dressed in a T-shirt of the Orange County punk rock band Social Distortion, Ulrich asked, 'Tell me, why do people just lie to [me]?'

It seems outrageous to consider this today, but in 1992 there was no small measure of fear and suspicion regarding the nature and habits of the acquired immunodeficiency syndrome. Just four years previously Guns N' Roses front man W. Axl Rose had penned the lyrics for the explosively incautious 'One in a Million', a song that sees its narrator speak of being unable to make sense of the 'immigrants and faggots . . .' who came to America, apparently, '. . . to spread some fuckin' disease'. (Whether or not these words represented Rose's personal views or were rather used to describe a character – admittedly an extremely well crafted one – remains a moot point.) It was also around this time that Sebastian Bach, the lead singer with also-rans Skid Row, filed his entry for the title of World's Stupidest Man by appearing onstage wearing a T-shirt emblazoned with the words AIDS KILLS FAGS DEAD.

But this gathering of some of the most famous – not to mention a number of the most sexually promiscuous – people on the planet did help cast light on a disease that in 1992 was seen by some as a plague for the twentieth century. Beneath the darkening sky of a gorgeous London spring evening, this significant achievement was made possible by the exalted levels of showbiz brilliance radiating from the stage.

'It really was a magical event,' is the opinion of then Guns N' Roses guitarist Slash. 'The spirit of that show was one of the best multi-band, multi-artist productions that I've ever been involved with. Everybody got along, there were no egos, the whole thing was brilliant. A lot of people put together these events for great causes but this was one of those things that went the way it was supposed to go and meant what it was supposed to mean. It was wonderful, one of the high points of the Nineties for me.'

The choice of venue itself was not without emotional resonance. It was on this very stage that just seven years earlier Queen performed what has often been acclaimed as one of the greatest live performances in the history of rock. The occasion was Live Aid, a fund-raising concert organised by Bob Geldof and promoter Harvey Weinstein to raise money for the people of Ethiopia, people that were not just starving but *being* starved. In aid of this, at 6 p.m. sharp on the evening of Saturday July 13, 1985, Queen strode onstage at Wembley Stadium and ripped into a twenty-minute set, the command of which was not so much complete as messianic. Honed by three days' rehearsal at London's Shaw Theatre, the band tore and swung through segments of songs such as 'Bohemian Rhapsody', 'Radio Ga Ga', 'Crazy Little Thing Called Love', 'Hammer to Fall', 'We Will Rock You' and closing track 'We Are the Champions'. This final song was fitting, because by twenty minutes past six no one who had seen the performance was in any doubt that this was so.

The following summer Queen would return to Wembley

Stadium for a two-night stand, the second of which would be their penultimate performance on British soil.

On the evening of April 20 the Freddie Mercury Tribute Concert was split into two distinct halves. The second half of the evening was given over to the members of Queen themselves who provided the music for a succession of impossibly famous people to join the band as guest vocalist for just a single number. Annie Lennox and David Bowie sang 'Under Pressure', with the latter proving what a terrible old ham he can be by reciting the Lord's Prayer (this presumably being the same Lord that saw fit to bestow AIDS upon the world in the first place). Liza Minnelli sang 'We Are the Champions' and Lisa Stansfield – pushing a hoover – sang 'I Want to Break Free'. For his part James Hetfield strode the stage singing 'Stone Cold Crazy', the Queen song Metallica had covered for the *Rubáiyát* double album released two years previously in celebration of the fortieth anniversary of Elektra Records. Onstage at Wembley Hetfield fronted a Queen line-up strengthened by the addition of Black Sabbath guitarist Tony Iommi. Out of step he may have been, but the delight on the singer's face was radiant just the same.

But for Hetfield and Metallica it was the first half of the show that was not so much problematic as it was emblematic of their musical inflexibility. During this opening section (as with Live Aid), bands were given the chance to play for twenty minutes or so. Onstage bands such as hard rock mediocrities Extreme played a set peppered with moments from Queen's own past, while Sheffield's shameless Def Leppard took cues from Queen by truncating their own songs into one bumper package of megahits. That Metallica are a better band than both Extreme and Def Leppard is not a difficult case to prosecute; but that Def Leppard and Extreme were better than Metallica at the Freddie Mercury Tribute Concert is an easy one to defend.

During the opening proceedings at Wembley Stadium that

evening, Metallica's cause was hardly helped by an introduction from Queen bassist John Deacon in a voice that sounded hesitant and shy. And while there was nothing wrong with what Metallica did next – they performed their three-song set of 'Enter Sandman', 'Sad But True' and 'Nothing Else Matters' with typical emphasis – the place and occasion in which they chose to do this showed that this was a band that has difficulty cutting their cloth according to the needs of special occasions.

To play 'Sad But True' six minutes into a concert that is intended to celebrate the life and music of one of rock 'n' roll's most irrepressible talents was simply perverse. As Hetfield sang that 'I'm your hate when you want love' and how 'I'm your pain when you can't feel', the observation once made by *Time Out* magazine that this was a band whose 'songs could use a bit of jollying up' seemed startlingly true. There must surely have been a proportion of people inside Wembley Stadium who wondered, 'Who invited this lot to the party?'

But while on April 20 this rigidity did not serve the band well, in other ways it remains one of Metallica's defining characteristics. That despite the success, this is a band who are *in* the mainstream without ever quite being *of* it.

2 – WHEREVER I MAY ROAM

Standing outside Le Dome brasserie, Lars Ulrich and Axl Rose watched a cavalcade of sports cars, SUVs and limousines nudge headlight-to-bumper along Sunset Boulevard, West Hollywood's *vena cava*. Eddie Kerkhof's restaurant, located at 8720 Sunset, a plectrum flick away from Tinseltown's most notorious rock 'n' roll haunts, was a popular meeting place for the entertainment industry's power players, and as Rose sucked on a Marlboro Red by the doorway, his live-wire companion offered a sarcastic running commentary on the beautiful people gliding by, all of whom were oblivious to the duo's presence.

'You know, people are going to be so surprised by this,' Ulrich told Rose. 'Everyone is going to be saying "I can't believe it, it'll never happen."'

As the pair returned to join James Hetfield and Slash at their patio table, their respective managers – Q Prime's Peter Mensch and Cliff Burnstein, and Guns N' Roses handler Doug Goldstein – could be found deep in conversation, their food untouched. With due respect to Le Dome's lauded haute cuisine, dinner could wait, for this elevated summit had been convened with one simple, if audacious, purpose in mind: to iron out the logistics involved in putting the world's biggest hard rock band and the world's biggest metal band on tour together.

†

Though the impetus to propel the Metallica/Guns N' Roses US touring juggernaut on to America's highways originated with the Guns N' Roses camp, the original concept belonged, inevitably,

to Ulrich. The little Dane had long harboured dreams of the
two groups uniting to deliver a historic touring package akin to
a Rolling Stones/The Who bill in the Sixties. Introduced by a
mutual business associate, music industry lawyer Peter Paterno,
the Californian bands had first met in 1987 and subsequently
bonded over lines of white powder and fingers of hard liquor
during Metallica's five-month residency in Los Angeles recording
the . . . *And Justice for All* album, with the San Franciscans gamely
keeping pace with the younger band's well-documented appetite
for self-destruction. In his self-titled 2007 autobiography, Slash
recalled James Hetfield requesting the use of his bedroom for a
romantic dalliance with a young lady at one typically rambunctious
party at his apartment on Hollywood and Franklin. 'I had to get
in there to get something, so I crept in quietly and saw James
head-fucking her,' the guitarist remembered. 'He was standing
on the bed, ramming her head against the wall, moaning in that
thunderous voice of his . . . "That'll be fine! That'll be fine! Yes!
That'll be fine!" '

The evening during which the two bands shared a stage for the
first time was an equally unrefined affair. The Los Angeles-based
heavy metal magazine *RIP* had hired the Hollywood Palladium
to host its fourth anniversary party celebrations on November
9, 1990, hand-picking LA cock-rockers Bang Tango, sepia-toned
oddballs Masters of Reality, San Francisco's Faith No More, Dave
Mustaine's Megadeth and Ulrich's long-time heroes Motörhead
to deliver a state of the hard rock nation address. Unbeknown to
the crowd gathered inside the beautiful 4,000-capacity art deco
building, the magazine's king-maker editor Lonn Friend had
not only persuaded Ozzy Osbourne to make an unbilled guest
appearance with Faith No More on their cover of Black Sabbath's
'War Pigs', but had also cajoled members of Guns N' Roses, Skid
Row and Metallica into uniting to form a one-off super-group for
the occasion.

The longer arms of the clocks in the venue's dressing rooms had ticked thirty minutes into November 10, when a visibly 'refreshed' Ulrich, Slash and Duff McKagan stumbled behind Skid Row vocalist Sebastian Bach on to the Palladium stage. Taking the opportunity to introduce four men who needed no introduction to the partisan crowd, Friend revealed that the quartet wished to be known as Gak – Hollywood slang for cocaine – a little in-joke which presumably seemed significantly more amusing when coined in a bathroom cubicle earlier that same evening. In truth, had the four men onstage spent rather more time with instruments in their hands instead of $20 bills up their noses in the days leading up to the show, the twenty-five-minute set which followed might have been marginally less shambolic. As it was, Gak's debut bow bore all the grace and artistry of a three-legged terrier attempting to write out its home address in excrement on a Hollywood sidewalk.

The quartet fumbled through an out-of-tune, out-of-key version of Guns N' Roses' 'You're Crazy' before committing assault and battery on Metallica's 'For Whom the Bell Tolls'. Axl Rose then took over on vocals for a stab at Skid Row's 'Piece of Me' before Bach re-joined the stramash to trade vocals with Rose on a version of Nazareth's 'Hair of the Dog'.

The set's closing minutes bore witness to the most telling performance of the night. Ulrich beckoned James Hetfield from the bar to play rhythm guitar on 'Whiplash', an invitation he would come to regret as he watched his friend's face register first bemusement then embarrassment and then granite-faced anger, Hetfield's eyes narrowing to slits as it became abundantly clear that vocalist Bach's familiarity with the Metallica standard extended only to screaming its title. Hetfield's mood was in no way improved when, as the song ground to an ignominious conclusion in squalls of feedback, a laughing Axl Rose approached the mic, and addressed the crowd saying, 'We tried to tell him that nobody knew the song!'

'He's into being a lumberjack tonight', Rose laughed, teasing the Metallica man over his decision to show up to the party in a blue plaid shirt.

'I'm a lumberjack and I don't give a shit,' Hetfield sang in response, his bristling demeanour completely contradicting his words.

'Whiplash' might not have been the most sophisticated song in Metallica's armoury, but, as an unabashed love letter to the San Francisco metal community which had first clasped his band to its bosom eight years earlier, its lyric still had a profound resonance for Hetfield. Seeing it transformed into lumpen pub rock cabaret stung the proud Bay Area émigré. Kirk Hammett was duly summoned to the stage to strap on his Flying V as Hetfield told the crowd, 'I'm going to sing it this time. The other guy fucked it all up.' Two choruses in, with the song now taking flight, Axl Rose stage-dived into the crowd and a smile was restored on the face of Metallica's redoubtable front man.

But it was close. Things could have gone either way.

Fifteen months on, seated around a table laden with gourmet French cuisine, Metallica felt they could afford to be magnanimous towards their LA brethren. Scores of shows deep into the Wherever We May Roam tour, the Metallica machine was operating at full hypnotising power, racking up multiple nights in North America's most capacious sports arenas – three nights at the 18,000-capacity Nassau Coliseum, five nights at the 17,500-capacity LA Forum – as sales of 'The Black Album' sailed north of four million copies in the US alone. Performing nightly on a special diamond-shaped stage, its 'snake pit' centre hollowed out so that a hundred fans might stand close enough to the epicentre to feel James Hetfield's beer-breath on their faces, the quartet understood instinctively that they had acquired an irresistible, unstoppable momentum. The idea that Guns N' Roses should close out each night of their proposed stadium tour was fine with Hetfield and Ulrich. And if Axl Rose insisted upon aping the organisers of 1991's inaugural Lollapalooza festival by granting organisations permission to erect booths promoting liberal causes in the parking lot at every stop on the tour, that, too, was okay with Hetfield, as long as everyone understood that he personally wouldn't be endorsing these causes. Provided that the bands were allocated equal time onstage and gate receipts were split evenly (and projected ticket sales suggested a gross of between one and 1.8 million dollars *per night*), as far as Metallica were concerned Guns N' Roses could do what they damn well pleased.

For Mensch, Burnstein, Goldstein and Bill Graham Promotions, the logistical headaches started here. The unusual nature of the tour presented unique problems. Since both bands were intent upon performing sets stretching to two and a half hours onstage, the event – making allowance for set changeover times and a forty-five-minute slot for an opening band – could potentially run to almost eight hours each day: furthermore, the fact that Metallica desired to take the stage after sundown each evening would mean that the concert could conceivably run two hours past midnight. For stadium managers and local law enforcement agencies this would create significant issues regarding crowd control, transport and noise regulations. Chicago, Cleveland, Philadelphia and Atlanta were among the cities who instantly rejected the opportunity to host shows: stadium managers in other key markets informed Bill Graham's people that a non-negotiable $4,000 per minute fine would be levied for shows exceeding curfew.

As if all this were not sufficiently daunting, above and beyond such work-a-day concerns, Axl Rose's mercurial reputation cast its own dark shadows on the venture.

On July 2, 1991, a riot had erupted at a Guns N' Roses show at the Riverport Performing Arts Center in St Louis, Missouri, when Rose walked offstage ninety minutes into the band's set, irked by confrontations with venue security. *Rolling Stone* magazine duly reported that the violence that followed led to sixty injuries, sixteen arrests, an estimated $200,000 in damage to the new amphitheatre, and 'the loss of most of Guns N' Roses' gear'. The St Louis city authorities subsequently issued an arrest warrant for the singer, charging Rose with four counts of assault and one count of damage to property. If convicted on all charges, the front man would be staring at four years in the big house. Of prime concern to stadium managers negotiating with Bill Graham's promoters in the spring of 1992 was the fact that, with Guns N' Roses committed to tours in Japan, Mexico and Europe, Rose had yet to be formally served with the warrant, meaning that he could be liable for arrest any given day on US soil. It could well be that the result of Rose being arrested for causing a riot would mean his non-appearance on tour with Metallica – and that might lead to another one.

'Promoters were calling us all the time asking about the Axl and St Louis matter,' Peter Mensch acknowledged. 'And we kept saying, "Don't worry. We'll sort it out before the tour starts." '

On May 12, with the issue still to be resolved, Lars Ulrich returned to Los Angeles following two sold-out Metallica shows at San Francisco's Cow Palace, to co-host a press conference with Slash at the Gaslight in Hollywood announcing the co-headline trek. The tour, Ulrich revealed, would kick off in the nation's capital on July 17, at the 57,497-capacity RFK Stadium, home of the National Football League's Washington Redskins, and close on October 6 at the 55,000-capacity Kingdome in Seattle, home to the NFL's Seattle Seahawks. While Slash hid behind his corkscrew curls and a glass of raw bourbon, Metallica's drummer slipped easily into the role of roustabout, promising the assembled media a tour that would be an epochal undertaking.

'I've always wanted to play with these guys, ever since we met them in 1987,' he said. 'I'm the one who had all the late-night conversations with the various members of Guns. Back in '87, we were the bigger band, then they became the biggest band in the universe. Now, in the hard rock scene of 1992, we're the two biggest bands. Taking the two biggest bands from one genre of music and putting them together is unprecedented.

'I don't think any of us realised, when we sat down and had our drunken talks about doing this tour together, how tough it'd be to get the three months of this happening. It's down to the persistence of the band members that this *is* happening, because if it was left to the managers, agents and accountants this would never have got off the ground.

'What we've always done in this band is take opportunities,' Ulrich continued. 'Up until the last two years we never got much help from the usual outlets, so our way of exposing ourselves was to go into situations where people weren't familiar with us. We've done 140 shows on our own all over the country, and yes, we could continue to do things by ourselves. But trying something different – like this tour – always appealed to us.'

In truth, the announcement of the tour was met with only polite interest outside the metal and hard rock press, because at the same time Ulrich and Slash were charming LA stringers in the Gaslight, a young band from Seattle were adorning the cover of *Rolling Stone* magazine for the first time, their front man sporting a white T-shirt on which the handwritten words 'Corporate Magazines Still Suck' were clearly visible.

Nirvana were the nation's most bewildered and reluctant new pop stars, a Black Flag/Black Sabbath-inspired punk-rock-style trio whose ascent to the top of the *Billboard* chart in January 1992 was as dizzying as it was unexpected. *Nevermind*, the band's second album and major label debut, was an adrenaline spike thrust gleefully into the heart of the pop mainstream, a collection of deliciously serrated underground rock songs which were simultaneously antagonistic and approachable, dead-eyed and delirious, channelling anger and apathy in equal measure. From the moment the album displaced Michael Jackson's *Dangerous* at the summit of the national charts, the US media was captivated and enthralled by the ragged Seattle collective, and their sensitive, brooding, sullen front man Kurt Cobain in particular. The edition of *Rolling Stone* of April 16, 1992, hailed its cover stars as the year's 'New Faces of Rock' and turned the spotlight on their home town's music scene, declaring Seattle 'the new Liverpool', while nominating Pearl Jam, Alice in Chains and Soundgarden as harbingers of a new wave of 'alternative' rock. As sales of *Nevermind* passed the five million mark worldwide, the scene's most critically lauded act looked destined to eclipse both Metallica and Guns N' Roses as America's new favourite rock band. Under the circumstances, Axl Rose's invitation to his Geffen Records label mates to open the Metallica/Guns megatour might have smacked of expediency, but the singer was a genuine fan of Cobain's band, as was Metallica's Kirk Hammett, who had long championed underground rock acts on Seattle's Sub Pop record label. Both camps were wounded and more than a little confused when Nirvana declined the offer, though no less confused than the Seattle band had been upon receiving Rose's entreaty to join the cockamamie caravan.

'It was a funny time for our band, because we were going through such a bizarre transition,' says Dave Grohl, then Nirvana's drummer, now the front man of Foo Fighters. 'Even as *Nevermind* was going gold and platinum we were still in a van with a U-Haul trailer and staying in back rooms [of houses belonging to friends/fellow musicians]. There was no overnight assimilation to our new-found rock stardom. We were still used to our lives as lowly underground musicians, but we were thrown into that weird world of being on television and the radio, and it was strange. That same year I went to see U2 in Montreal and Bono asked if Nirvana would tour with U2 in stadiums. And I just couldn't imagine our music translating. Now, decades later, I understand how music translates in an atmosphere like that: I get it. But at the time it seemed so foreign to us.

'Our band had a lot of respect for Metallica, for sure, we always did. Because it seemed like they had come from the same place: they may have lived a different lifestyle than we did, but they did it the right way, they were little bad-asses that changed the world one club at a time, and personally I had a lot of respect for them. But the Guns N' Roses thing was just too out of our world, it just didn't seem like it made any sense. To go out and play to thousands and thousands of people who'd have fucking kicked our asses if they'd known us in high school didn't necessarily seem like the right place for us to be at the time.'

The opportunity was duly passed along to Faith No More, who, at the time the tour was announced, were just setting out as the main support in Guns N' Roses' European stadium run. Long-time friends of Metallica, thanks to guitarist Jim Martin's high-school friendship with Cliff Burton, the wilfully provocative San Francisco quintet were fully cognisant of the pact they were entering into in signing up for the tour. 'Every band in the world might think they want to open for Guns N' Roses,' bassist Bill Gould told England's *Select* magazine that summer, 'but lemme tell you, it's been a real ugly personal experience having to deal with all the shit that surrounds this fucking circus.'

A circus the madness of which Metallica would have their eyes opened to soon enough.

†

On July 12, 1992, five days before the biggest tour of the summer was due to begin, Axl Rose was officially served with his arrest papers at New York's John F. Kennedy Airport as he disembarked from an in-bound flight from Paris. Two days later the singer stood in front of St Louis County Court Judge Ellis Gregory in a Clayton, Missouri, courthouse and pleaded innocent to the charges laid before him. A trial date was set for mid-October, and he was released on a $100,000 bail bond.

The final obstacle standing in the tour's way had now been negotiated. With the first three dates of the excursion – a date at Detroit's Pontiac Silverdome followed the bow at RFK Stadium – fully sold out, Lars Ulrich was in bullish mood as he held court in a Washington DC hotel suite on the eve of the opening night, playing down any suggestions that the Guns N' Roses vocalist's temperamental nature might impact upon the smooth running of the dates which stretched ahead.

'I always find it amusing that the minute you start saying "Guns N' Roses", everybody conjures up all these pictures that are the result of images and rumours,' the drummer told Robert Hilburn of the *LA Times*. 'I know a lot of people said the tour will never happen or Axl'll never show up, but I never had any worries. I know Axl, and that when he really wants to do something, he can do it. Both bands have enough mutual respect for each other not to drag each other down.'

Day one of the tour passed off without incident. Following a politely received aperitif from Faith No More, Metallica took to the stage as a glowering sun slid behind the Washington Monument, kicking off their eighteen-song set with 'Creeping Death' and closing with the irresistible 'Enter Sandman'.

'Metallica seems fully aware that this tour presents a marvellous opportunity,' observed Bruce Britt, reviewing the event for the *Los Angeles Daily News*. 'In a performance that could only be compared to Attila the Hun's tour of Mongolia, Metallica storm-trooped its way into the hearts of the crowd. Their set was simply superb – more than ninety minutes of non-stop musical mayhem. Musically the band goes toe-to-toe with any heavy metal act.'

The momentum of the evening began to dissipate in the

lengthy changeover period between bands. Almost two hours separated the closing notes of 'Enter Sandman' and the spiralling opening riff of Guns N' Roses' set opener 'It's So Easy' – two hours in which a restless crowd occupied their time by conducting stadium-wide food fights and bullying female audience members into exposing their breasts for leering cameramen to project onto the giant screens flanking the stage – and Axl Rose was greeted by an audience already mentally calculating the optimum point at which to head towards the Stadium-Armory Metro station for the last trains bound for suburban Virginia and Maryland. For their part, the RFK crowd faced a band almost unrecognisable from the feral street rats who had arrived on the scene just five years earlier proclaiming that rock music had 'sucked a big fucking dick since the Sex Pistols'. Izzy Stradlin, the quintet's punk rock conscience, had followed sacked drummer Steven Adler out of the band in November 1991, and Rose, Slash and Duff McKagan now stood at the core of an expanded thirteen-piece touring band featuring three backing vocalists and a three-piece horn section. ('I'm getting more and more confused about who's who in Guns N' Roses,' Faith No More's Roddy Bottum told reporters, with waspish wit. 'There's Dizzy and Iggy and Lizzy and Tizzy and Gilby and Giddy . . . Shit man, onstage now there's a horn section, two chick back-up singers, two keyboard players, an airline pilot, a basketball coach, a coupla car mechanics . . .') On moments that the group struck a groove the new-look Guns N' Roses possessed the cocksure swagger of the mid-Seventies Stones, a mixture of sexuality and sin that could not be denied. But too often the momentum of the set was slowed by expansive solo spots and newly extended song codas. Rose constantly exhorted those watching to 'wake the fuck up', but by the time Guns N' Roses' traditional set closer 'Paradise City' brought the evening to a not at all premature climax, its anthemic chorus was echoing off banks of empty, up-turned seats.

The opening night set a template for the first week of the tour. When *Rolling Stone* magazine pitched up at Giants Stadium in East Rutherford, New Jersey, on July 18, the contrasting fortunes of the co-headliners was all too obvious to writer Tom Sinclair.

'Midway through Guns N' Roses' two-and-a-half-hour Giants Stadium set,' he wrote, 'a frustrated Axl Rose tried to goad the capacity crowd into showing more enthusiasm. "It's not that fuckin' hot," he chided them. Rose was talking about the weather, but he could well have been offering a capsule review of GN'R's show . . . but if truth be told, even if GN'R had been in top form all night, they couldn't have topped Metallica's galvanizing set. On song after anthemic song, Metallica achieved a pristine brutality that was riveting . . .To paraphrase the group's recent hit, after Metallica, nothing else mattered.'

'We're out there grabbing some of their fans by the throat and going "Wake up you motherfuckers!" ' James Hetfield told reporters. 'This ain't no fantasy shit, no rock 'n' roll fucking dream.'

Rose's frustration with the way the tour was unfolding boiled over when the circus returned to East Rutherford for a second bow on July 29. Sashaying to the lip of the stage to initiate Guns N' Roses' electric cover of Bob Dylan's 'Knockin' On Heaven's Door', the singer was struck in the crotch by a cigarette lighter thrown from the audience. In obvious discomfort Rose dropped his microphone and hurled his white cowboy hat to the floor, leaving Duff McKagan to complete the song. The following day, an announcement was made that Rose had suffered 'severe damage to his vocal cords' – presumably not from an errant Zippo – and as a result, the next three shows on the tour – in Boston, Columbia, South Carolina and Minneapolis – would have to be rescheduled.

The tour resumed on August 8 at Montreal's Olympic Stadium. Metallica rolled into town early, as Lars Ulrich had promotional duties to attend to at local TV and radio stations. Outside the offices of French-language station Musique Plus the drummer signed autographs for waiting fans and promised a spectacular evening ahead.

For one of the young autograph-seekers, meeting the drummer was a particularly special treat. Laurence Langley played drums in a Metallica tribute band named Battery, who that same night had been booked (along with a Guns N' Roses tribute act) to play Montreal rock club La Brique at an unofficial after-party for the stadium show. Having seen Battery's flyers pinned to notice boards in rock clubs from Long Beach to Long Island, Ulrich was familiar with Langley's band and asked his young doppelgänger if he had tickets for the Olympic Stadium show. Hearing that he did not, the drummer promised Langley that he would arrange for tickets and VIP passes to be left for him at the stadium's box office. When Ulrich hammered out the opening pattern of 'Creeping Death' at 7 p.m. that evening, deep in the 53,000-strong crowd Langley matched his hero beat for beat.

Metallica had tweaked their set slightly during their enforced lay-off – with 'Welcome Home (Sanitarium)' pushed forward to become the third song of the evening, swapping places with 'Fade to Black', which had been relocated to follow Jason Newsted and Kirk Hammett's mid-set solo instrumental showcases. As sheets of pyro announced *Ride the Lightning*'s controversial ballad, however, Langely's air-drumming halted mid-stroke.

'The flames went up as James was supposed to come in with the riff, and Jason and Kirk and Lars kicked all in but the riff never came,' Langley recalls. 'We were thinking "Oh, that's cool, James is pausing, and holding back." And then the pause went on a bit longer, and there was no sound. Kirk and Jason were looking over their shoulders towards Lars behind his kit, and he was standing up trying to peer through the smoke and fog from the pyro in order to see what was happening. Then Kirk and Jason walked back to the drum kit and talked to Lars for a few seconds and they all left the stage. We were like, "What the Hell is going on?" '

Huddled together in the wings, Ulrich, Hammett and Newsted were informed of the reason for the delay. Hetfield had stepped into the path of an onstage pyrotechnic and been engulfed in a tower of flame when the device detonated: his left hand and arm suffered second-degree burns, with Newsted noting that Hetfield's skin was 'bubbling like on the Toxic Avenger'. As the singer was rushed to Montreal General Hospital, his band mates returned to the stage to explain the situation to their bewildered audience. In their Montreal hotel Guns N' Roses too received the news, with the show's promoters requesting that the LA group move their set start time forward to help appease disappointed fans. As the band was ferried to the Olympic Stadium the musicians discussed ways by which they could extend their set. It was their singer, however, who held the power of attorney, and he had yet to leave his room.

'Not only did we not go on early enough to fill the void left by Metallica, we went on three hours later than our own scheduled stage time,' says Slash, recalling the mind-boggling state of insular arrogance in which Guns N' Roses were embedded. 'And once we did, Axl ended it early.'

Guns N' Roses were forty-five minutes into their set when Axl Rose halted the show and told the audience, 'We got it together in Europe only to have it fall apart here. If anyone is interested, this is going to be our last show for a long time.' The set resumed with 'Double Talkin' Jive' and 'Civil War', after which Rose threw down his mic, and stormed offstage, leaving his band mates and the audience staring at one another in confusion.

'I'm sure he had his reasons,' noted Slash, 'but neither I nor the crowd, as far as I know, knew quite what they were.'

'And that,' said a disbelieving Kirk Hammett, 'was when all hell broke loose.'

Axl's truculence was the final straw for the Montreal crowd. As organisers pleaded for calm, a section of the audience began systematically breaking the stadium apart, looting the merchandise stalls, ransacking the bars and hurling chairs through the plate-glass windows of the corporate boxes. Horrified by the tsunami of rage sweeping across the arena, in the bowels of the stadium Lars Ulrich, Kirk Hammett and Jason Newsted sought out their tour mates and found the LA band relaxing in their dressing room 'acting like nothing happened'.

'Axl's down there with a cigarette-holder in one hand and a glass of champagne in the other,' recalled an incredulous Newsted. 'He said, "My voice is giving me trouble." '

'We could hear the stampede overhead, and knew that there was no going back on,' Slash confessed. 'I can't say that I was surprised when the audience started rioting.'

'By the time we got outside,' recalls Laurence Langley, 'the crowd were already tearing everything apart: turning over cop cars, smashing windows and just going crazy. It was an incredible scene, it was kinda shocking. People weren't beating each other, so it didn't feel dangerous, but it was just like this group effort to destroy everything around them: 50,000 angry French Canadians trying to tear the stadium apart.'

Three hundred riot police officers were deployed to quell the disturbances, firing tear gas into the crowd in a bid to regain control. Four subway stations were shut down and running battles spread across the district. When the smoke cleared, twelve rioters were in police custody and the tour's Toronto date became the fourth show postponed.

'I felt like an ass,' Slash later admitted. 'I couldn't look James, Lars, or anyone from the band in the eye for the rest of the tour.'

'But things were always cool between me and Metallica, and they still are,' Slash insisted to one of this book's authors in 2014. 'Although I was embarrassed by a lot of what was going on, they realised that what was happening wasn't being driven by me.'

✝

With their injured guitarist back in the fold, Metallica's touring party decamped to Denver to regroup and consider contingency plans. As when James Hetfield had broken his arm in a skateboarding mishap in 1986, it was decided that a replacement rhythm guitar player would be drafted into the band as emergency cover. Laurence Langley's band Battery were in Cleveland on August 10 when they received a phone call from Q Prime asking if their front man Harvey Lewis might be interested in applying for the part-time vacancy.

'We were freaking out, as you can imagine,' laughs Langley. 'They sent Harvey a ticket to Denver and sent a limo to pick him up at the airport. When the driver turned up, he said, "Hey, sorry, we have to wait to pick up another guy who's auditioning with you." And Harvey said, "Oh yeah? Who's that guy?" The driver said, "His name is John Marshall." We knew John because we'd played supporting Metal Church, and obviously we knew that he'd sat in with Metallica when James broke his wrist skateboarding back in '86 on the . . . *Puppets* [Damage Inc.] tour so Harvey was immediately, like, "Hmmm, well, I guess I'm not getting this gig!" '

As expected, when the tour resumed at Phoenix International Raceway, in Avondale, Arizona on August 25, Marshall, Metallica's former guitar tech, was positioned stage right with Hetfield's Gibson Explorer held tight around his midriff. As a childhood friend of Kirk Hammett, Marshall was entirely comfortable in his new role, and commendably unfazed by his temporary promotion to the big leagues. Nothing, however, could have prepared him for the carnival of excess which now enveloped the touring party. By this point, Guns N' Roses were spending $100,000 a night on lavish backstage parties of an excess not seen since the fall of ancient Rome. Organised by Axl's sister, Amy, and half-brother, Stuart, each happening had its own theme – 'Sixties Night', 'Roman Orgy', 'Greek Night', 'Casino', 'Pool Party' –

each more extravagant and vulgar than the next. Metallica's own celebrations, though less ostentatious, were no less decadent.

'We used to have these things called "minges",' Hammett reveals. 'What they were was parties that we would get together on days off in cities that we were in. We'd either rent a club or a building. I remember we even had a minge in a run-down church. Basically to set up the minge we would go to a strip bar the night before and tell all the girls, "Hey, we're having a party tomorrow," and give them the address. They would come over the next evening. We'd have a keg, the whole crew and all our friends there and we'd have parties on our days off. Absolutely sex, drugs and rock 'n' roll. We also, for a while, would do "imports". Importing would be taking a girl from, say, Cincinnati and bringing her into Atlanta for a few days. Then importing her back to Cincinnati. We would do that a lot. We really had a lot of fun on the road. We came from that school of thinking. The Sixties and the Seventies, that's what people did. They'd go out and party and hang out with chicks and have fun.'

As the tour entered its final week, *Kerrang!* magazine dispatched one of its star writers to San Diego, for a front-line report. A biker, some-time security guard and former punk rock vocalist, the then twenty-eight-year-old Londoner Mörat was no wide-eyed innocent, but the trip proved an eye-opening experience. Outside San Diego's Jack Murphy Stadium, the writer was approached by a middle-aged Guns N' Roses fan who offered him a 'good time' with herself and her two sixteen-year-old daughters in exchange for a backstage pass. 'You'll just love them,' she promised. 'They have long dark hair, beautiful skin. We'd do anything.'

When this unsavoury invitation was politely declined, the lady tried one last desperate gambit. 'We have horses!' she shouted, as the young writer walked away.

'It was pretty horrible,' Mörat recalls, 'really repellent and objectionable. People were just so desperate to be anywhere near the band, and obviously some of the crew were taking advantage: you'd see these under-dressed under-age-looking girls wandering around with passes featuring the letters DFA . . . the joke was that those letters stood for "Does Fuck All".'

'There's a lot of people who aren't very smart on this tour,' Hetfield sighed, when the journalist caught up with him backstage. 'They're just fucking stupid. We need a break.' Asked for his thoughts on his tour mates, the singer offered the opinion, 'We're not the best of buds.'

'I sit here and don't look at them and I don't deal with them,' Hetfield stated. 'Lars loves that shit. He's kinda like the drunk PR guy sometimes. He handles that section. He likes to hang out with a bunch of drunk rockers. It'll get to be on the tour where, during the drum solo, Lars will announce, "All right, we'll all go drinking down at the blah, blah . . . some strip joint or some rock club. Every fucker and their mom will show up there, y'know, so why the fuck would you wanna go down there? Have a quiet beer and you'd just get mobbed. There's bodyguards standing around you, and because there's bodyguards, people wanna get at you. Go in some Country and Western bar and shoot pool and no fucker bugs you at all. All that shit just seems like a waste of time.'

When the journalist sat down with Metallica's 'drunk PR guy', Ulrich was every bit as unrepentant about enjoying his summer as Hetfield was dismissive: 'Out of the four of us, I'm the one that's probably having the most fun doing this,' he admitted. 'The other guys kinda run away from it. I think the other three guys are the ones that have changed more than I have, because we used to all four be equally into this.'

Racking out thick rails of cocaine as he spoke – 'You could actually hear him chopping [lines] on the tape,' Mörat recalls. 'During the interview he was denying doing cocaine while offering me some.' – Ulrich was in bullish mode as he faced up to the writer's accusations that Metallica had become the kind of band they themselves used to hate.

'I can definitely sense that in Europe, much more than in America right now, it's all "Oh my God! What's going on with little, dear old Metallica?"' the drummer noted perceptively. 'What's going on is there's shitloads more people showing up and there's more motherfuckers buying the records than ever before. You've got somebody like Kurt Cobain saying he can't deal with all this. Well, go break up!'

It was put to Ulrich that his band, once the underdog's choice, was now attracting an audience of 'bank clerks' – a somewhat ill-judged accusation, suggesting as it did that bank clerks were less likely to appreciate the band's art than a hardcore fan base comprised of what? Convicted criminals? Tattoo artists? Scaffolders?

Mörat's rebuke caused the drummer's voice to rise in agitated response.

'We didn't go out on purpose to attract fucking bank clerks,' Ulrich spat back, glossing over his own resolutely white-collar origins. 'Sure you can say "Enter Sandman" is not like "Metal Militia", but "Enter Sandman" was the natural thing that came out of us in [1991].

'I can see what you're saying,' the drummer conceded. 'Metallica are definitely not on the edge.' But even here, with drugs coursing through his system that in other musicians would have turned their brains to mush, the drummer remained perceptive, adding, 'but that's because the mainstream has moved a lot closer to the . . . edge than [it was] five years ago. To that bank clerk, Metallica's still the most fucking extreme thing he could get into!'

As true as the drummer's words may be, there was an obvious flipside. With Metallica having dragged the mainstream in their direction, they band had vacated the spot they once occupied on the lunatic fringe. This property was now home to a host of

angrier and even more provocative groups. What's more, one
of the most controversial of its number was about to join the
Metallica and Guns N' Roses caravan.

In a brazen example of biting a hand bearing food, Axl Rose
had finally had reached breaking point with Faith No More. The
opening act had continued insulting Guns N' Roses as the tour
crawled across North America, and (for once, not unreasonably)
the mercurial front man decided that enough was enough and
had the band removed from the bill.

'We said a lot of shit [about Guns N' Roses] and didn't realise
how bad it was until we got caught,' admitted Faith No More
bassist Bill Gould. 'Axl was real straight with us but it was an ugly
scene. He said "It's like I went away and came back home to find
you guys fucked my wife. I only like you guys, Nirvana, Jane's
Addiction and two other bands, and all of you hate me." '

By the time the Metallica/Guns N' Roses tour set up shop
at the Jack Murphy Stadium, Ice T's Body Count had been
installed as the day's opening act. As if the tour hadn't quite been
controversial enough, the San Diego Police Department were
furious that Body Count might elect to play the song 'Cop Killer'
onstage in their city. In an attempt to head off such an eventuality,
the rapper was threatened with prison in a letter from San Diego's
chief of police. Ice T regarded this white sheet of paper as a red
rag and duly wiped his arse on the letter onstage. Very suddenly
indeed Metallica appeared rather more domesticated than their
drummer would have liked to have believed.

'Body Count added a real air of danger to proceedings,' the
watching Mörat recalls. 'Because for all that the headline bands
liked to think they were edgy, the reality was this corporate circus.
I'd never been in the middle of such a fake world. I remember
at one point there was a girl in a wheelchair backstage and Lars
said to me "Watch me turn the charm on with her" and I'm like
"You don't have to turn the charm on, you should just be a nice

fucking person." There was an underlying feeling that there was something wrong with the whole circus – with the egos and all the posturing and bullshit.'

The tour limped wearily to its conclusion at the Kingdome in Seattle on October 6, 1992. From sea to shining sea, the headliners had played in front of a total audience of almost 1.2 million people, grossing over $32 million from the twenty-five shows. They had endured riots, skin-grafts, chaos and all manner of aspersions. But despite the drama and tension that had engulfed the caravan from the start, Metallica still considered the excursion to be a success, as being another mountainous challenge successfully negotiated.

'Whenever I hear any mention of that tour,' said Jason Newsted, 'one word comes to mind: victory. It felt victorious.'

'It was pretty difficult. But overall, it was good for us, I think,' James Hetfield mused when he returned home to San Francisco. 'We did snatch a lot of Guns N' Roses fans by the neck and kinda showed them what this was all about. I guess they thought Guns N' Roses were the heaviest thing on the planet, and they fuckin' found out wrong.'

'It was this epic, potentially fantastic, adventure,' says Slash, 'and even with all things considered, it was an event. Regardless of what was going on, it was something that people went to see. And it was something that people will never forget.'

✝

Tensions between Metallica and Guns N' Roses rumbled on long after final peals of feedback rang out at the Kingdome. On November 17, 1992, the San Francisco band released Adam Dubin's epic 236-minute 'Black Album'/Wherever I May Roam documentary *A Year and a Half in the Life of Metallica* as a double VHS pack. Unvarnished and not always flattering, amid the footage of studio high jinks and on-tour japery, included in the finished product was an interview Dubin conducted with

Hetfield, asking the singer for his thoughts on touring with Guns
N' Roses. Hetfield mimed putting a pistol to his head and pulling
the trigger. Another segment of the film featured Hetfield reading
Axl Rose's tour flyer aloud, to discernible sniggers from band and
crew members.

'Axl "Pose" dressing-room requirements – absolutely no
substitutions,' Hetfield reads. 'One cup of cubed ham . . . it's got
to be cubed so it can go down his little neck. One rib-eye steak
dinner. One gourmet cheese tray. Pepperoni pizza – fresh: I think
that's just for throwing around. Cans of assorted Pringles chips
. . . bottle of Dom Perignon.'

'That's where the money's at, right there,' Hetfield sneers,
tossing the document aside. 'Just crap.' As the flyer hits the floor,
it is met with Hetfield's boot stamping upon it with genuine force.

Axl Rose reserved his right of reply until Guns N' Roses
brought their Use Your Illusion tour back home to California in
April the following year. Addressing the crowd at Sacramento's
Arco Arena on April 3, the singer did not pull his punches,
labelling Hetfield a 'racist' (alleging that he had issues with Ice T
'and any black man') and calling Ulrich 'a stupid little cocksucker'.

'So we're kinda like around the Bay Area, right,' Rose began,
to initial cheers, 'Good, so it's like we're here on somebody else's
turf in a way. We used to think that we were home boys or
something. Let me talk about maybe your good friends Metallica
for a minute . . .

'Let me tell you a couple of things about Metallica,' the singer
continued to a now hushed audience. 'First off, they do a lot of
bitching for a band who got paid about twenty to thirty per cent
more than fucking what they deserved at a show, 'cos they didn't
bring that much . . . I thought I was friends with these people . . .
I'm going to dedicate this to people who like to run fucking little
videos with people saying "Fuck you, this isn't the Guns N' Roses
tour, this is Metallica" or saying things like "Oh shit, it was a joke

because we're friends" . . . This is for you Lars, and you James, – this is called "Double Talkin' Jive Motherfucker"!'

'It's very difficult for me to relate all this to the Axl that I knew,' shrugged Ulrich when informed of his old friend's onstage rant. 'Because when we relate the Axl who called me a "cocksucker" to the Axl that I knew, when we sat down alone and spent time together, just hanging out, we got on well. I quite liked the guy.'

Hetfield was more dismissive.

'Who knows what he's on about?' he said. 'He likes to complain. The only valid thing he'd have to say about that racist stuff is we wanted Motörhead and he wanted Ice T, or Body Count, after Faith No More left the tour. We needed a support act and that was his hot new band that he wanted to crawl up whoever's ass to get to. So we fought about it, and ended up splitting the dates. That's it. I don't listen to Ice T or Body Count; not my favourite band, you know? It seems that because I don't like rap music, that makes me a racist. A black guy doesn't like Country and Western, is he a racist? What the fuck? You've got to have compassion for everything?'

'[The tour] was different,' Hetfield later noted. 'It was hard going, dealing with Axl and his attitude. It's not something we'd want to do again.'

Nor would they need to. Within three weeks of their stadium tour ending, Metallica were back on the road on their own terms, headlining multiple nights at arenas with a capacity of 10,000 to 15,000 throughout Europe. Jason Newsted's UK tour diary, written for *Kerrang!*, painted a picture of a contented, united band bonding over wine-tasting sessions, shopping trips and late-night blues jams in five-star hotel rooms. Checked in as Bill Bollox (Ulrich), Dwight Guy (Hetfield), Philbert Denasex (Hammett) and Travis Bickle (Newsted), on November 4, the band convened in the bar of a Manchester hotel to watch the results of the 1992 US presidential election as they came in.

'Clinton wins,' Newsted noted simply. 'I hope it's for the best.'

While in England, the quartet – or more specifically Hetfield and Ulrich, as was accepted practice – began piecing together ideas for their biggest headline show to date, an open-air event to be staged in the 60,000-capacity National Bowl at Milton Keynes, fifty miles north-west of London, on June 5 the following year. Testament to their burgeoning status, the band would hand-pick their supporting cast. As a gracious 'thank you' to the band who had fed and watered him on his very first trip to England, Ulrich insisted that New Wave of British Heavy Metal veterans Diamond Head would be given the honour of opening the show.

Tickets for gig number 287 on a tour now being billed as Nowhere Left To Roam went on sale shortly after the drummer's twenty-ninth birthday on December 26. By late February, more than 29,000 Metallica fans had handed over £19 for their watermarked invite to the ball at the Bowl. On March 2 John Jackson, the band's agent, faxed Ulrich with his thoughts as to how a further 31,000 fans might be persuaded to join the party.

'When you look out at the audience at Milton Keynes, you may not be able to tell if there is 45,000, 50,000, 55,000 or 60,000,' Jackson noted. 'But I will know.'

The agent's proposal was a simple, yet brilliant, piece of theatre. Jackson suggested that Metallica should invite Megadeth – 'a band you may have heard of', he noted in a droll aside – to play alongside the headliners for the first time since a concert on New Year's Eve 1985 at the San Francisco Civic Auditorium.

'Having Megadeth fly in on a one-off for this show will immediately make this one show unique,' wrote Jackson, 'especially as the British press and our fans know of the history of Dave Mustaine and Metallica. The British media will whip the show up into an EVENT.'

'Yes, I do represent Megadeth,' Jackson concluded, 'so yes, I am biased, but this bias has never overshadowed what I believe is the best for METALLICA. I hope that what I have said makes sense. Maybe you could give Peter [Mensch] your decision tonight, or I could check out Rolf Harris's availability as I'm sure he will bring in the Mums and Dads . . . '

Milton Keynes never would get the opportunity to hear the sound of a wobble-board amplified through a 50,000 watt PA. Instead, on June 5, 1993, under an overcast sky, Dave Mustaine followed Diamond Head and The Almighty on to a stage the foundations of which he'd helped to construct in a Los Angeles garage a decade earlier. In doing so he announced – somewhat prematurely, as it went – 'The ten years of bullshit is over between Metallica and Megadeth.'

Backstage, predictably, Lars Ulrich was all smiles.

'I'm in a really great mood,' the drummer told MTV's *Headbangers Ball*. 'The fact that we can come back to England and play to 60,000 people in one go is incredible. I think it's going to be good. We want to take a couple of years away from the spotlight, so we want to give people something to remember here.'

As darkness fell, and Ennio Morricone's 'The Ecstasy of Gold', as ever, Metallica's introductory music of choice, rang out across Buckinghamshire's only man-made amphitheatre, Ulrich embraced his manager Peter Mensch, and made his way over to his band mates for the short walk to the stage. Mensch and Cliff Burnstein said goodbye to the BBC documentary film crew that had been tailing them throughout the day and traced the drummer's steps. Ulrich's 'Black Album' mission statement – to 'cram Metallica down everybody's fucking throat all over the fucking world' – had been fulfilled.

'They wanted to make an album that could stand up against the first Led Zeppelin records or [AC/DC's] *Back in Black* or *Highway To Hell*,' Mensch reflected. 'And they absolutely did that, they made a classic.'

3 — HERO OF THE DAY

It was inevitable that there would be a comedown. After rolling through 202 cities, dotted throughout thirty-seven countries, over a period of twenty-three months, the Wherever We May Roam tour finally skidded to a halt at the Werchter Festival in Belgium on July 4, 1993. At the conclusion of a raucous 'So What', its joyful obscenities screamed skywards by a massed chorus of crew members, friends and family, a topless James Hetfield strode to the lip of Metallica's custom-built stage and sprayed the audience with champagne while Lars Ulrich and Jason Newsted hoisted aloft a fan's homemade banner hand-painted with the words 'Have a Nice Vacation'. Hetfield, Ulrich, Newsted and Kirk Hammett then linked arms before bowing deeply to the 75,000-strong crowd and exiting stage left.

No one remembers very much of the rest of the evening. Ian Jeffery, the band's tour manager, had arranged for the presentation of a cake – tastefully iced with a coiled marzipan snake that echoed the cover of 'The Black Album' – and more champagne, but the after-show party was a subdued affair, less a celebration than a wake. As American Independence Day drew to a close, the prospect of imminent freedom from the tour bubble filled band and crew alike with mixed emotions.

'I'm not looking forward to going home,' Hammett readily admitted. 'This is what I'm here to do: I'm here to play guitar, to play shows, that's my vocation in life. Going home and doing nothing makes me feel guilty, like I'm a bum.'

Back home in San Francisco, as post-tour depression sank in, Hammett crashed hard. Phone calls from friends went unanswered, social invitations were spurned, guitars lay unplugged and unplayed.

It was, Hammett recalls, 'very difficult', to reintegrate into domestic life. So, one afternoon, the guitarist pulled on a beanie hat, turned up the collar of his jacket, and headed out in search of a cure for his summertime blues.

Having grown up in the area, Hammett knew San Francisco's Mission district well. As a kid he practically lived at the San Francisco Comic Book Co. on 23rd Street, just blocks from his family home on 20th and South Van Ness. As a teenager, he had spend entire weekends at the Grand Theater cinema on 23rd and Mission, watching obscure European horror films and cult B-movies at all-day screenings. And as an adult, he now knew exactly on which block to queue in order to score heroin.

'It's easy, you go down to 16th and Mission, which is a popular copping place,' he revealed. 'You have these Mexicans going "Mota! Cheeba!" – Mota being marijuana and cheeba being heroin. [For] twenty-five bucks you get a balloon and you smoke it or snort it.'

'I was curious,' says Hammett, 'just curious. It [heroin] was very popular with a lot of musicians and a lot of friends I had. They talked it up really well . . . I was just out for adventure.'

Back at home, Hammett opted to smoke the drug. Minutes later, the guitarist was on his hands and knees in his bathroom, depositing the contents of his stomach into his toilet bowl.

'It was not the drug for me,' he says. 'It just turned me into a grumpy old man. I puked my guts out, then I felt sluggish and loud music did not sound good to me. Picking up my guitar and plugging it into an amp, I couldn't deal with it. I tried it [heroin] a few times. [But] It kept me away from everything that I really, really loved and I didn't think that the high was particularly enjoyable anyway.'

Having rejected one of rock 'n' roll's more predictable escape routes, Hammett decided upon a rather different tack. In the autumn of 1993, as his thirty-first birthday beckoned, the guitarist in the world's biggest heavy metal band decided to go back to college, enrolling at San Francisco State University to take classes in film, jazz and Asian studies. 'You can only be what the public thinks you are for so long before it becomes boring,' he noted.

Elsewhere in the city, the business of Metallica was, inevitably, still occupying Lars Ulrich's time. Interviewed backstage at Milton Keynes on June 5, the drummer had revealed that the band had started the process of 'cleaning the attic out' in order to collate a live album and video set documenting the Wherever We May Roam tour. With the band's passports now tucked away at home, the task of sifting through hundreds of hours of live recordings fell to him. 'It's not something that's going to sell as many as the last record,' Ulrich emphasised. 'It's for the fans that have been there, our offering to them.'

When it was unveiled on November 23, 1993, this 'offering' served not so much as a full stop on the first decade of Metallica's recording career as an exclamation mark. Packaged in a box emulating a flight case for equipment, everything about *Live Shit: Binge & Purge*, from its content (three CDS and three VHS cassettes, documenting shows in Mexico City, Seattle and San Diego, plus a trivia-packed booklet, a mock Snakepit pass and a 'Scary Man' stencil) to its price tag (£75 in the UK, $89.95 in the US) served to identify its creators as a band of considerable substance and stature. Given the success of Metallica's self-titled fifth album and the scale of the tour undertaken in its name, it is understandable that the band's first live collection would be a heavyweight affair. The fact that Metallica had been on the road for almost two years and had performed for an estimated 4.3 million people proved yet again that this was no ordinary band. But *Live Shit's* . . . self-congratulatory, self-aggrandising nature sat uneasily alongside the quartet's reputation as being the

Band of the People. This status also took a hit from a price tag that carelessly crossed the line between chutzpah and bare-faced cheek. Not that Ulrich saw it that way, of course.

'The reason it costs $89.95 is not so we and Elektra can walk away with big fat bank accounts, it's basically to cover the fucking costs of about two and a half million bucks,' the drummer insisted. 'Our management did a survey and discovered that this is the most expensive packaging anybody has ever put together. You've got everything in there, nine hours of music, seventy-two-page book, backstage passes, stencil, keys to our houses . . . so fuck, take it or leave it!

'I think it's turned into a great way of getting the last three and a half years out of our systems,' the drummer added. 'Now the slate really is completely clean. We wrote the album, made the album, toured the album and here's the documentation of the album's music on the road. Now we can take our nine months or whatever off and start with a clean slate. Everything about this tour is gone. It will enable us to completely let go of everything from the last few years, and when we begin to approach the next album we can do so without any lingering, left-over baggage.'

An exercise in unashamed dick-swinging it may have been, but as a package aimed at the kind of Metallica fans who lived and breathed the band with an intensity to match Ulrich's, there was much to appreciate and admire about *Live Shit . . .* While the filmed content might suffer from Wayne Isham's stock MTV direction, the power, presence and personality of the music on the audio CDs is undeniable. Culled from a five-night stand at Mexico City's Sports Palace arena on February 25, 26 and 27 and March 1 and 2, 1993, Metallica sound ferocious, focused and utterly fearless. The eighteen-minute version of 'Seek & Destroy' may be indulgent and unnecessary, exceeded only in pointlessness by the combined nineteen minutes afforded to Hammett and Newsted's solo instrumental showcases, but when the quartet truly take flight, as they do here on spectacular versions of 'Whiplash', 'Sad But True' and 'Harvester of Sorrow' in particular, Metallica sound majestic, and insatiably intense. The transitions between the 'Black Album' material and songs sourced from the band's earlier releases are seamless, making a mockery of the idea that with their fifth collection the quartet had somehow compromised their art in pursuit of mainstream glory. If the *Metallica* album was so out of step with the records that preceded it, why do the songs flow together so persuasively? It's impossible to hear 'Wherever I May Roam' run into 'Am I Evil?' and 'Last Caress' and argue convincingly that one is listening to a mainstream rock band, much less one knowingly neutered for the mass market. Like the man who pulled its components parts together, *Live Shit* . . . might occasionally seem a little too pleased with itself, but it is an audacious statement from a band utterly aware of its own value as one of the best-loved and most successful musical acts in the world. That, in America, the box set found its way into enough homes to register an entry into the *Billboard* 200 at no. 26 only served only to validate this confidence.

Though little was made of the fact at the time, to the members of Metallica the *Live Shit: Binge & Purge* box represented not just the culmination of the 'Black Album' campaign, but also the fulfilment of the record contract with Elektra Records to which they had put their signatures in A&R man Michael Alago's Manhattan office in the summer of 1984. The terms of the deal signed that afternoon stipulated that the San Francisco band would record and release seven albums for the label. Nine years later the quartet had in fact released only four full-length studio albums – *Ride the Lightning* (1984), *Master of Puppets* (1986), . . . *And Justice for All* (1988) and their eponymous, all-conquering 'Black Album' – but they had also given the label the *$5.98 EP: Garage Days Re-Revisited* mini-album, as well as two VHS releases in *Cliff 'Em All* and the two-part *A Year and a Half in the Life of*

Metallica, collections the band and their management regarded as being equivalent to full-length albums. In the eyes of the San Franciscans the release of the expansive (and expensive) *Live Shit* . . . compendium signalled the conclusion of their first major label contract. With sales of 'The Black Album' still buoyant, Metallica believed they could negotiate a new contract with Elektra from a position of supreme strength. Acting on the quartet's behalf, lawyers from the firm Manatt, Phelps and Phillips proposed to the label that their clients enter into a new joint venture and partnership agreement with the company, waiving album advances in exchange for a profit-sharing arrangement predicated upon a substantially improved royalty rate. Elektra president Bob Krasnow was open to the idea, but negotiations between the two parties were thrown into disarray when in the summer of 1994 Elektra was taken over by the Warner Music Group, a division of the Time Warner media corporation. Time Warner's chief executive officer, Robert Morgado, appointed Atlantic Records head Doug Morris as president of the new conglomerate. The resulting boardroom earthquake saw Krasnow, Metallica's oldest ally at the label, resign from the company he had been at the helm of since 1983. Negotiations between the label and band stalled with immediate effect.

Metallica's response was unexpected and bold, a power play that blind-sided their bosses. On September 27, 1994, the band's lawyer Jody Graham Dunitz filed a lawsuit at the California Superior Court petitioning that the group be released from their contract with Elektra. Metallica's motion was based on a clause in the California Labor Code that permits an employee to be freed from a personal-services contract after seven years. The law had been cited in cases where Hollywood actors wished to liberate themselves from prohibitive studio contracts, but had yet to be invoked in court in cases centred on the music industry. Similar suits by former Eagles front man Don Henley and soul singer Luther Vandross, against Geffen Records and Epic Records respectively, had been settled out of court. Once again, it seemed as if Metallica were intent on setting a precedent.

In a statement issued to media organisations, Lars Ulrich criticised Robert Morgado for 'greedy and arrogant' behaviour, claiming that the Warner Music Group man had reneged on promises made by Bob Krasnow.

'Our faith in this company has been flushed down the drain,' Ulrich said. 'Elektra used to have a reputation as a label that treated artists with respect. Now it's just another place where arrogant business people break promises.'

'For the last ten years,' Ulrich told a reporter, 'our thing has been very pure, very clean, very straightforward. But there comes a point where you have to realise that you're taking it up the ass, and I don't like the feeling very much.'

In early December the legal battle shifted to New York, as litigants and other key players in the case were summoned for pre-trial witness statements. Inevitably it was Ulrich who headed east to represent the band, filing daily reports for Hetfield, Hammett and Newsted as the legal positions became increasingly entrenched. Exasperated by the posturing and prevarication, the drummer convened a meeting with Peter Mensch, Cliff Burnstein and Doug Morris and noted, 'All the people who can fix this are in this room. We don't need to deal with lawyers, with the food chain. Let's talk this through.'

'We went back and forth for about two hours and came to an agreement that everybody felt comfortable with,' Ulrich recalled. 'I pulled my hand out, [Morris] shook it, and there was the deal.'

In January 1995 Elektra and Metallica issued a joint statement announcing the resolution of the dispute. The terms of the settlement were not disclosed, but beyond what the drummer identified as '2,000 pages' worth of clauses that nobody gives a fuck about', the deal saw the band re-sign with Elektra on a significantly higher royalty rate and, crucially, secure the rights to the master recordings of their entire catalogue.

By this point work on the first Metallica album to be released under this new arrangement had begun in earnest. For those listening attentively, the first signs that the beast was emerging from its slumber had come forty-nine minutes into the quartet's set at the twenty-fifth anniversary of the Woodstock festival in Upstate New York the previous August. For an audience soaked from a day's torrential rain, Metallica unveiled a snippet of a new song, then bearing the working title 'Outlaw', secreted into 'Seek & Destroy'. A one-off festival show for the band, Woodstock 2 drew an audience of 350,000 music fans to Winston Farm in Saugerties, New York with a bill that saw veteran artists from the original Woodstock line-up (Joe Cocker, Crosby, Stills and Nash, Santana) share stages with emerging acts (Green Day, Collective Soul) and established arena bands (Red Hot Chili Peppers, Aerosmith).

Sandwiched between headliners Aerosmith and Nine Inch Nails, Metallica resolutely refused to buy into the faux nostalgia of the event. The band issued a bespoke T-shirt featuring their 'Scary Man' image with dollar bills for eyes and the words 'Hippy Shit' scrawled underneath. Onstage the band began a set that was being broadcast live in to tens of millions of American homes – not to mention broadcast live on radio in the UK – with James Hetfield shouting the words 'Fuck you!' before a single note of music had been played. When those notes did come, they sounded the opening riff of 'Breadfan', an impossibly obscure B-side originally recorded by Welsh progressive-metal act Budgie. In a mischievous mood, Hetfield later introduced 'Seek & Destroy' as a new song brought to the band by Jason Newsted but even those clued in on the front man's joke were surprised to hear the *Kill 'Em All* standard dissolve into an extended blues riff jam after its second chorus.

Whether or not anyone bar the band onstage were aware of

the fact, this was the watching world's first preview of what would become Metallica's next album, *Load*.

Hetfield and Ulrich began assembling the bare bones of their group's sixth album in May 1994, less than ten months after calling time on the Wherever We May Roam tour. As was now standard practice, the pair first sifted through Hetfield's extensive 'riff tape' collection in order to cherry-pick ideas that might form the spine of new songs. Both men were agreed that this new material should sound looser and less rigidly defined than before. They desired songs that were grittier, more soulful and more human. As winter descended, a raft of new tracks began to take form. Working in a basement studio installed in Ulrich's hilltop Marin County home – a facility dubbed 'The Dungeon' – the duo began the process of committing arrangements and guide vocals to tape. On November 28, 'Streamline' (later to be known as 'Wasting My Hate') became the first new Metallica demo in four years. Two days later, a second song, 'Load' (subsequently re-titled 'King Nothing') was recorded. Three further tracks – 'Devil Dance,' aka 'Devil's Dance'; 'Fixer', later extended to 'Fixxxer'; and 'Mouldy', soon to be 'Hero of the Day' – joined their siblings before the New Year chimes rang out. By Easter a further eight tracks were laid on two-inch tape. 'The ideas kept on coming,' Ulrich noted, sounding as surprised as anyone by the relative ease of the creative process.

'All this material had built up on the road,' Hetfield explained. 'There were bags and bags of tapes with riffs on them . . . stuff we had accumulated from five years of not writing. First it was like, "Okay, let's stop at twenty songs." Then we'd get going and say, "All right, we'll stop at thirty." It was fucking crazy.'

'Before you start working on a new record, you wonder if you can still deliver,' Ulrich added. 'But once James and I lock in and start work together, it's pretty much unstoppable. The bottom line is, playing and writing with James still gets my dick as hard now as it did in 1981.'

On May 1, 1995, Metallica officially commenced recording their sixth album. Having gained the quartet's respect and trust during the torturous birth of 'The Black Album', Bob Rock's services were retained for production duties. But in a break with tradition, for the first time the band elected to record on home turf, at The Plant studios in Sausalito, a facility at which albums such as *Raised on Radio* by Journey, *Sports* by Huey Lewis and the News and Van Morrison's *Beautiful Vision* had been recorded. Given the discipline he had instilled in the group during their nine-month stint at Hollywood's One On One studios, Rock's initial advice at the outset of the process took his charges by surprise: 'Don't record, just rehearse,' the Canadian suggested, 'and when it feels right I'll record you.' The musicians were encouraged to experiment with tunings and instrumentation, textures and tone, to indulge their instincts and interact organically, rather than be hemmed in by what they had come to believe to be the 'proper' way to make a record.

'We're almost having fun in the studio,' Ulrich noted, as the process got under way. 'It's going very quickly, but the key word is that it's also very relaxed. We're going in and doing basically what we hoped for in our wildest imagination, which is not getting caught in some anal torment of precision and tightness. The new songs we're writing just called for a looser, livelier type of thing and we set our goal with this record to try and capture more the spirit of the songs than worrying about the technical stuff. We've been talking about that for months and months and months, and what usually happens when it comes time is that we put our tail between our legs and start shitting bricks! But this time everything we talked about actually happened, so we're like, "Wow, this is pretty cool."'

So relaxed and productive were the initial months at The Plant that in August Metallica felt able to break from the session to accept an invitation to cross the Atlantic for a fourth appearance at Donington Park, this time in a headlining slot.

The promoters of the Monsters of Rock festival desperately needed a favour from the Bay Area quartet. With the rise of grunge and alternative rock, traditional metal bands had taken a battering, and in 1995 the number of viable contenders to headline England's only metal festival was vanishingly small. In 1988 headliners Iron Maiden had drawn a record crowd of 107,000 people to the East Midlands for their debut appearance on Donington soil. Seven years on and even this most redoubtable of warhorses was looking ready for the glue factory. With their classic line-up dissolved and charismatic front man Bruce Dickinson replaced by journeyman Blaze Bayley, in promoting their tenth studio album, *The X Factor*, Steve Harris's band was reduced to single-night stands in modest theatres such as the Town and Country Club in Leeds and the Apollo in Manchester. As for other potential candidates for the festival's prime slot, the ground was similarly barren. Judas Priest were operating in reduced circumstances following the exit of front man Rob Halford, Guns N' Roses were in disarray following guitarist Slash's departure, AC/DC had seconded themselves to a Canadian recording studio and Aerosmith, surfing a wave of success on the back of 1993's ten-million-selling *Get a Grip* album, were ruled out by virtue of having headlined the previous summer.

So dire were the straits in which the Monsters of Rock festival found itself during this period that in 1993 the event had been shelved because of this lack of a credible headline act. To do the same again just two summers later would signal to the music industry that metal as a commercial force was finished in the UK.

While the notion of his men in black being re-cast as metal's own white knights doubtless appealed to the sentimental side of Lars Ulrich, the drummer was aware that Metallica no longer needed to operate beneath the umbrella of a corporate festival franchise in order to sell tickets in the UK. The success of the band's appearance at the Milton Keynes Bowl had proved that. Fully aware of this power, Lars Ulrich let it be known that his band would headline Donington in 1995 but only if the festival's organisers ceded complete control of their operation. The deal was this: Metallica would select the bill and running order, and the event would be branded not as the Monsters of Rock but as Metallica's 'Escape from the Studio', a name sufficiently open-ended that it could be trademarked and re-employed for future happenings.

With these terms agreed, it was a relaxed and high-spirited touring party which billeted itself in west London in the final week in August.

At one point during the week Ulrich could be found in a central London newsagent seeking out a copy of *Metal Hammer* magazine, which just happened to have his likeness as its cover image.

'Where's the Satanic Metal section?' he joked, bouncing through the aisles like a meerkat raised on a diet of methamphetamine and Sunny Delight. Finding the magazine, the drummer brandished the title under the nose of an understandably bewildered Japanese tourist browsing the shelves alongside him.

'Check it out, that's me,' Ulrich explained. 'See? Famous, huh? Pretty cool, huh?'

This light-hearted mood was maintained throughout the trip. On August 23, the quartet warmed up for their excursion to the East Midlands with a 'secret' show for fan club members and media at the 1,000-capacity Astoria 2 club on London's Charing Cross Road, premièring two new songs, '2 x 4' and 'Devil's Dance'. The band claim this concert to be the best they have ever played.

Three days later a chartered helicopter deposited the quartet on the Donington site.

'The weather's good and the vibe is good,' noted Ulrich. 'Walking around here, I'm so happy and everyone else seems to be happy too. Is that bad when you're in a metal band?'

Backstage a host of familiar faces greeted the incoming party.

The Escape from the Studio '95 line-up included Slash's new band, Slash's Snakepit, Warrior Soul, Corrosion of Conformity, Skid Row and White Zombie. The thrash movement was represented by the mighty Slayer and Bay Area neophytes Machine Head. Occupying the 'special guest' slot – a fact that did not go down well with a number of the other bands – was Northern Ireland's Therapy?, then riding high on the back of their million-selling *Troublegum* album.

Ulrich explained the bill's selection process in untypically straightforward terms. 'We looked in our record collection and thought, "What's my favourite record of the moment?" It's COC,' he said. 'What was my favourite record last week? It was Warrior Soul. We've got a bunch of friends in bands, we've got a bunch of people we like hanging out with and there are a bunch of albums we like listening to, so we put them all on.'

For all the love being shared backstage, however, the headliners were not shy of stamping their authority on the day, and in doing so making sure that other acts were aware of their station.

'We'd played Donington for the first time in 1994 and had a fantastic day, so we wanted to come onstage to Thin Lizzy's "The Boys Are Back in Town", as a reference to the previous year,' recalls Therapy? front man Andy Cairns. 'Obviously there was a link with us both being Irish bands too. But Metallica's tour manager got wind of this and said we couldn't use the song, as it was part of *their* intro music. We were also told not to use James Hetfield's "ego ramps" at the front of the stage, which were for Metallica's sole use.

'Of course, the first thing that Michael [McKeegan, Therapy? bassist] and I did was to walk straight down there,' Cairns laughs. 'It wasn't out of disrespect to Metallica – we were all Metallica fans and it was a great honour to play with them – but that was just our belligerent nature then. It didn't seem to do our relationship any harm: we did more shows with them and Lars and Kirk would be in our dressing room whenever the "party favours" were being shared out. But the key phrase [when taking cocaine with the pair] was always "Don't tell James!" '

At 8 p.m. the orchestral swells of 'The Ecstasy of Gold' resounded around Donington Park for the fourth time in eleven summers. Before Ennio Morricone's composition reached its stirring conclusion, however, the music ground to a halt, as if a stylus had been forcibly dragged across a vinyl record. In its place, an announcement was made over the PA.

'Attention concert-goers! Due to the recent death of heavy metal Metallica has been cancelled. Please leave quietly and drive home safely.'

As the message was absorbed by a jeering crowd, a sea of middle fingers was raised in the direction of the stage. A split second later, however, this universal signifier of discontent was transformed into a hand gesture inextricably bound up with heavy metal culture, the 'devil's horns', as the heroes of the day sprinted onstage to the strains of 'Breadfan'. 'Master of Puppets' and 'Wherever I May Roam' followed before James Hetfield addressed his audience for the first time. But when he finally did so, the singer's words were accompanied by a broad smile.

'Looks like we're going to have ourselves a good motherfucking time,' Hetfield roared. 'Everyone's sweating a little bit out there, aren't they? Giving it the fucking old Metallica yahoo, right? So, it's been a little while since we've seen y'all, huh? It's good to see you maniacs again. We've got some fucking heavy shit for you, man, can you fucking handle it?'

The crowd at Donington Park indicated that they could handle that just fine. This audience then listened attentively to the brace of new songs and roared their appreciation as the headliners paid tribute to their supporting cast with a cheerfully sloppy medley that incorporated the riffs from Corrosion of Conformity's 'Human', Guns N' Roses' 'Sweet Child of Mine',

White Zombie's 'More Human Than Human' and Slayer's 'Black Magic' alongside Whitesnake's 'Slow and Easy' and, perhaps inevitably, Deep Purple standard 'Smoke on the Water'. *Kerrang!* magazine would later churlishly label this playful behaviour 'pointless', arguing that Metallica were 'prick-teasing' their audience. But this po-faced criticism sat at odds with the general consensus, and, perhaps less surprisingly, with the opinion of the band's biggest fan.

'As one-off shows go, it went much better than expected,' was Lars Ulrich's considered view. 'We had our shit together and it kinda kicked.'

And with that self-assessment, the tourists went home satisfied.

✝

In November James Hetfield was compelled to stage another escape from the studio, this time alone. Metallica's stoic front man had on his mind matters upon which he wished to concentrate away from the feverish atmosphere of The Plant. His long-estranged father, Virgil Hetfield, had informed his youngest son that he had advanced-stage cancer and was not expected to beat the disease. Still seeking to forge a meaningful relationship with the man whose absence had caused him so much pain in his teenage years, James now had to face up to the prospect of life without either of his parents.

In search of solitude and serenity, Hetfield signed up for a hunting trip to Wyoming, in winter one of North America's most inhospitable and hostile territories. The excursion would require the man who penned the lyrics to 'The Four Horsemen' to saddle up for a two-day trek through snow and rain.

'The ride out was brutal,' Hetfield would later recall. 'It was about ten straight hours of riding over a 10,000-foot [deep] pass in the middle of the night. It's pitch black and snowing and you're freaking out . . . Some wild shit happened up there . . . it inspires you. Your mind is totally clear. You can get way into yourself.'

Alone in the wilderness with his thoughts, Hetfield began to reflect upon his relationship with his father and others close to him, as well as with those who would only ever know him through the music he made. As he did so, lyrics began to come together in his mind. Keen to commit these words to paper, Hetfield realised to his annoyance that his fifteen-pound survival pack contained neither pen nor pencil. He did, however, have ammunition boxes full of lead-tipped bullets. And so, sitting in the dark in his tent, Metallica's lyricist used live ammunition to jot down notes and phrases that would provide the emotional core of his band's next record.

Returning to The Plant revitalised, Hetfield hoped to secure space and time to lay flesh upon these bare bones. But on his return to the studio the singer discovered that his journey into the wild had not only unblocked his creative pores but had also opened up the recording session in an unexpected manner: Kirk Hammett informed Metallica's alpha male that in Hetfield's absence he'd tracked rhythm guitar parts for a Metallica album for the very first time.

The idea came from Ulrich. In the studio the pair shared an unusual relationship. While Hetfield was responsible for rhythm parts that he would overdub as many as six times on each song, Ulrich would coax from the band's lead guitarist some of the finest solos in the history of metal. Apropos of nothing one day, the drummer suggested that Hammett might like to track a couple or three rhythm parts as well. The horror with which this suggestion was met could scarcely have been exceeded had Ulrich encouraged Hammett to take advantage of Hetfield's absence by setting fire to the singer's house. But with both Ulrich and Bob Rock insistent, Hammett set to the task with typical diligence, fashioning complementary splashes of colour and tone which might accentuate, rather than subtract from, Hetfield's riffs.

On another day, Hetfield might have viewed this incursion into territory very firmly delineated as his own *very* sacred turf as a hostile takeover, a challenge to his authority and a betrayal. But with his mind refreshed by the bracing Wyoming air, he responded to the news with a request to hear the tracks his band mate had recorded. As Bob Rock cued the music, everyone in the room held their breath.

The look on Hetfield's face at what he was hearing signalled a measure of displeasure and discomfort. But both producer and band mates knew that this was not the time to provoke a confrontation. Instead it was made clear to the front man that if he felt that Hammett's playing detracted in any way from his own intentions for individual songs then the additional guitar tracks would simply be erased. Reassured by this, over the days that followed Hetfield would approach Rock and ask for a third, fourth or fifth listen to this song, or that song, sitting in silence as Hammett's nuanced playing coalesced with his own more regimented style. With each successive listen, he found the balance more appealing.

'I wanted the guitars back in your face again,' he recalled. 'I like the way *Kill 'Em All* just had fucking guitars up your ass and the drums were not the leader of the group. I think that on "The Black Album", everyone wanted to be up front. But something has to be back there, and it ended up being the guitars, which were given a wider, thinner sound and pushed back. On this album the drums drive the rhythm instead of leading the band, and there are these two guitars playing different things right up front.

'It was what was needed for the record,' he continued. 'The looseness just wasn't coming across. No matter how many fucking Martinis I had, I could never get [my own replicated] guitar tracks to sound different [from one another]. It was the same guitar player playing it, fucked up. It wasn't a fucked up guitar player trying to play it right!'

With this Rubicon crossed, work proceeded harmoniously at The Plant through the winter. Ahead of the Christmas break, the band unanimously decided upon an office outing, one at which they themselves would provide the entertainment.

On December 24, 1995, Motörhead's indestructible front man Ian 'Lemmy' Kilmister turned fifty. Ten days earlier friends and family had staged a celebratory party for the great man at the Whisky a Go Go, at which Metallica elected to perform as unannounced special guests. They did so in the guise of The Lemmys, a Motörhead tribute act, resplendent in long black wigs and shades, sporting drawn-on moustaches, bullet belts and freshly inked fake Ace of Spades tattoos. 'The fucking look on people's faces,' laughed Lars Ulrich. 'Classic.'

The gig would be Metallica's first appearance at LA's most rock 'n' roll venue since a pair of shows on March 27, 1982, supporting Saxon. At the second of those two performances, the band had played four cover versions that they attempted to pass off as their own songs. Back at the Whisky thirteen years later, they would play six covers, none of which they could ever pretend were their own, starting and finishing the set with the deathless 'Overkill'.

'I remember that there were these rumours flying around that Metallica were going to show up,' recalls Los Angeles-based photographer Lisa Johnson. 'It was a landmark occasion. Not only is Lemmy a legend, but he was kinda the first in our world to turn fifty, you know? None of us thought we'd live to see fifty, and here's Lemmy celebrating that birthday. So it was pretty special.

'The Whisky was packed with about twice as many people as it actually holds. We were all looking at the stage wondering what was going to happen, who was going to come on, and suddenly these four weird-looking guys come on. And everyone was, like, well, we don't know *who* that is, but it's certainly not Metallica. But then we all realised that these people were all dressed up to

look like Lemmy, and it *was* Metallica onstage. It was definitely a
special occasion, a lot of fun as well.'

'That was the biggest compliment anybody has ever paid me,'
Lemmy later noted. 'But they got their tattoos on the wrong arm,
every one of them.'

†

Given the relaxed, yet productive, pace at which matters were
proceeding at The Plant, Elektra Records doubtless considered that
they were giving Metallica a more than generous deadline when
they set May 1, 1996, as the date for Metallica's sixth album to be
mastered in New York City. This was surely reasonable; the band,
after all, had entered the facility exactly one year earlier. But the
label underestimated the elastic nature of time on Planet Metallica.
Despite the quartet having elected to focus upon just fourteen of
the twenty-seven songs demoed in Sausalito, by the second week
of April three of those fourteen songs were bereft of vocals, with
many more still awaiting additional guitar embellishments from
Hetfield and Hammett. The sessions had now relocated to New
York, where, somewhat farcically, Q Prime had been forced to
block-book no fewer than three recording studios for the band:
two rooms at Right Track Recording on West 48th Street and an
additional room at Quad Recording, across the street at 723 7th
Avenue. Even more ludicrously, with the band staring down the
barrel of a mastering engineer's starting pistol, flights and upmarket
lodgings had already been booked in Manhattan for members of
the international press corps, with journalists – including one of
the authors of this book – poised to interrupt the sessions on a
daily basis for the purpose of conducting interviews with the band
about an album as yet unfinished.

Given the circumstances, the quartet appeared remarkably
at ease when juggling promotional and studio duties at Right
Track. When an unmastered CD of new songs was slid into the

studio's stereo system for representatives of *Kerrang!* magazine, Kirk Hammett could not resist the temptation to add air guitar flourishes to the mix while Hetfield, Newsted and Ulrich sang along in the manner of drunken sailors. On a first listen the album, now christened *Load*, sounded immense. Not just that, it was also looser and more expansive than any collection to which the band had previously put its name. Curiously *Load* sounds like the kind of album the group might have made had they never incorporated Ulrich's love of the New Wave of British Heavy Metal into their genetic code, a paean to bands beloved of Hetfield at a time before his head was turned by a permanently over-driven Danish drummer. As *Load* unfolded in New York City, attentive ears could hear the influence of (among others) Aerosmith, Ted Nugent and even Lynyrd Skynyrd.

As if this were not disorientating enough for the writers and photographers on assignment from a number of the world's leading rock publications, the appearance of the four men responsible for the songs filling the room was also disconcerting. Each musician had been shorn of his long hair, and while black clothing remained the default setting, their threads now bore the logos of designer labels rather than of army surplus stores. In addition Hammett had a silver labret dangling below his lower lip. When asked by *Kerrang!* photographer Ross Halfin to change into a suit, a 'Made In SF 11-18-62' tattoo was clearly visible across his midriff.

'When someone says "Metallica" they think heavy metal, thunder and lightning, long hair, drunk kids,' Hammett noted. 'But times have changed and the kind of person who listens to metal doesn't necessarily look like that. And why should we? Why should we conform to some stereotype that's been set way before we ever came into the picture?'

'It's been five years since we did the last record, and there's been a lot of changes in our lives over the past five years,' Ulrich added. 'We're just not kids any more. I will not bullshit anyone and stand in a black Annihilator T-shirt in a photo session, because it's not what I wear when I walk around. I don't wear a leather jacket any more, so why put one on in a photo session? This is how I look, this is how I am, this is how I'm comfortable, this is me in 1996.'

'Do people think that I go for a piss in the morning, look in the mirror and go, "Hey, I'm a rock star?" ' the drummer asked. 'That just doesn't happen. I realise how spoilt I am and I know I've been incredibly lucky, but I also know that I deal with all this incredibly well. I have lost the plot once or twice, but I've always managed to get myself back on the ground. There's no fucking fake bullshit here.'

Today, and for the next two years, Ulrich will employ the word 'greasy' to describe the new Metallica album. He'll reject suggestions that Metallica have gone 'alternative' – 'Why the fuck should we want to fit in, given the success we've had doing our own thing?' he asks, not unreasonably – and is equally dismissive when it's put to him that, having displaced metal's old guard in the Eighties, his band now stand as the dinosaur rock band against whom the next generation must rebel.

'We've had that for years,' he says with an exaggerated stage yawn. 'When we put "Fade to Black" on *Ride the Lightning* people were saying Slayer were the alternative to Metallica because we were playing this acoustic garbage. People should get off their asses to topple us. Like, here's a guitar – blow us away if you think you can.'

'When "The Black Album" came out no one knew who Kurt Cobain was,' he adds. 'Just fucking think about that for a bit.'

Mention of Nirvana's late front man turns the conversation towards alternative rock, and the band's decision to headline the coming summer's Lollapalooza festival, due to begin in Kansas City, Missouri, on June 27. Originally established in 1991 by Jane's Addiction front man Perry Farrell as the North American equivalent of such free-wheeling European events as the Roskilde and Glastonbury festivals, this was a production that had been responsible for launching artists such as Green Day, Nine Inch Nails and Rage Against the Machine into the mainstream. But whereas once Lollapalooza was the most critically adored of all the happenings of the American summer, by 1996 the 'alternative nation' suddenly appeared as short on talent as metal had at Donington just a year earlier.

Exit grunge, enter Metallica, to top a bill that featured contributions from Soundgarden, Screaming Trees, Waylon Jennings, Cocteau Twins, Rancid and the Ramones, among others. In the clamour to question the San Franciscan band's motives for accepting the Lollapalooza gig, many critics failed to notice that this compilation of artists was actually rather inspired.

'In 1992 Lollapalooza was the alternative to our tour with Guns N' Roses,' Ulrich acknowledges, 'but to me Metallica and Lollapalooza in '96 doesn't seem that strange. It was getting a little stagnant, because how "alternative" is Lollapalooza when in America the alternative is the mainstream?'

'People think way too fucking much about our motivation,' is James Hetfield's terse reply when it's suggested to him that Metallica headlining 'alternative' rock's flagship event might appear to be a calculated attempt to re-position themselves amid the churn of a changing market.

Compared to his animated drummer, Hetfield is a rather taciturn, imposing presence in the studio today – 'Lars thinks he's tough, whereas James *is* tough,' Kirk Hammett sums it up neatly. Four days before the band decamped to New York, it transpires, the singer's father Virgil passed away, and Hetfield is still processing his loss. When the singer does open up to journalists – identifying two new songs, 'Until It Sleeps' and 'Bleeding Me' as being directly inspired by his father's illness – he will do so eloquently and with no little humility.

'A lot of people die in a bus accident, and you don't get to say goodbye to them,' he notes, referring to his band's collective loss of Cliff Burton in 1986. '[In the case of my father] I got to [say goodbye]. It's tough to deal with, "Wow, I got no parents." I'll sit down with the band members, their parents, at dinner. And I'm, like, by myself. It's really freaky.'

'But Metallica is the fucking world to me,' he insisted. 'It always has been and that's not going to change. Whoever becomes my partner through life has got to deal with that. I'm married to Metallica.'

†

Metallica's sixth album was released in the US on June 4, 1996 (and one day earlier in the UK). In an inspired piece of guerrilla marketing the group conspired to launch the album with three free shows, outside Tower Records stores in the Bay Area cities of San Jose, Concord and Sacramento, announced on local rock radio stations that same day. Though bureaucracy scuppered the Concord show – with Q Prime being unable to secure the necessary noise permits – the appearances in San Jose and Sacramento went ahead as planned, and saw the world's biggest metal band pulling up into shopping mall parking lots in both cities in order to hammer through a six-song set played on the back of a flat-bed truck for disbelieving fans. As those same fans poured into the record shops to obtain a freshly minted copy of *Load* for themselves, James Hetfield watched on like a proud parent.

'You know, when everyone's stopped talking about fucking haircuts and make-up and all the other shit, there'll just be the album,' he noted.

In truth, though, many fans formed their initial opinions about *Load* before even hearing a note of the music contained within. On the album's inner sleeve Metallica appeared in tailored shirts, eye-liner and – in Lars Ulrich's case – a fur coat Liberace might have rejected for being too ostentatious. The iconic logo

Hetfield had first scrawled out on school exercise books had been altered too. Where, many fans wondered, have 'our' Metallica gone?

From the album's opening notes, it is immediately evident that in the second decade of their recording career Metallica were bound for new horizons. And when Hetfield bellows 'Now it's time to kiss your ass goodbye' one minute into the chest-beating, bar-brawl swagger of 'Ain't My Bitch', it is equally clear that the band is not about to apologise to followers old or new for this decision.

For all that it divided Metallica's audience, one accusation that cannot be levelled at *Load* is that its creators opted to play safe. From its striking, hipster cover – a photograph by Brooklyn-born artist Andres Serrano, created by mixing the artist's own semen and bovine blood between two sheets of Plexiglas, intended to convey the exhilarating pain of rebirth – to the photographs within and on to the songs themselves, this is an album wholly encumbered by respect for Metallica's personal heritage. From the Southern gothic atmospherics of 'Until It Sleeps' to the sparse, plaintive, country-style drawl of 'Mama Said', there is a clear willingness to experiment and expand, a conscious decision to break free of old formulae. At its best – on the epic 'The Outlaw Torn', the slow-burning, seething 'Bleeding Me' and first single 'Until It Sleeps' – *Load* is the sound of men putting away childish things, a daring and liberating re-imagining of Metallica's none-more-bleak worldview. When Hetfield addresses the passing of his father on 'Until It Sleeps' – his brusque roar softened to sing 'It grips you, so hold me, it stains you, so hold me' – Metallica have never sounded more bruised or human. And when 'Bleeding Me' opens with the new day rising optimism of Hetfield's belief that 'I'm digging my way, I'm digging my way to something, I'm digging my way to something better', the band's capacity for reinvention appears limitless and impossibly thrilling.

The problem with *Load*, however, is that these masterful epics are surrounded by much that is mundane and mediocre. '2 x 4' is shamefully weak, a My First Riff garage boogie that should have never have been developed beyond use as a finger-loosening exercise at sound check. The plodding 'Cure' is equally uninspired, the promise offered by a menacing spoken word intro dissipating quickly in a quagmire of lyrical clichés and directionless chugging. Worse still is 'Ronnie', a strong contender for the worst song recorded by Metallica in the Nineties, which manages to take an intriguing subject (a shooting at a school in Washington State in 1995) and somehow transform it into a sub-Skynyrd redneck rumble. It's hard to imagine how months of trawling through Hetfield's riff tapes allowed this achingly tedious, fingers-in-the-belt-loop stomp to ever surface.

While it's true that much of the album benefits from a little distance – 'King Nothing' and 'Hero of the Day' are much, much better songs than anyone gave them credit for in the summer of 1996 – the inescapable truth is that Metallica's sixth album is handicapped by its authors' inability, or more accurately, unwillingness, to pare back the material at their disposal.

Up to this point in their career, Metallica had never written a song which *didn't* end up on a Metallica album. Prior to *Load*, Lars Ulrich's keenly developed ear for a home-run-riff equated to a batting average higher than any other band of their type. But with no one to oppose and follies to indulge, questions other than 'How can we best interpret this collection of songs?' were allowed to enter the equation. One wonders, too, whether the feel-good fecundity of the sessions at The Plant caused the usually meticulous Bob Rock to feel the love rather than hear the noise. If not, then one wonders just why his normally forensic A&R instincts were as blunted as the evidence on *Load* would suggest.

Despite a cache of commanding songs and a position atop the rock food chain, with *Load* Metallica (at least in part) succumbed to ignoble failure. With the 78-minute-59-second album debuting at no. 1 in the UK, the US (a position it would hold for three weeks) as well as in Australia and eight other countries, the full impact of this mis-step was not immediately apparent. But as weeks turned into months the notion that metal's most unstoppable force might be fallible after all was hard to ignore.

Almost as hard to ignore was Perry Farrell. As Metallica's tour headlining the Lollapalooza bill hovered into view, Farrell attempted to distance himself from the monster he had created by telling everyone who would listen that Metallica's stewardship of the festival would herald the death of nothing less than the alternative nation. A gathering designed to celebrate diversity and fringe music, he argued, should not have at its core a main-stage line-up comprised solely of white men who played guitars.

Given that in previous years Lollapalooza had witnessed acts as diverse as Ice Cube, The Jesus and Mary Chain, Nick Cave & The Bad Seeds, Sinéad O'Connor, Lush, George Clinton and Boredoms, it was hard to disagree with Farrell's point, though Ulrich was keen to shift the blame for the line-up elsewhere.

'We didn't make the bill,' he protested. 'If it was up to me I'd have Oasis, Tom Waits, George Michael, Buddy Guy . . . there'd be no barriers at all. I keep telling people that this isn't about Metallica taking over Lollapalooza.'

'As it was told to us, they'd specifically asked for us to be included,' Soundgarden guitarist Kim Thayil counters. 'I like to think that's that true, but, of course, people in this business tell you all sorts of things so you never really know for sure. But what I do know is that it was a great bill, a fantastic bill. We already knew Metallica – we'd hung out with them over the years and played with them as well [at the 1991 Day on the Green festival] – but you also had the Ramones – I mean the Ramones! Tens of thousands of people every day were able to see the Ramones. How amazing is that? And of course you had Screaming Trees,

Rancid, I think the Cocteau Twins were on the bill [at the behest of Kirk Hammett] . . . it was just a really exciting and imaginative bill.'

Of the four members of Metallica, the bohemian, intuitively open-minded Hammett was the man most attuned to the spirit of the festival. The guitarist had attended at least one Lollapalooza show every summer since its inaugural staging in 1991 and had actually jammed onstage with both Primus and Ministry. Lars Ulrich and Jason Newsted pointed to their own busy schedules to explain why they hadn't previously attended, while James Hetfield surprised no one by making it known that this liberal, alternative road-show was not his natural habitat.

'I saw some pictures of a guy [a member of the Jim Rose Circus Sideshow] hanging a rock off his dick.' Hetfield explained. 'I thought, "I don't need to see that."

'I don't understand the elitism of it all,' Hetfield added dismissively. 'I thought the whole thing about it was supposed to be weird shit going on. The part I like most is we're hated again. I kind of miss that. People like us too much now.'

When the tour finally started at the Longview Lake, Kansas City, on June 27, it was hard to escape the feeling that much of the pre-Lollapalooza hype had been generated purely to shift tickets, especially when, on the eve of the opening date, the *Lawrence Journal-World* newspaper in Arizona reported that the Tucson stop on the tour had sold only 3,000 of its 50,000 tickets in its first week. But so much hot air and blinding light left Metallica unmoved. The quartet rolled through the twenty-two shows as they always did, in a self-contained caravan, with their own production, lights, crew and backstage area. Needless to say, the Metallica faithful turned up in their thousands. When *Billboard* magazine ran its weekly Boxscore Top 10 Concert Grosses column in its August 24, 1996 issue Lollapalooza had two dates in the Top 10 – with the July 30 show at The Gorge in Washington State having sold all 20,000 tickets (for a gross of $700,000) and the July 17 show in Phoenix grossing over $600,000 at the box office with over 17,000 tickets sold in a 22,000-capacity venue. The view from the Metallica camp as it rolled back home towards California was clear: 'Crisis? Behave.'

'There was a kind of feeling in 1995 that Lollapalooza was kind of *our* festival, because we'd played it that first year,' says Kim Thayil. 'By that I kind of mean that there was still this division between the kind of world that Metallica were seen to represent and the kind of world that we were seen to inhabit. But I think that year's [event] really went a long way to breaking down those walls, and it did so in an organic and natural manner. There was nothing forced about it. It was so great. And of course as you get older you realise that these divisions are meaningless anyway, and I think looked at in hindsight that bill makes such perfect sense. I'm very proud to have been a part of it.'

4 — CARPE DIEM BABY

As the sun signals noon on a late summer afternoon in Paris, no member of Metallica has seen the morning. For one of this book's authors however, it had been an early start. At 6 a.m. at Waterloo Station a Eurostar train bound for the Gare du Nord in the City of Light awaited, and so too did an audience with Metallica.

The band's hotel is in the centre of the city, and is a place of hushed magnificence. It has by now been a very long time since Metallica slummed things, although like their presence in the mainstream itself, the sight of their physical selves in five-star lodgings can sometimes appear incongruous. Despite having been a millionaire for a number of years, on the road in the US in support of 'The Black Album' James Hetfield could still be heard complaining about the cost of a grapefruit breakfast – $14! – in the kind of hotel where menus comprise a single sheet of paper tucked into a firm leather folder. When he swaggered down to the hotel bar on that same tour and in this very city – dressed as usual in his de rigueur uniform of black – he was told by the maître d' that to be served an overpriced beer he would first have to put on a tie. Informed that the front man was not in possession of a tie, in an exchange of Jeeves-esque condescension beloved of maître d's the world over, Hetfield was loaned one – a pink number. With perfect insouciance, this 'Leader of the Free World' put on the tie and was thus served with a drink. Moments later an American patron who *did* appear entirely at home in the lap of five-star luxury approached Hetfield and told him that he didn't 'have to go to this extreme to look ridiculous' and that he '[looked] like a child'. As the stranger returned whence he had

come, Hetfield muttered, 'Wear a tie, don't wear a tie. Fuck you.
I'll come down here naked next time.'

(A seasoned world traveller from childhood, Lars Ulrich,
naturally, is the member of Metallica most comfortable amid
such finery. This said, in years to come the drummer will instruct
his handlers to book him into Claridge's, London's most exclusive
hotel, with the words, 'I want to stay at Selfridges.')

In one of the two-Michelin-starred restaurants here, a starter
of carpaccio of beef costs thirty francs, and a main course of pasta
no bigger than a golf ball carries a price equivalent to that of
a Fabergé egg. Fortunately such gastronomic sophistication –
entirely lost on a twenty-five-year-old music journalist – is on
Metallica's tab, as it is on Metallica's time. Because when one finds
oneself in Metallica's orbit, time belongs to them, and them only.

Hammett, Hetfield, Newsted and Ulrich convene gradually
on the hard floors of the vast expanse that is their hotel lobby.
The band may be currently on tour in Europe, but after each
show the musicians return by private jet to this spot. It is a rather
old-fashioned way of touring, and one practised by only the most
exalted of groups. The practice was – inevitably – conceived by
Led Zeppelin in the Seventies, who after any concert within a
two-hour flight of Los Angeles would return to the Hyatt Hotel
– 'The Riot House' – on Sunset Boulevard in order to partake in
the kind of antics that are still being spoken of forty years later.

Outside Metallica's hotel there stands a coach. Security men
– bodyguards – stand discreetly on the street as their four charges
ascend the steps at the vehicle's side door. Hetfield, dressed in a
long-sleeved T-shirt that has a bastardised Coca-Cola logo and
the word 'Satan' on the front, sits alone on a double seat. He
is approached by Hammett. The pair swap stories about the
quantity of alcohol each man had drunk the previous evening,
at separate engagements. From the front of the vehicle an engine
purrs into life and as the fifty-two-seat coach inches its way into

the glacial crawl of Saturday traffic, Metallica's working day has officially begun.

The sights roll by. The Eiffel Tower stands imperious in the distance. In two years' time France is to host the football World Cup, and as the coach passes by the partially constructed shell of the Stade de France one of the band's minders pushes his face up against a coach window and in a pronounced London accent tells all that this is the place where England are going to win the World Cup. As the throb of Paris cedes ground to the city's outskirts, the coach picks up speed en route to its destination, a private airport at which waits Metallica's private jet.

For the visiting journalist, the experience is at first intimidating. Travelling with a band whom one has never before met can be a disconcerting experience, especially if that band is a personal favourite. Perhaps if the group were younger, or less well known, it would be easier to impose oneself upon them in the hope of at least giving the impression that you were not just A. N. Other music journalist. But this is Metallica.

Today's flight is bound for Belgium, where this evening the quartet will appear at the Flanders Expo arena in the city of Ghent. As French immigration officials board the aircraft in order to inspect each passenger's passport, hundreds of miles away a crew of a hundred people are occupied with the ten-hour task of assembling an 'in-the-round' stage the size of an ice hockey rink and a lighting rig that weighs twenty-seven tons. This caravan is transported from city to city in nineteen trucks and carries with it its own generators, as the venues lack the kind of juice required to energise such a spectacle. Speaking of which, each night the show concludes with what appears to be a technical calamity, where lighting trusses collapse to the ground and a technician hurtles across the stage consumed by flames. In the pre-Internet age this frankly stunning sight excites and astonishes up to 15,000 people every time the band performs.

In Paris the plane prepares for take-off. But really this is a plane in the sense that the TARDIS is a police phone box. Inside, the aircraft is partitioned into two living rooms; a communal area towards the front – in which James Hetfield sits in a spacious armchair – and a more private dwelling towards the rear. Fridges appear to have been stocked by the patron saint of alcoholism. As the aeroplane taxis onto the runway, Metallica dare their English guest to stand up during take-off, knowing full well that the laws of physics will compel him to hurtle backwards towards the rear of the vehicle. This invitation is politely declined. Uninterested either way, Hetfield leafs through a music magazine. He happens upon a piece about Soundgarden front man Chris Cornell that features a quote about how on the band's recent Lollapalooza tour Metallica opted to play 'secondary' cities in order that they could play larger metropolises on their own arena tour. Reading this, Hetfield mutters the words 'dumb ass'.

With the plane now airborne and level, the Metallica front man retreats to the plane's second room to answer questions posed by a journalist who, at this point, is consumed by nerves. Despite a strong opening, the general consensus regarding the recently released *Load* album is no longer emphatically positive. Photographs of Kirk Hammett wearing eye-liner and of the lead guitarist French-kissing Lars Ulrich have not been well received. Whispers float through the air that potential second night 'holds' in venues across Europe have not been booked. Regardless of the overall creative success of Metallica's sixth studio album – the results of which are varied – there can be little doubt that its propulsion away from the sound of 'The Black Album' is evidence of a band that still possesses a restless and beating artistic heart. But it is also undeniable that for the first time, at least publicly, dissension has begun to smear the greasepaint of Metallica's public face. There is no surer sign of this than Ulrich's claim that his band was a metal act 'eight or nine years ago' – surely the clue was in the name – while Hetfield himself says 'absolutely' the opposite.

Asked if this represented a genuine difference of opinion, the front man answers, 'Yup.' He adds, 'It's okay to disagree in the press. I think one thing and [Ulrich and Kirk Hammett] think another. I think they're afraid to be called heavy metal and I'm really not afraid of that. People call you what they will anyway. On [*Master of*] *Puppets* it was "Are you a thrash metal band?" So I think the reason they're afraid of it is that it puts you in a hole. I say we're a heavy metal band, but we're also a rock band, we're a ballad band, a crushin' fuckin' slow Sabbath [type] band. We've got so many parts to Metallica and I'm not afraid to be called any of the fuckin' things.'

In print, James Hetfield sounds irritable here, perhaps even angry. But he isn't. Eating a bowl of breakfast cereal served to him by the aircraft's one stewardess, he is laconic and even droll. On the subject of Kirk Hammett's current 'Cuban pimp' look, the front man says he thinks maybe Kirk has lived in San Francisco a little too long. On the charge made by Pantera front man Phil Anselmo – whose own band's *Far Beyond Driven* (1994) set stole the crown from 'The Black Album' as being the heaviest record ever to attain the no. 1 spot on the US *Billboard* Hot 200 – that Metallica had lost both their teeth and their way, the response is 'I guess he's run out of fucking comedy material' and that anyway 'coming from a man who just fuckin' OD'd [Anselmo had recently had a substantial mishap with a vial full of heroin] it doesn't sound like he's got his shit together too well', an observation that caused its author to laugh, and to laugh hard.

'I can understand that [Anselmo] maybe doesn't like the record,' comes the more considered opinion. 'But what I can't understand is why he wants to talk about us at a Pantera show.'

But if Hetfield was able to dismiss Phil Anselmo with a forearm smash and the words '[what he has to say] doesn't really bother me too much', on the wider subject of an uncommonly lukewarm reaction to *Load* on the part of Metallica's larger constituency, the front man suddenly found that he had more meat, and more gristle, upon which he is forced to chew.

At first the topic is met with a resonant chuckle and the observation that 'in our business – as with any business to do with entertainment – there are going to be people who slag you and who don't like everything you do.' But this rather boilerplate response is quickly embellished by the admission that 'yeah, when someone starts slagging you off when they don't really know what the fuck they're talking about, we can't really write a letter back to every fuckin' guy explaining and justifying what you're doing in your fuckin' life, you know? If they've taken the time to sit and slag you, then I guess they must be pretty fuckin' bored in their [own] life. So we're getting slagged for some of the things we're doing. But we've been slagged before; this isn't a new thing. When "Fade to Black" came out on *Ride the Lightning*, it was like "Oh, you've sold out!" How many times can you sell out? I think some of these people think we've sold out on every record we've done.'

A generation on from the afternoon when Hetfield spoke these words above the Franco-Belgian border, they still carry the authority of a man who is convinced to the point of defiance regarding the course on which Metallica was set. In this he was largely, if not entirely, justified. And for all the talk about a disappointed and at times dismayed fan base, during its initial residency on the *Billboard* Hot 200 *Load* still sold in excess of four million copies, seven million worldwide. In fact Hetfield might well have answered every charge put to him aboard a private jet he personally co-owned with a simple, three-word response: 'Crisis? What crisis?'

In the intervening years, however, and benefiting from the blessing of hindsight, Hetfield's opinion on *Load* had not so much hardened as calcified. A band 'absolutely has to evolve, but let's have it naturally,' he says, adding that for him this period in Metallica's history 'didn't seem natural'.

'Why did we need to reinvent ourselves?' comes the question. 'What's wrong with what's going on here? [We were] trying to be something we weren't, I would say [and this stylistic change of gear] confused us even more musically . . . On *Load*, we tried to mix a bit of this and a bit of that and it just didn't seem to work. It had long songs that were just ploddy and went nowhere. There's quite a few great songs [on *Load*]' but they could have been greater.

'Lars and Kirk drove on those records. The whole "we need to reinvent ourselves" topic was up [for discussion]. I'm a team player most of the time and I know Jason and I did not agree [with] what was going on. But if we're going to make this work, let's [all] get into it and try and make this work. But it was very image-based. Image is not an evil thing for me, but if the image is not you then it doesn't make much sense to me. I'm okay playing a role where I'm acting, and doing something "cool" in a video, but not on the record itself. I think they were after a U2 kind of vibe, the reinvention of Bono, him doing his alter-ego thing. But I couldn't get into that. The whole "now in this photo shoot we're going to [look like] seventies glam rockers". Like what? I would say half – *at least* half – the pictures that were to be in the [CD] booklet, I yanked out. The whole cover thing, the whole image, it went against what I was feeling.'

For Metallica the first seeds of disunity had now been sown.

✝

Two months to the day after Metallica flew from Paris to Ghent, the band was in London. The quartet had flown in from Utrecht in Holland to play a part in the inaugural MTV Europe Awards, a live transcontinental event presented by ex-Take That singer

Robbie Williams – at the time an artist similarly occupied with what for him was the ultimately overwhelmingly successful matter of reinventing himself – and staged at Alexandra Palace.

Despite having twice been gutted by fire since its construction in 1873, 'Ally Pally' remains an architectural wonder positioned majestically on top of a hill that affords magnificent views of London's eastern corridor. In 1936 the building, erected to rival south London's Crystal Palace, became the site of the first live BBC television broadcast, the transmitter of which still points skyward to this day. Sixty years on and the 'People's Palace' was once more the site of a 'Televisual Event' – albeit one of a more specialist kind. For Metallica, as for every artist present that evening, the brief was simple: turn up, nibble canapés in the same room as Simply Red, The Fugees, Smashing Pumpkins and Oasis, play their single – in this case 'King Nothing' – and have your music broadcast live to an entire continent of viewers. What could possibly go wrong?

Plenty, as it happens. Metallica's sound man, 'Big' Mick Hughes, first learned of his employers' change of plan when he was summoned to the group's dressing room and asked the times not of 'King Nothing' but of two other, distinctly off-piste compositions. Come the evening itself, Hughes was the only person who had any idea of just what was about to be unleashed. Moments before the San Franciscans take to the stage the audience is 'treated' to a backstage link from English comedian Julian Clary. An otherwise talented performer, at the MTV Europe Music Awards Clary carries himself with the air of a man who believes himself to be above it all. As his in-ear monitor informs him that Metallica's short set is about to begin, he offers the viewing public a dismissive flap of the back of his hand and the words, 'Get on with it now, it won't be long and we can go home.'

Metallica are now onstage in a live broadcast. The camera glides over the heads of the people in the main hall and settles on

James Hetfield. As it does, the front man leads the band not into
'King Nothing' but instead into four minutes' worth of music
with lyrics that cover infanticide, bestiality, hebephilia, rape,
drug use, one use of the word 'cunt' and several variations of
'fuck' and 'fucking'.

'I've got something to say,' he sings as the band smash into
their cover of the Misfits' gloriously tasteless 'Last Caress', 'I killed
your baby today [and] it doesn't matter much to me as long it's
dead.' This established, Hetfield then goes on to reveal 'I raped
your mother today.' In little more than ninety seconds 'Last
Caress' is done, but Metallica are not. Leaning into the microphone, Hetfield serves up a rhetorical question for the millions
of by now open-mouthed viewers from Stockholm to Sicily. 'So
fuckin' what?' he snaps, before turning his head in order to deposit
a mouthful of phlegm on the Alexandra Palace stage. Faster, clearly,
than the technicians in the MTV VT truck outside can cut to an
unscheduled commercial break, Metallica are now headlong into
their cover of the Anti-Nowhere League's impossibly offensive 'So
What'. As if spitting loose a mouthful of broken teeth, Hetfield
informs everyone that 'I've fucked a sheep, I've fucked a goat, I
rammed my cock right down its throat' before asking, 'So what?
So what? So what, so what, you boring little cunt.' As the song
smashes to its conclusion – in front of an audience in which a
number of people are holding sunflowers – Hetfield throws his
microphone to the ground and without a by-your-leave Metallica
have gone. As everyone watching asks themselves, 'Did that really
happen?' MTV finally cuts to the commercial break its controllers
wished had begun five minutes earlier.

At least in principle Metallica's exhilarating outburst on
a television broadcast that was no more likely to permit foul
language than was Songs of Praise would be a moment for which
they are still celebrated, if only because rebellion for its own
sake is still worth the candle. But after being caught flat-footed,

MTV quickly regained control of the situation; the innumerable repeats of the 1996 MTV Europe Music Awards were excised of Metallica's contribution. On the whole the channel had fortune on its side. The band themselves made nothing whatsoever of the incident and did not speak of it (or were not asked about it) in the press. To go with this, at the time MTV was at best a fringe channel in the UK. And with the Internet not yet a widely used tool of instant communication, those in mainland Europe that did see the original broadcast didn't think anything of keeping their thoughts to themselves. Tallied up, these factors mean that one of the most explosive moments of the group's career went unnoticed by even their most hardcore devotees.

But while at Alexandra Palace Metallica proved that, as with artists from Pete Townshend to John Lydon, it was unwise to believe that they were as yet fully house-trained, elsewhere the group continued on a march that to many spoke of premature middle age. In the summer of 1997 Metallica returned to The Plant studios in Sausalito, California, to finish recording the songs that had not featured on *Load* the previous year. With producer Bob Rock once more attempting to inspire his charges, Metallica secreted themselves in this wood-panelled studio emerging exactly three months later with thirteen completed songs. This collection, fittingly, would be called *Reload*.

Preceded by the single 'The Memory Remains', *Reload* was introduced to its waiting public on November 17, 1997, and one day later in the US (where albums are released on a Tuesday). Fans of the band may well have been thinking, 'We wait five years for a new Metallica studio album and two come along more or less at once,' but at the same time the volcanic expectations that preceded the release of *Load* were not repeated here. Metallica's constituents were not jaded, but as a whole neither were they quite the swivel-eyed fanatics that had galloped to record shops in 1993 to drop £75 on the *Live Shit: Binge & Purge* box set.

This, though, seemed to Lars Ulrich just fine.

'I've stopped trying to calculate anything,' he said on the subject of how he expected *Reload* to be received by listeners who at this point were still a number of weeks away from hearing it. 'I can't predict or hope or wish any more for anything. I don't know what anybody else is thinking about anything. I think the only difference between me now and a few years ago is that I'm a lot less concerned with what people think and I'm also a lot less interested in defending Metallica, or trying to get people to understand my way of looking at [the subject]. As you probably know, I used to spend a great deal of time explaining the way we looked at certain things and all this stuff. I'm not so bothered about doing that any more.'

Coming from the mouth of the normally irrepressible Ulrich, such apparently phlegmatic sentiments sound forlorn and even despondent. That a man who just years earlier was happy – determined, even – to conduct no fewer than six interviews a day before hopping onstage in order to tub-thump his way through a three-hour set of fiendishly complicated music should be reduced to such apparent apathy is striking. It might be that the drummer was simply having a bad press day, but if so this was the first one on record. It could be that the Dane was simply fatigued by the endless questions about Metallica's changing nature. But then such questions had been chasing him for years, and when they were not he would happily chase *them*. Could it be, then, that Ulrich's despondency is informed by a lack of confidence in his band's new material?

The real problem faced by Metallica during the period of *Load* and *Reload* was not that the band misplaced their mojo for writing songs, but rather that the sheer volume of material recorded for both albums meant that the wood was lost to the trees. The band's Achilles heel wasn't so much the writing, but rather the total absence of editing. The logic was this: that Metallica had

written and recorded twenty-seven songs for two studio albums
– they even allowed Jason Newsted to feature as co-writer on one
song – and so they were going to release twenty-seven songs over
two albums even if the weaker material sapped the strength of
the listener's capacity to appreciate the stronger tracks. Had the
best songs from both albums been compiled into one release –
although the sounds of both albums are quite different from each
other, a point never made – then the resulting CD would surely
have been a collection about which people still enthuse today.
But of course, this was never considered.

'I'm an artist and I don't write shitty songs,' was Ulrich's
chuckled response to the notion that a spot of judicious editing
might have been in order. On the specific point that *Load* and
Reload would have be better served in unity as one shorter
album Ulrich conceded that that was 'an interesting idea', before
admitting, 'It wasn't one we ever considered.' At this point in the
conversation Metallica's English PR appears on the line to tell the
journalist that Lars might have to leave the line soon as he is in
fact in make-up at the video shoot for 'The Memory Remains'.
His response is quick.

'I'm not in make-up! Real men don't wear make-up!'

Reload features no songs that are as awful or as acutely
misjudged as '2 x 4' or 'Ronnie', but it does feature moments
so stodgy that one wonders whether it is intended to be listened
to or used to grout the bathroom. That its overall feel is more
unified than its predecessor means it doesn't shift moods like a
day-release patient who has forgotten to bring his medication
to the family picnic: this is compromised, however, by the fact
that at an over-long seventy-eight minutes the collective whole
is boring.

This, though, is the bad news first. In places *Reload* carries
much that is good and some that is great. Opening track 'Fuel'
kicks out the jams in a manner that suggests this might be the

start of something rather special indeed. And for Metallica, most unusual. Instead of first wading through forty-eight bars of riffs and drum fills, the song begins with James Hetfield's voice urging, 'Give me fuel, give me fire, give me that which I desire.' Ostensibly a song about one man's appetite for petrol fumes and speed, this is not a subject matter that augurs well for those who viewed Metallica as being the one metal band who could be relied upon not always to be thick. But Hetfield knows better than many that it is not a song's subject that counts so much as the manner in which the subject is conveyed. And as the front man seems to literally *spit* out the words 'turn on beyond the bone, swallow future, spit out home, burn your face upon the chrome', the listener is reassured by the finesse with which he transcends so many obvious pitfalls.

The peaks of 'Fuel' are matched by 'The Memory Remains' (which features a guest vocal contribution from an alarmingly broken-voiced Marianne Faithfull) carried aloft by an intangibly precise sense of finality and foreboding. Two songs later Metallica revisit their past in the form of the not encouragingly titled 'Unforgiven II'. While not repeating its predecessor's glory, it nonetheless showcases how in the years since the release of 'The Black Album' its creators had learned to arrange their music with subtlety and depth when circumstances required this. Elsewhere, despite presumably attempting to coin the worst song title in the history of recorded music, 'Carpe Diem Baby' proves just how effective Metallica could be at merging verses and choruses into one rather minimalist whole, not least when attempting to stretch their own ideas beyond their natural limits.

Most impressive, and most unusual, of all is 'Low Man's Lyric', a song which begins in a restrained manner and stays that way for the seven minutes and thirty-seven seconds it takes to make its point. To a melody that is more folk music than heavy metal, and to instrumentation that includes the sound of a hurdy gurdy, Hetfield tells a never quite in-focus tale of acute loss and inevitable and continued personal failure. 'The trash fire is warm,' he reveals, adding, 'but nowhere [is] safe from the storm.' As the song progresses it seems as if this pitiful and forlorn figure might have found a chance of redemption. But, no, this isn't to be, with the fault lying with the narrator and him alone. 'So you bring this poor dog in from the rain,' he says of whoever it may be that has attempted to lessen his burden, 'though he just wants right back out again.'

With the release of *Reload* the debate continued as to whether Metallica were still equipped to deliver music of the quality to which they had put their name in the past. But while the voices in this debate rose to a clamour louder than anything on *Kill 'Em All*, few seemed interested in the state of the band's lyrics. Those who did care to consider this would see that on *Reload* Hetfield's ability with a pen was soaring. On 'Prince Charming' (which, with a chorus cribbed almost wholesale from 'The Four Horseman', is far from a musical classic), he takes the unspecified and threatening *other* witnessed in songs such as 'Harvester of Sorrow' and 'Sad But True' and bestows upon it more identifiable characteristics. 'The marks inside your arms spell me, spell only me' he reveals, continuing, 'I'm the nothing face that plants a bomb and strolls away.' On 'The Memory Remains' Hetfield is once again concerned with death and madness, but this time in the form of the declining fortunes of one once famous. As a 'nowhere crowd [cries] the nowhere tears of honour', a fading starlet raises a cigarette 'up to lips that time forgets while the Hollywood sun sets behind [her] back'. As all this unfolds, the lyric describes a band playing somewhere in the distance as a life recedes 'ash to ash, dust to dust, fade to black'. That Hetfield could manipulate words into arresting couplets had been evident since 'Battery' in 1986. But on *Reload* his capacity for conjuring up specific and often deeply moving images is often exquisite.

When *Reload* was released just weeks before Christmas in 1997, however, the talk was all about stagnation. Even *Kerrang!*, normally the band's most reliable of tub-thumping supporters, saw fit only to afford the album a tepid three-K (out of five) review.

'I don't read the *Kerrang!*s of the world every week,' Lars responded, unconvincingly. But on the subject of his group's changing sound he remained typically resolute, saying, 'I think that, if anything, hopefully Metallica will be looked upon and remembered as [a group] that didn't have their guard up in the way that other hard rock bands [did], and that as we went through all these different metamorphoses – whether people liked them or not – they were pure and natural and were the honest thing to do . . . [but] I am surprised at people's surprise over some of the things that have happened to us over the last couple of years, because I thought we always wore all those potential changes and all that stuff on our sleeves. Us going away for five years [from the recording studio following the making of 'The Black Album'] what the fuck did they expect?

'But I have to tell you,' he continues, 'that I do like the fact that people have a problem with what we're doing, because that causes debate and when debate starts then people sit and talk about all different types of things and then hopefully something good will come out of that debate. I kind of welcome that and I think it's healthy in an incredibly stagnant hard rock scene of 1997. And if we're the ones that end up pushing those envelopes and getting people to look at some of these things – not necessarily to agree with all of the points [Metallica are making] but at least respecting or acknowledging different points of view – then I think that's really healthy.'

†

Despite its tepid critical reaction, *Reload* still found millions of friends. It was the third Metallica album in succession to debut at no. 1 on the *Billboard* Hot 200 and, as with its predecessor, sold a not insubstantial four million copies to American listeners during its initial run (and, again, seven million copies throughout the world). Of course, compared to the band's monolithic fifth studio album, this was relatively small beer. But 'relatively' is the operative term. With the exception of Def Leppard's blockbusting *Hysteria* – an album which in North America actually *exceeded* the sales of its similarly ubiquitous predecessor, *Pyromania* – virtually all bands who spent time in the stratosphere on one album inevitably saw their circumstances reduced on subsequent releases.

And anyway, as the drummer-as-spin-doctor was on hand to explain: he thought that 'if "The Black Album" came out today I don't think it would do as much as *Load* [or *Reload*] did. I don't think there's as many people that listen to rock music as in 1991, 1992 and 1993. That's definitely a fact. Rock music is a dying breed. It's that simple.'

Of course, reports of rock's demise have over the years been innumerable and, at least at this time, invariably premature, something which Lars Ulrich – ever the keenest student in the class – should have understood. That said, a glance about the guitar-strewn mainstream of North American and European rock music at this time does suggest a strong case for despondency. In platinum terms the pop-punk movement that had been elected by the youth of America to replace the darker hues of the alternative nation – time on which had been called by Kurt Cobain firing the finishing gun in 1994 – had failed to extend beyond the charms of Orange County's The Offspring and the Bay Area's own Green Day. The world's most popular guitar band of this time was arguably west London's Bush, a group comprised of nice men who made music that today is remembered by no one. In terms of metal, the pickings were even slimmer, with thrash metal now discoloured by the sepia-toned tinge of yesteryear and the movement's heirs apparent (notably Pantera and Sepultura) busy stretching the creative value of their sound while at the same time cutting its commercial cloth. A new kind of sound was beginning to emerge with groups such as Korn and Deftones, but such stirrings had yet to coalesce into a recognisable movement, let alone one that could be given a name.

Not for the last time, in this sense Metallica could count themselves fortunate. Despite this being a time when many other artists questioned the group's authority, none of them had the capacity to steal their crown. This was also the period during which Metallica's personnel found itself occupied by matters other than the band to which they had dedicated their adult lives. In 1997 both James Hetfield and Lars Ulrich became fathers for the first time – the front man to daughter Call Tee and the drummer to son Myles – developments which forced the band to pare back its annual live commitments to a relatively sparse ninety shifts. But despite a smaller invoice for jet fuel, a number of these were of totemic significance, such as a debut appearance at Madison Square Garden and a first outing at the Reading Festival, the original spiritual home of British heavy metal. To complete this set, Metallica were finally able to honour a commitment to appear on NBC's ground-breaking and prestigious *Saturday Night Live* that had been on hold since Hetfield broke his arm in a skateboarding mishap more than a decade earlier.

But if the San Franciscans themselves weren't convening in as many enormodomes as was the norm, at least the band's music was still being performed live. The Nineties were a period that saw the emergence of a curious phenomenon, that of the tribute act, without which no group can be said to be truly legendary. And Metallica were among the first bands to attract this most sincere form of flattery.

Laurence Langley's Battery may not have flown by private jet or headlined Giants Stadium in East Rutherford, New Jersey, but the little group named after the first song on *Master of Puppets* were capable surrogates. Such was the positive word emanating from clubs across the US and Canada that it reached Metallica themselves. Langley was told on more than one occasion that whenever Ulrich happened upon one of the group's flyers at a club visited after one of his band's shows, he would without fail carefully fold it and place it carefully into his jacket pocket. The two parties finally found themselves in the same room in 1994, the day before Metallica's superbly named Shit Hits the Sheds tour began its summer crawl south and west across the US. The San Franciscans and Canadians broke bread by drinking cognac in a club in Buffalo, New York.

Four years later Battery's course would collide with the band from whom they earned their living in a more sensational manner.

'I remember it was a Thursday night,' recalls Langley today. 'We got a call from our agent at the bar we were playing that night – because we didn't have cell phones back then – that our road manager took. After he'd finished speaking to whoever was on the other end of the line he waved us all over. He said, "You're not going to believe this [but] Metallica want you to open for them." And, of course, we were, like, "What? Why? What do you mean?" And he just said, "All I know is that Metallica is doing a series of shows and they want you to open up for them. I'm getting a call back on Monday with all the details." '

Langley and Battery spent the weekend longing for this news to hatch, hoping that it was true but fearing 'that it was a joke', to such a degree that they breathed not a word of the development to anyone, including their significant others. But by the flipside of that weekend the band would learn that they were to play a fundamental part in one of the most fabulous ideas to which Metallica have ever put their name.

Over the course of just seventeen days, in September 1998 the San Franciscans convened once more at The Plant and, with Bob

Rock again cracking the whip, recorded eleven cover versions by artists ranging from English gristle punks Discharge to Middle-American roots rocker Bob Seger, taking in perennial favourite the Misfits and Diamond Head, legendary turns Black Sabbath, Thin Lizzy, Lynyrd Skynyrd, obscurities from Mercyful Fate and curiosities from the hands of Blue Öyster Cult and Nick Cave & The Bad Seeds. Armed with a collection of songs that covered many different styles and techniques, the one overriding quality coursing through the sixty-five minutes' worth of covered material was a playfulness reminiscent of 1987's *Garage Days Re-Revisited*.

On the campaign trail for *Reload*, Ulrich had let it be known that it was his band's intention to release 'four albums in four years', despite the fact that not a single journalist believed him ('Lars, it took you months to finish *Reload*, and half of those [songs] were written two years ago,' was one writer's justified response). Just seven weeks after its recording, Metallica unveiled their third album in as many years. Released on November 2, 1998, *Garage Inc.* included not just its creators' most recent studio recordings, but also a second CD on which was imprinted every cover version the group had previously committed to tape, from their 1984 version of Diamond Head's 'Am I Evil?' up to and including the four songs recorded for the occasion of Lemmy's fiftieth birthday in 1995.

As a concept *Garage Inc.* is both cute and effervescent, a perfectly judged vessel in which to frame a band's own musical identity. People who work out of corner offices at major record labels would describe the collection as a 'stop-gap release'. But the loving flourishes with which Metallica stain the canvas of what is in effect a studio album in its own right elevate their creation above such dismissive phraseology.

Even so, with the album finished and soon to be on the shelves, its authors were not beholden to undertake anything more strenuous than a round of interviews and perhaps one or two music videos with which to promote it. But this being Metallica, such minimalism was unlikely to wash.

Instead, when it was suggested by Q Prime employee Marc Reiter (perhaps half in jest) that the band should help push their curious new collection towards the light by performing a short series of club concerts, an idea was suddenly on the wing. It was proposed that in order to promote *Garage Inc.* Metallica should undertake a tour of the kind of clubs in which they had not appeared for almost fifteen years.

'Any other band would say, "You're crazy!" ' recalls Reiter. ' "I'm going back to that shit hole?" [Instead] They say, "We're in!" Not only that, but [Ulrich insisted] that it's *the* club [at which the group used to play]. I'm surprised he didn't ask us to track down the bouncers and bartenders that were there then too.'

But there was a problem. In returning to 'the clubs' Metallica desired only to perform a selection of the songs from each of *Garage Inc.*'s two CDs. Those lucky enough to have secured a Wonka-Factory-rare ticket for an audience with the genre's biggest band in the most reduced of surroundings would justifiably wish to hear songs other than those originally recorded by Budgie and Discharge. Duly, Metallica and Q Prime considered the best way of appeasing the nightly clamour for songs such as 'Creeping Death' and 'Nothing Else Matters'. It was Cliff Burnstein who proposed a most delicious solution: to have a Metallica tribute band as the tour's support act.

And so it was that on November 17, 1998, Battery crossed Province lines from Quebec to Ontario in order to embark on five-date hop from Toronto to New York City by way of Chicago, Detroit and Philadelphia. The venues in which the Canadian and American bands appeared may not have been each city's most intimate – the Aragon Ballroom in Chicago posted a not exactly bijou capacity of 4,500, for one – but suffice to say that had the excursion taken place in the Internet age resale prices for each ticket would in dollar terms have exceeded the number of people gathered in each venue.

As recalled by Langley, the all-too-short tour sounds like the very best of times. Upon meeting James Hetfield in Toronto – 'Hey Battery guys! What's up?' came the greeting – Langley asked what songs his band was permitted to perform, to which the answer came, 'anything that's a Metallica original'. So for five nights Battery would open their set with 'Creeping Death' and find themselves received by Metallica's audience as if they were Metallica themselves.

'There was an unbelievable feeling of acceptance right away,' recalls Langley.

On the afternoon of the show at the State Theater in Detroit, the opening act was approached by the ever likeable 'Big' Mick Hughes who told them that as he wasn't 'getting his fix of old-school Metallica' for the rest of tour he would personally oversee their sound. Three nights later in Philadelphia Lars Ulrich told a local rock radio station that following that night's appearance at the Electric Factory they were 'going to have a little party with Battery', and that listeners should tune in to the station later that night to learn the location of this happening. As it turned out, the event took place at a two-pump petrol station at which Metallica sat at trestle tables and signed autographs for literally thousands of fans. For their part, the members of Battery were also interviewed for the radio station that broke the news of this most unusual of post-concert activity.

For the final night of the tour, on November 24, Battery found themselves at 209 West 52nd Street amid the chaos of Midtown Manhattan. Better known as the Roseland Ballroom, this was the site where fourteen years earlier Metallica had made their first appearance in the borough of Mahattan and had unleashed upon a capacity crowd of 3,200 people a set of such power and precision that the next day they were offered a record deal by Elektra Records. In the intervening years it is bizarre to think that the band played Manhattan on only two further occasions, once at the Felt Forum in 1986 and then eleven years later at this facility's larger room, Madison Square Garden. Back at the Ballroom, Metallica made their way to the stage before their allotted hour, in order to interrupt Battery's set with threats to cut off the tribute act's long 'hippie hair' with garden shears.

Just one week after it had begun, the Garage Inc. Tour (such as it was) was over. With the venue now empty, Battery were invited into Metallica's dressing room for photographs that each member still cherishes to this day. Ulrich was dressed in the robe he wears after his post-performance shower; Hammett's torso was naked save for the bandages that he still wore following an operation to remove his appendix shortly before the tour began. As the Canadians were about to leave, Hetfield told his visitors to wait just a moment. He told the group's front man, Harvey Lewis, that he had something for him, and slid across the floor a hard-bodied guitar case. Unclasping the latches, the singer opened the case and saw inside a James Hetfield signature ESP guitar replete with an autographed certificate of authenticity.

'That's for you,' said Hetfield. 'I've been using that one each night on the tour. Take it and kick ass.'

†

While the popular narrative of Metallica in their thirties is of a band that could find nothing worthy of their union's second act, a review of this, the most creatively hectic yet subsequently overlooked period of the quartet's existence, is essential. With an abundance of creativity, a willingness to explore fresh ideas, a desire to traverse new musical terrain and a devil-may-care attitude o the clamour of voices rising in protest, the San Franciscans shed themselves of old, dead skin. A number of the band's songs and calculations from this time might be below spec, but their refusal to be pinned beneath glass or preserved in aspic remains remarkable. Many among the band's audience would have loved Metallica to have conformed to type and 'gone back' – 'Why is it that people always want to "go back"?' wondered James Hetfield – to refashion 'The Black Album' or re-imagine *Master of Puppets*, but they would not have loved these efforts in the same way, or with the same incandescence as before. And while there were those who hated what Metallica became in the Nineties, this too is no bad thing: because the opposite of love isn't hate, it's indifference.

'I think the thing about Metallica during this time was that for the first time in their careers they no longer had anything to *oppose*,' says Brian Slagel, the LA-based owner of Metal Blade Records and the man whose 1982 compilation album *Metal Massacre* first brought the name Metallica (or Mettallica as it was misprinted on the sleeve) to the world's attention. 'Up until "The Black Album" they always had something that they could stand against and gun for. They were the outsiders, you know. But then they won the war and suddenly there was nothing else in their firing line. In a way I think the music they made in the Nineties is a reaction to this new reality.'

Of course, it wasn't always fun and games, and it wasn't often well received. On February 1, 1999, the band released their version of Thin Lizzy's take on Irish folk standard 'Whiskey in the Jar' and for the first time in their career garnered reviews that were not tepid but universally hostile. Faced with such a level of opprobrium, the band simply selected a number of the most vituperative reviews and published extracts from them on the single's front sleeve. Later that year, the quartet looked out from the stage at Woodstock 1999 in Rome in Upstate New York and saw a sight that looked like the Somme. Headlining the four-day event's third night, they opened their set with 'So What'. The chaos inherent in the song's lyric had already been realised in physical form. Earlier in the day Limp Bizkit had disgraced the stage, with their front man Fred Durst helping raise the temper of a crowd already agitated by poor conditions and extortionate prices for concessions (including a reported $9 for a bottle of water). As the group played songs that were soon to be described by Moby as being 'rape rock', even Durst could see that things were getting out of hand. But when he addressed the crowd with the words, 'Don't let anybody get hurt,' it was as if he was unable to stop himself: 'I don't think you should mellow out [though],' he quickly added. 'That's what Alanis Morissette had you motherfuckers do.' (Immediately after his band's set Durst was arrested but not charged.) Compared to this, Metallica's rather quotidian headline set could only really register as an afterthought, albeit one for which the group were handsomely remunerated before being spirited away from the festival site minutes after bidding those less fortunate a good evening. Twenty-fours later Woodstock 1999 concluded in a crashingly predictable fashion, with a riot that saw part of the stage set on fire and a number of sexual assaults on female audience members, including rape.

'I think [Woodstock 1999] was probably the worst gig we played all summer,' Hetfield would confess at the end of that year. 'The tempos were all fucked up, vocally there were fuck-ups [and] the stage was a piece of crap.'

But in the year that saw people obsess over a Millennium bug, the computer glitch that might cause aeroplanes to fall out of the sky and cruise missiles to take their place, Metallica once again found new ways of expressing themselves. In this case, they threw a party as though it was 1899.

Despite the assertion of Cliff Burton that '[Johann Sebastian] Bach is God', classical music was one musical genre about which Metallica had otherwise remained silent. This, though, was set to change with the seed of an idea that had been planted nine years previously by a man with whom the San Franciscans had only the slightest acquaintance.

Michael Kamen was a composer born in 1948 in New York City whose music provided the scores for films such as Terry Gilliam's *Brazil*, David Cronenberg's *The Dead Zone* and Alan Parker's *Pink Floyd The Wall*. Kamen also worked with Pink Floyd on *The Wall* album in 1979, as well as collaborating with artists such as Kate Bush, Eric Clapton, Bob Dylan and Herbie Hancock. In 1991 Kamen was invited to oversee the addition of a string section to 'Nothing Else Matters', a version of which came to be known as 'The Elevator Mix'. Assuming that was the end of that, the composer was surprised to discover on meeting the band at a subsequent awards ceremony just how enthused Metallica were about his work on what was already their most gentle song. 'You know,' he told them, 'you guys should really work with an orchestra, your music is really suited to that.' And then he bid the band farewell. Five years later, in 1997, Michael Kamen heard from Q Prime that Metallica was ready to go to work on his idea. The composer had just one question: what idea?

But Metallica, as Metallica always do, made things happen. Kamen not only scored the orchestral parts that would meld, harmonise and sometimes scrap with Metallica's own music, but he also assumed the role of conductor of the orchestra with which the three-man string and one-man percussion section would play. The orchestra of choice was the San Francisco Symphony ('SFS'), a collective that Lars Ulrich was not slow to describe as being 'one of the most respected symphony orchestras in the world'. These component parts in place, this marriage would come together with a speed and effectiveness that seems extraordinary.

It took just three days to twist the band and orchestra into one cohesive unit. In fact the first day's preparation took place without the 104 musicians that comprise the SFS, and instead centred around Metallica, Michael Kamen and producer Bob

Rock, who by now must have been contemplating just what the band was going to throw at him next. The conductor wondered aloud if 'So What' would feature as part of the set list, before improvising his own lyrics for the song. To hear a man with an ear attuned to such a degree that he is able to identify that one musician in an entire orchestra is playing 'Call of Ktulu' one half note lower than the others sing 'so fucking what . . . take your grandmother and fuck her . . .' is to get a sense of just how far removed from his natural habitat he really was. With a sense of comic timing that suggests he might have made it as a Marx Brother, Ulrich asked 'Whose fucking idea was this?'

The next day the band transferred their operation to the lovely Berkeley Community Theatre for two days of rehearsals with the orchestra. At first the two parties sound a world apart, but soon enough common ground is found, until, that is, the musicians whose names to date do not appear on the sleeves of a Metallica album are off for a legislated break. 'I'm joining their union,' says Andy Battye, James Hetfield's Rotherham-born guitar technician.

The pressure is enormous. Not only must the band and the symphony learn to play with each other through twenty-one songs – two of which, 'No Leaf Clover' and 'Minus Human', are brand new – but Metallica must also learn to conform to the time-keeping disciplines required for Michael Kamen to keep the two camps in the same musical bars, a proposition Hetfield admits is 'difficult'. But despite a ticking clock that must seem as if it has a bomb attached to it, spirits are high. Hetfield, for one, revels in his role as laconic raconteur. He'll admit that classical music didn't interest him at all and note that when Michael Kamen 'makes the sign of a pentagram [with his conductor's baton] that's when I come in'.

The next evening 3,491 people (a number of whom had attended specifically to hear the orchestra rather than the band) roar into life as 104 musicians and one conductor walk on to the stage. Thirty-four seconds later and Michael Kamen leads the musicians into a live orchestral rendition of 'The Ecstasy of Gold'. As the sound from a lone French horn hovers and hangs gallantly in the air, beneath it the other musicians begin the swell of noise that will be joined by those who have paid to be here tonight at the first sight of the four members of Metallica walking onto the Community Theatre's elegantly dressed stage.

'With the orchestra you've got so many colours with all these cool instruments going on,' says Hetfield of this four-times-in-a-lifetime experience (the group would repeat their two-night Berkeley performance with different orchestras at Madison Square Garden and Berlin's Velodrome), 'You're creating those crescendos, and the building and breaking of them in there, because live Michael Kamen was doing it. He's the guy whose [conducting] mixes live, that's his gig.' As Hetfield stepped on to the stage in Berkeley, it was to a platform busy with working musicians, a scene unlike anything with which he had previously been engaged.

'Sonically, I shut [the orchestra] out,' he says, while adding that 'visually . . . you had to be a part of that.'

'We were very adamant on that point,' he says. 'Because we didn't want the orchestra to be some backdrop behind us making noise. We wanted [them] to be part of it. So in certain songs I was sitting in [among the members of the SFS]. Jason was running by knocking music stands over, sheets [of music] flying. You could go into [one of the] sections and rock out with them a little bit.' But with all this going on, 'if I'd have [their music] in my ears too, it would have been complete sensory overload. So I didn't get to enjoy the Full Monty that night. I kind of just had to see afterward how the pieces of the puzzle came together. And it was a puzzle.'

Released just thirty-eight days before the end of the century as both a double live CD and concert DVD, *S&M – San Francisco*

Symphony & Metallica – is a collection that on paper did not threaten much but in reality delivered more than the most optimistic listener might expect. No little credit for this should go to Kamen, a man whom Kirk Hammett described as being 'for all intents and purposes a member of Metallica' for the duration of the project. Were his score heard without the accompaniment of four heavy metal musicians it would impress as a creative piece in its own right. Melded to Metallica, the music brings flavour from the band and vice versa.

It isn't all entirely convincing. The main body of 'Master of Puppets' is simply too frenetic and busy to afford the kind of space in which so many musicians might operate with any freedom. 'Enter Sandman', 'Sad But True' and (surprisingly) 'Wherever I May Roam' are little more than the sound of towering hit singles that have been flooded with strings for no real creative advantage. And while these selections are enjoyable enough, there is nothing radical, let alone definitive, on offer during these moments.

The same, though, should not be said of *S&M*'s highest peaks, the majority of which tend to come during renditions of Metallica's newer songs. 'No Leaf Clover' is a short-form masterpiece, one of the band's finest songs secreted away on an album that fans have come to think of as existing in a realm separate from other releases. Anchored by a lyric concerning misplaced optimism in the face of inevitable calamity, in sparse verse Hetfield tells of one sufficiently ebullient to 'pay no mind to the distant thunder', someone that wiser heads recognise as being a 'sucker for that quick reward', who fails to recognise that 'the soothing light at the end of [the] tunnel' is in fact 'a freight train coming your way'. The lyrics offer yet more proof that as the Nineties drew to a close Hetfield seemed some way from running dry of finding good ways to deliver bad news.

Best of all, though, comes midway through *S&M*'s second half. As heard on *Load* 'The Outlaw Torn' is a song of a determinedly hulking menace that utilises space in a manner new to its authors. Married to Michael's Kamen's score, however, the composition assumes a whole new power. Nine years earlier, in Vancouver, Bob Rock had listened to James Hetfield and Lars Ulrich's early-day demo of 'Sad But True', and hearing in it elements of the monolithic power of latter-day Led Zeppelin, declared it 'Kashmir for the Nineties.' Here, though, the producer was almost a decade premature. For it is at this point, with the assistance of the San Francisco Symphony, that Metallica finally ascend to such a level, in a song that nudges its way to just seconds shy of ten minutes. The track seems to saunter into focus, later receding into a valley between the first of just two choruses and Kirk Hammett's squalling guitar solo. At this point, remarkably little is going on as the orchestral score prepares to slowly cause a tranquil sea to bubble and froth. And as 'The Outlaw Torn' does bump its way into troubled waters, the violence this heralds is allowed to shoot out in all directions. 'You make me smash the clock and feel, I'd rather die behind the wheel,' sings Hetfield, dragging his voice across that 'die'. As the musicians go smashing into the chorus, the lyric takes the form of a warning: and a plea. 'If my face becomes sincere, beware' and 'when I start to come undone, stitch me together.'

Metallica have never sounded more powerful than this. As *S&M* closes out with a version of 'Battery', the ferocity of which sees orchestra and band duke it out like cobra and mongoose, and with backing vocals from Jason Newsted that suggest he's caught his hand in a threshing machine, the band triumphantly call time on a most imperious album, and this most unusual decade.

5 — TURN THE PAGE

In March 2000 radio stations across North America began playing a brand-new Metallica song in the middle of their day-time schedules. Audiences were informed that 'I Disappear' was to feature on the soundtrack of the forthcoming action movie *Mission: Impossible II*. It was also made public that the film's producer and leading man, Tom Cruise, had personally approached Q Prime to request an exclusive Metallica recording for a blockbuster that Hollywood's trade press were already tipping as the summer's most bankable release. If long-term Metallica fans were surprised to hear that the quartet had acceded to Cruise's overtures, where previous offers from film-makers had been rebuffed, their reaction was as nothing in comparison to the shock waves which reverberated within the Metallica camp the first time they heard their stand-alone track live on the radio. The reason? This particular version of 'I Disappear' had not been cleared for release.

Even as senior staff at the law firm of King, Purtich, Holmes, Paterno and Berliner began drafting cease-and-desist letters for immediate delivery to station managers from Anchorage to Pensacola, an internal inquiry was established to identify the source of the leak. It did not need to be said that the culprit would be punished with immediate effect.

Metallica had written, arranged and recorded 'I Disappear' in the course of just one week with Bob Rock at The Plant in December 1999. Prior to the studio session, Tom Cruise had arranged for his private jet to fly to San Francisco to collect Lars Ulrich for a personal tour of the film set in Monument Valley and had then scheduled a private screening of the film in rough-cut form. After being led by director John Woo through the film's plot, Ulrich determined that his band's contribution to the soundtrack should embody the epic scale and spectacle of the production. When their own 'rough-cut' version of 'I Disappear' appeared on US radio, Ulrich and Hetfield were still locked in discussions as to which of two versions of the song would best serve the needs of both band and film.

Beyond the question of who had leaked the recording, Q Prime were initially puzzled as to how the track had been disseminated to programme directors from coast to coast without recourse to Elektra's traditional distribution methods. The answer, when uncovered, was alarming in practice and terrifying in principle.

The song had been sourced from a new online digital distribution platform named Napster, developed by a nineteen-year-old freshman student at Boston's Northeastern University named Shawn Fanning. The teenager had written the programme in response to his college room-mate's daily complaints about the unreliability of Internet sites offering MP3 music files for download. His bright idea was to empower a community of like-minded music fans to trade digital files via a simple peer-to-peer network. Once the Napster programme was downloaded, users were plugged in to this global community and were afforded access to one another's music libraries, enabling the rapid exchange of files. Fanning's idea proved hugely popular, and in just nine months, some five million people had downloaded the programme to their own desktops, making it the fastest-growing programme in Internet history. The company's CEO Eileen Richardson proudly dubbed it 'the MTV of the Internet'. There was, of course, one crucial difference: MTV paid the artists whose videos it played a royalty. Napster did not.

The wider music industry reacted aggressively to Napster's rapid growth. On December 7, 1999, the Recording Industry

Association of America filed a lawsuit against the company, accusing it of 'operating a haven for music piracy on an unprecedented scale'.

'Napster is about facilitating piracy and trying to build a business on the backs of artists and copyright-holders,' RIAA senior vice-president Cary Sherman said in a statement released to the press.

In response Richardson refuted the RIAA's claims and maintained that Napster's primary motivation was to enable emerging artists to reach a broader audience.

'There's no chance, if an artist doesn't want their music on the Internet, that we want to put it there. Absolutely, positively not,' Richardson said. 'It would be nice if the recording industry would work with us, instead of against us. We've asked them, begged them, for a list of artists that don't want their music on the Internet – they will not, and cannot, produce it.'

Metallica became the first band to publicly confront the file-sharing platform. On April 13, Howard King filed a lawsuit in the United States District Court pitching Metallica, E/M Ventures (the partnership established between Elektra and the band in 1994) and Creeping Death Music (the quartet's publishing arm) against Napster and three American universities whose computer networks permitted the use of Napster's programme.

'Plaintiffs are the owners of copyrights in songs and sound recordings created by the recording artist known world-wide as "METALLICA",' lawyer Howard King's statement began. 'Including its first album, "*Kill 'Em All*" released in 1983, Metallica has released 9 albums, including 2 double albums and has sold more than 50 million albums through normal retail channels in the United States alone. METALLICA's 1991 self-titled album "Metallica" has sold more than 12 million copies through normal retail channels in the United States, making it the third largest selling album since the retail sales tracking service, Soundscan, was formed in 1991. "Metallica" continues to sell almost one million copies per year. Metallica has been nominated 9 times for Grammy Awards by the National Academy of Recording Arts and Sciences, winning 5 times. Until now METALLICA was compensated for the creation of its creative property, by the sales of compact discs, tapes and recordings, embodying those works and ancillary related products.'

The suit then alleged that Napster 'devised and distributed software whose sole purpose is to permit Napster to profit by abetting and encouraging the pirating of the creative efforts of the world's most admired and successful musical artists', noting that 'these acts take place without the knowledge or permission of the plaintiffs, who do not receive the compensation to which they are entitled pursuant to their copyrights.'

'With each project, we go through a gruelling creative process to achieve music that we feel is representative of Metallica at that very moment in our lives,' Lars Ulrich added in his own statement. 'We take our craft – whether it be the music, the lyrics or the photos and artwork – very seriously, as do most artists. It is therefore sickening to know that our art is being traded like a commodity rather than the art that it is. From a business standpoint, this is about piracy – aka taking something that doesn't belong to you; and that is morally and legally wrong. The trading of such information – whether it's music, videos, photos, or whatever – is, in effect, trafficking in stolen goods.'

On the afternoon of May 1, having first tipped off local and national media as to their intentions, King and Ulrich drove out to Napster's headquarters in San Mateo, California, and hand-delivered to the company thirteen boxes of paperwork listing the names of over 335,000 people who, they claimed, had pirated Metallica's original material using their software. As television cameras and digital recorders were thrust in their faces, the duo demanded that the company block these people from access to Metallica's work. That same afternoon Ulrich gave an interview to the BBC's *Money Programme* in which he laid out the fundamentals of his band's complaints and maintained that Metallica had the stomach for the anticipated fight ahead. 'If we have to start knocking on doors and confiscating hard drives, then so be it,' said the drummer. With these words, Ulrich became a hostage to fortune.

The publicity stunt backfired horribly; the backlash was as immediate as it was severe. In making a public show of criminalising 335,000 music fans – of which the vast majority were college students and fans, or at least potential fans, of his band – the drummer came across as pompous, smug and humourless, and as a bully at that. One now erstwhile supporter swiftly set up a website called PayLars.com to allow music consumers the opportunity to donate $1 for each officially released Metallica song downloaded, to 'make up for all the revenue the band thinks it's losing'. Another website created a short animated film which features a vicious pasquinade of the little Dane ranting about the injustice of online piracy while a Neanderthal-styled James Hetfield squats like a silverback gorilla and (amid bags of money) grunts 'Money good! Napster bad!'

The band's peers were no less unrelenting in their own public condemnations. 'We happen to be of the school of thought that it is nice to have more, not less fans,' The Offspring commented. 'It's not like Metallica need any more money than they've got,' said Deftones front man Chino Moreno.

'I saw that idiot from Deftones saying shit about me,' a visibly bristling drummer responded. 'Is that the best argument people can come up with? Hearing people saying that was a little annoying for a few days and now it's somewhere between funny and sad. It's sad and pathetic. Do we need more money? No, we're fine. Thank you for asking about my financial situation but I'm taken care of for ten fucking lifetimes. I'm cool, everything's fine. Is it possible this could be about something else?'

It's now June 3, and Ulrich is delivering these words while seated in the lush gardens of one of Los Angeles' most iconic and well-appointed hotels, the Sunset Marquis on Alta Loma Road. The drummer, and his band, are in Los Angeles today in order to première 'I Disappear' at the MTV Movie Awards. But such is the mounting clamour of angry voices being trained in his direction that Q Prime have taken the unusual step of flying one of *Kerrang!*'s London-based writers – now one of the authors of this book – eight time zones west in order that Ulrich might better address the issues underpinning their lawsuit to a publication that in the past had rarely been unsympathetic to Metallica's cause.

'There are very few forms of media where we can sit down like this and explain exactly what's at stake here,' the drummer explains, as he perches upon a white sun lounger adjacent to the hotel's outdoor Jacuzzi. In his hand is a packet of Camel Ultra Light cigarettes; a bottle of Evian water glistens at his feet. 'I don't care if people don't like me personally, but this is an important issue. Most of my comments on this have been reduced to thirty-second sound bites which is why [the only thing people seem to be asking is] "Do they really need more money?" '

'I read *Kerrang!* every week,' said the drummer who three years earlier claimed that he did no such thing, 'and I've seen all the comments from artists who're opposed to our stance. This Napster thing affects all artists and artists should have their own opinions. This shouldn't be about kindergarten snidey remarks. I respect the right of Billy Corgan or the guy from The Offspring or Fred Durst to give away their music for free, but please respect my decision not to. Who can argue with that?'

The interview begins in earnest with Ulrich recalling the day on which he was informed that radio stations were playing an illegally acquired work-in-progress version of 'I Disappear'.

'We had a couple of different versions of "I Disappear" and

we hadn't really decided which one we were going to go with and all of a sudden I get this call that these three or four versions of the songs are being traded around the world,' he says, his voice rising steeply. 'We felt that it was morally wrong and we had to take a stand. I find it strange that people who know Metallica, and how we like to control what's come from us, think it's weird that we're going after this. We don't pick fights, but we felt that a line had been crossed. In those situations you don't sit down and second guess the consequences or the public perception of those actions. Metallica has always been about dealing with our own shit and when somebody fucks with us we deal with it.

'It's our music, we own it, we write it, we pay for it, we should control where it goes and to whom and when,' he adds. 'That's it in a nutshell.'

Just six weeks on from the day his lawyers filed their court action against Napster, on this afternoon Ulrich will describe the case, and the intense media scrutiny to which it has been subjected, as 'a bit of a mindfuck'.

'In my wildest imagination I didn't dream that this would turn into what it's turned into in the last six weeks,' he says.

'Look, [my moods are] up and down on this every day. Some days I feel it's so overwhelming and I sit there and ask myself "Why am I doing this?" And I have to remind myself that I'm doing it because it's the right thing to do. You have to remember, this isn't just about music: the reason that music is out of the box first is that it's the shortest amount of digital information that's tradable. But, according to the information we're getting, we're probably twelve to eighteen months away from a situation where the day that a movie opens in theatres, it can be downloaded for free on computers all over the world, and the day that Tom Clancy writes a new book it'll be up on the Internet for anyone who wants it. I mean, that's fucked-up stuff. And that is a fight, I believe, worth fighting for.

'I have good days with it and bad days with it: I have days where I'm energised and days where I sit there going, "I'm a total fucking loser." But I always come back to the same point: when we believe we're right and it's the right choice we find the energy and we find the resources. And I tell you, for the last six weeks this has taken up an average of four hours of my day, doing interviews and doing research and whatever: these are four hours I could be playing with my son. It's a pain in the fucking ass, let there be no question about it.'

Talk turns to Ulrich's by now infamous May 1 trip to San Mateo. Igniting his first cigarette of the day, Ulrich exhales loudly, before attempting to explain an act the memory of which is already threatening to overshadow every scrap of goodwill ever extended to his band.

'The reason we gave Napster those names is because they asked us to provide evidence of people violating our copyright,' he explains patiently. 'We believe that Napster have the technology to find those people themselves, but their whole thing is about setting Metallica up against our fans, and that's where we feel that they're really fucking with us. They had the ability to get that information themselves. And the other thing that we believe that Napster has the ability to do, which they won't, is to block the ninety-six Metallica master recordings – not the live tracks, or the bootlegs. We know they have the technology to do that, but the problem becomes that if they let us take our songs off then everybody else, bar the Offsprings and Limp Bizkits and whoever, will take their stuff off too and then the $15 million that these venture capitalists have invested in Napster will go down the toilet. The people behind Napster aren't doing this because they have nothing to do with their time, they're doing it because one day they believe they will turn Napster into a multi-multi-multi-million dollar venture that they will profit from greatly. But the profits that they make will be dirty money.

'One of the biggest misconceptions about Metallica is this whole thing of, "We're doing it for the fans." No, we're not fucking doing it for the fucking fans, we're doing it for ourselves. The reason fans relate to what we're doing is because our music and what we do isn't [polluted by] what somebody else expects or wants from us, that's been the party fucking line from the start. Yes we sign autographs and we're accessible and we don't put ourselves on pedestals above our fans, but we don't do this for the fans.

'If anyone doesn't want to be a fan of Metallica because of this, then I'm saddened, but I'm not going to change my stance. Everybody talks about the Metallica backlash but "I Disappear" has been the most requested song on radio for five weeks and we've sold 400,000 tickets for our twelve US dates this summer, so I'm wondering if this backlash is from the same people who had fucking heart attacks when we cut our hair four years ago or when we got Bob Rock to produce "The Black Album" or when we wrote "Fade to Black" or made a record with a symphony orchestra?'

Clearly, at this point the drummer is in full flight. But while Ulrich may be right about those that are complaining about his actions, he is wrong about the nature of this complaint. It is at this point that the journalist points out to him that these are not equivalent circumstances, and not just that, but to believe that they are is to profoundly underestimate the intensity of feeling marshalled against him.

The subject of the drummer's appearance on BBC television's *Money Programme* is raised, and the resolute Dane is momentarily silent as he's told that his comment – 'If we have to start knocking on doors and confiscating hard drives then so be it' – is one of the more insane and ill-advised statements ever made by a rock musician. With the possible exception of Axl Rose, he's told, it's impossible to conceive of another rock star behaving in such an extraordinary manner.

'I've definitely said some things that are wrong and I'm aware of it, believe me,' Ulrich groans. 'I've said couple of things that I've retracted and a couple of things that I've regretted. This has been a very, very tough six weeks for me and sometimes I get irrational and say things that are out of line. I'm learning things on a daily basis. Obviously, Metallica aren't going to go out and start fucking chasing after people on that level. But at the same time, what's happening is illegal. People have all this crap about invasion of privacy: okay, so if I'm in the privacy of my own home . . . if I rape my twelve-year-old daughter in the privacy of my own home does it then make that okay? You're doing something illegal in the privacy of your own house, right? We're trying to fight this fight on many different levels. There's the legal arguments and then there's trying to educate people and try to make people understand that they're doing something that is wrong.

'Of course, there are naysayers and, of course, we realise that everybody has passionate opinions about this thing. If my music should be free to everyone, should your magazine be free to everyone who wants it? Can I call up my lawyer and ask him to work for me for free because I want him to? Where is the line here? I mean, the marketplace dictates that CDs cost $16. Do I think that's too much? Probably. Do I dictate those prices? No, I don't. And if I don't, do I have the right to just take it? I bought a Suburban [SUV] a couple of months ago and it was $43,000. If I think that $43,000 is too much to pay for that [SUV] does that give me the right to just grab the keys and steal it? Of course not.'

At this point, the conversation is temporarily stalled as ex-Take That singer Robbie Williams strolls past the outdoor Jacuzzi, greeting Ulrich and then shouting 'Metallica rock!' when the drummer asks if he has anything to say to the readers of *Kerrang!* Later the actor Billy Bob Thornton will stop by also. This is more than celebrity glad-handing, with Thornton having been photographed publicly sporting a faded Metallica T-shirt from a period long before they became famous. Later still Ulrich will boast of his friendship with actor Sean Penn and his recent skiing trip to Aspen with rap-rocker Kid Rock. It's clear, and indeed appropriate, that the drummer should feel entirely at ease in elevated company. But a flash of the boy he used to be surfaces when it's suggested that he might like to hear the thoughts of some genuine rock fans in regards to the manner in which he has conducted himself since the skirmish with Napster began.

'Believe me, I've read them all,' he laughs. '"Bugger off, Lars, and get some drum lessons" was one of the better ones.'

The idea that the online exchange of digital music files is simply the twenty-first-century equivalent of trading tape recordings, the practice of which introduced Lars Ulrich to the bands that changed his life, is given similarly short shrift by the drummer.

'Yes, but then it was from a friend or neighbour and the copies were on a shitty cassette that clearly was not up to par with the original vinyl,' he laughs. 'Now you can get perfect digital copies which are as good as the original. I can't accept that's the same thing.

'There's a lot more issues at stake here. If people grab songs from the Internet and then don't buy that record, it's going to be really tough for new artists to break through record-company channels, because when the record companies see that the sales aren't going up, they'll withdraw their support. There's two important facts here. The first is that no band has broken out from the Internet alone; the second is that in the forty-eight hours that we were monitoring what was being traded on Napster, there were 1.4 million Metallica downloads, and not one single download of a band that wasn't signed to a record label. Napster isn't really affecting our sales at the moment, and I'm not sitting here pretending that I'm on a moral crusade for the baby bands. I'm just saying that there will be a domino effect at work.

'On a deeper level this issues says a lot about where our society is at right now. People have this relationship with the Internet and think that if something is on it they have a right to it. That's wrong, it's a privilege to have that access. Why is it only people who have computers [can] have the right to free music? Should all music not be free then? Can we just throw open the doors at Tower Records and do away with the cash registers? There's some imbalances here that just make no sense.'

At this point the journalist's scheduled forty-five-minute appointment with Ulrich is at an end, and a limo is waiting at the hotel entrance to spirit the drummer off to Sony Studios in Culver City where the MTV Movie Awards will shortly begin taping. Over the course of the interview the drummer has been, by turns, defensive, bullish, arrogant, insightful, apologetic and patronising. But, sensing a certain anxiety on the writer's part as the clock ticks away, the Dane exhibits a thoughtfulness and kindness that speaks well of him. He asks whether his visitor thinks he has everything he needs for the story he must file upon returning to London, and without waiting for an answer, bounds to his feet and excuses himself to speak with a representative of his management company. In seconds he's back.

'Okay, I've told them to put Kirk [Hammett] in the other car and you can come in the limo with me so we can talk more,' he says. 'The driver will drop you back. This is important stuff, so I don't want to cut it short.'

As his car glides out of Beverly Hills, Ulrich is asked if he has any final message he might care to pass along to a young music fan who has been downloading Metallica material from Napster.

'I'd say, please respect the fact that we have these ninety-six master recordings of original songs that are available on our CDs and don't download them,' he answers. 'You can give the middle finger to me and do it, and think I'm a fucking dick, or if you're a true Metallica fan, you can respect the fact that this is what we want to do with our music. If you don't respect that, then fuck me, I'm the asshole.'

The Metallica vs. Napster court battle would rumble on for a further thirteen months, until July 2001, when the software company reached an out-of-court settlement with the band. That same month US District Judge Marilyn Patel, presiding over the RIAA's long-running dispute with Napster, ruled that the company should shut down all music downloads until it could prove that its technology for blocking copyrighted material was 100 per cent effective. It was the beginning of the end for Shawn Fanning's enterprise.

What Lars Ulrich understood in 1999, and what virtually no other recording artist seemed to recognise, was not so much what Napster represented in the present but what its business model might mean for the future. Any musician today who does not regard the quotes printed above as being anything less than prophetic is a fool. The trouble facing Ulrich in his fight was the roles in which the combatants were cast. Inevitably, the drummer was the spoiled rock star interested only in money; predictably, Fanning and his venture-capitalist backers – and the drummer was wise to articulate the presence of money-men in the shadows – played the part of liberators striking a blow for the squeezed masses. This was nonsense. Yes, of course Ulrich had become rich beyond measure from his endeavours – no attempt was made to hide this fact. But can anyone seriously suggest that this was his intention when forming Metallica nineteen years previously? If it was, playing music that no radio station would air and refusing to make videos was a perverse way of going about it. If money was the motivation, he would surely have moulded Metallica's music to what he believed were the desires of the marketplace, just as so many other bands had been happy to do. The fact that in 1999 no one could remember the names of these bands provided a pretty solid clue as to the difference between them and him. If further evidence were needed – and, sadly, it was – the courageous and correct revelation that 'we don't do this for the fucking fans' is all anyone should need to hear.

Clearly Ulrich did not play a tactical blinder. But the essence of his argument was, and is, right. If Billy Corgan from Smashing Pumpkins or Dexter Holland from The Offspring wished to give their music away for free, then they were entitled to do so. But a musician who takes the opposite view should not be criticised for the fact that his music has already made him rich. Not only is this not the point, it is not even *a* point. That Metallica's own privately funded research revealed that in a forty-eight-hour period the only music downloaded from Napster came from bands already signed to labels – again, punching holes in the notion that this was in some ways an altruistic endeavour – should have terrified the music industry. Instead, far too many people occupied themselves mocking the messenger while failing to heed the message.

Anyone who still believes that Ulrich's zealous and sometimes foolhardy crusade against Napster was wrong in both principle and practice might care to compare the music business as it was then to how it appears now. Today the scene is one of almost total ruin. While one might not care to shed tears for the fate of people who work at record companies – or did work at them, at least – the effects on bands themselves are equally stark. Labels are signing far fewer acts, and of those they do sign more are being 'dropped' and at a faster rate than ever before. A look at the headline acts of European summer festivals reveals a dwindling pool of older bands – a fact that, ironically, has served Metallica well – whose status is preserved because of the fact that with a few notable exceptions (Arctic Monkeys, say, or Biffy Clyro) the industry no longer has the infrastructure to support the slow growth of a group from under-card act to headline attraction. Yes, there are more bands in existence today than was the case in 1999.

But these bands come, and then go, quicker than ever before.

Napster was the invention of people who regard quantity as being more valid than quality. It was not merely that the site failed to place financial value on the songs and albums it offered its subscribers, but rather that it failed to ascribe value of *any* kind. The logical conclusion of such a mindset is a world where music is entirely disposable.

But as Lars Ulrich pointed to the future, the world merely stared at his finger.

†

In the midst of endless debates about copyright, entitlement, corporate greed and personal responsibilities, the 2000 Summer Sanitarium tour came as a welcome return to work for four men who had suddenly found their band's day-to-day business a topic of national and international debate. At the summit of a five-band bill featuring Korn, Kid Rock, Powerman 5000 and System of a Down, Metallica were able to forget about courtroom depositions and focus instead upon the rather more liberating business of playing over-amplified instruments for the delectation of the Metallica family.

The tour was not without incident. After an Independence Day show in Baltimore, James Hetfield aggravated a chronic back injury while water-skiing and was ordered to sit out the next three dates. Into the void stepped Jason Newsted, assuming lead vocal duties on standards such as 'For Whom the Bell Tolls', 'Creeping Death' and 'Seek & Destroy', and directing operations as Korn's Jonathan Davis, Kid Rock and System of a Down's Daron Malakian and Serj Tankian got to fulfil childhood dreams of fronting the biggest band in the business.

A six-month period of what Hetfield gleefully called 'FUK OFF time' stretched ahead of the group as the run closed out with a brace of shows in Lexington, Kentucky, on August 8 and 9. For

Newsted, the break represented an opportunity to put the final touches to a collection of songs he had been finessing in his home studio for the best part of a year.

Newsted had been jamming at The Chophouse with San Francisco teenagers Brian Sagrafena and Dylan Donkin since the summer of 1995, letting the tapes run for hours to capture improvised soundscapes influenced by the likes of Jane's Addiction, The Beatles, Soundgarden and Jeff Buckley. Initially, as with his on–off side projects with musician friends such as Devin Townsend, Robb Flynn, Andreas Kisser and Tom Hunting, the sessions were all about getting high on speaker fuzz, adrenaline and batches of Northern Californian herb. But when Donkin and Sagrafena returned from a road trip to Mexico in summer 1999 with eight fully formed songs, Newsted began to see genuine potential in his young friends. One song in particular stood out for Newsted, a classic, timeless pop song called 'Colder World' on which Donkin's vocals reminded the bassist of a young John Lennon. Newsted played the tape over and over, blown away by how much his friends had progressed since he last saw them. He proposed that the trio should knuckle down at The Chophouse and draw their free-form jams into more cohesive forms. In May 2000 the three musicians set up in The Site studios in Northern California with a producer friend, and set about documenting their collaborations, with assistance from Kirk Hammett, ex-Faith No More guitarist Jim Martin and members of the San Francisco Symphony orchestra whom Newsted had met during Metallica's *S&M* album sessions. Newsted felt that this music needed to be heard, and as tapes of the project, now titled Echobrain, circulated among staffers at Q Prime's New York offices, he was given to understand that Peter Mensch and Cliff Burnstein shared his enthusiasm. Hetfield was quick to disavow him of this notion.

James Hetfield had blown up at Newsted before, during

sessions for the *Load* album, when a San Francisco radio station aired songs that the bassist had recorded with Devin Townsend and Tom Hunting under the band name IR8. When Metallica re-grouped at One On One Studios in North Hollywood on September 27 to record interview segments for a *Classic Albums* feature on the making of 'The Black Album', Hetfield let it be known that the Echobrain tapes must remain under lock and key at The Chophouse. When Newsted voiced his dissent, arguing that Hetfield's iron grip on Metallica was proving suffocating to him, Hetfield looked his friend in the eyes, shrugged and said simply 'Other arrangements can be made.' The bassist threw a fit.

'There are certain things I do not allow someone to say to me,' he recalled. 'Seriously, I don't care if it's my father. There is no way that I will let anybody talk to me in a certain way. He was being very vicious. "You can't have this band while you have Metallica." I'm fucking thirty-eight years old at this point, we had earned each other how many fucking tens of millions of dollars helping realise each other's dreams. I helped feed his kids, he helped support my nephew, whatever. We did all that shit then he says to me, "Other arrangements can be made." That's the line right there.'

'You're going to talk to me like that after everything that I've fucking been through for this band . . .' he fumed. 'I saved you motherfuckers, don't forget it. Don't forget it. You think that was easy shit? I saved you fuckers, I brought you back to life, I resuscitated you and you talk to me like that? "Other arrangements can be made? Somebody else can take your place?" '

In November the four members of Metallica were interviewed for a feature in *Playboy* magazine. Still seething about Hetfield's confrontational stance at One On One, Jason Newsted's mounting sense of injustice was all too obvious to writer Rob Tannenbaum.

'It sounds like this sabbatical is frustrating to you,' he

suggested. 'Yes,' Newsted replied. 'James and Lars started this thing together. They came through all of the hardships. And they have serious, written-in-stone feelings about the band, about how it needs to be run. That's very, very hard to swallow sometimes. I guess our understanding is that we don't want to be like other bands, where people go off and do side projects. I have made some incredibly wonderful music with other musicians. It would just floor people – it has floored people. But I just can't release it.'

'James and Lars won't let you?' Tannebaum probed.

'It's not Lars,' was Newsted's blunt response.

'I just can't get caught up in these meltdowns,' said Ulrich, attempting to distance himself from the gathering storm clouds. 'I've got some issues in my family life, with my wife, that are a little more weighty than, like, whatever James Hetfield and Jason Newsted are bickering over.'

'We're getting really close to some things we shouldn't be talking about,' Newsted admitted. 'I would like him [James] to see that this music is truly a part of me, like his child is a part of him.'

Metallica's alpha male, however, appeared wholly unwilling to soften his stance.

'Where would it end?' James Hetfield mused. 'Does he start touring with it? Does he sell T-shirts? Is it his band? That's the part I don't like. It's like cheating on your wife in a way.'

Ever the diplomat, Kirk Hammett tried to find a middle way between the immovable object and the unstoppable force.

'I've spoken with Jason for hours on end,' he told the man from *Playboy*. 'I'm upset for him. James demands loyalty and unity, and I respect that, but I don't think he realises the sequence of events he's putting into play.'

'I just hope,' said Hammett, 'we can survive this in one piece without tearing each other's fucking throats out.'

6 — FRANTIC

On January 8, 2001, Jason Newsted told James Hetfield, Lars Ulrich and Kirk Hammett that he was leaving Metallica. The bassist had spent three months considering his decision – a good deal more time than his band mates did before offering him the job back in 1986 – and by the time he convened with them for the first time since Christmas he was certain of it. This was not a negotiation. Newsted was out of Metallica. He was a dot. He was gone.

It is tempting to review the decision of the Michigan-born musician to finally sever ties with the band and think, 'Good for you.' In one sense Newsted had never been forgiven for being the beneficiary of the tragic circumstances that brought him to Metallica in the first place; over time this source of resentment had calcified into spite. Too many were the occasions that Hetfield, Ulrich and (to a lesser degree) Hammett were able to use their always 'new' bassist's fundamental kindness and decency as a rod with which to punish a 'whipping boy done wrong'. The fact that he was never afforded full partnership in the group meant that when factions arose they did so with the numbers uneven. It never occurred to James Hetfield that had Newsted been a figure of greater authority he would have been an ally in the power-struggles with his drummer and lead guitarist over the matter of the band's public identity in the years of the *Load* and *Reload* albums.

While his band mates threw back vodka and whisky, Jason Newsted was forced to swallow his pride. This he managed to do without ever seeming to compromise his own dignity or sense of personal identity. A man whose destiny to one day stand onstage as a member of Metallica seemed pre-ordained, Newsted was the very embodiment of the 'team player'. It was with grace that he rationalised his band mate's constant rebuttal of the riffs he would submit for use in songs – over the course of fifteen years his name appears on the writing credits of just *three* Metallica compositions – reasoning that while he may not have supplied the source material heard on the band's albums (and thus neither did he reap the rewards of songwriting royalties) he saw it as his job to help fully realise whatever songs were chosen by the band.

But when James Hetfield's need for absolute control strayed outside the perimeter of the Metallica compound, Newsted found himself suffocating. As diktats were issued as to what he could and could not do under his own musical wing, the bassist found himself resenting a man he had previously not only respected but also idolised. At this point, the game was up.

'As [the band] became more popular we were taken away from actually plugging in [and playing music],' he recalls. 'In my eyes, that was the demise. Less and less time plugged in with volume, looking at each other, making music. It didn't have the same heart for me . . . I don't know what they were doing instead. I was playing. I was making music for other people. I never stopped; I still haven't. I play drums more than Lars does any fucking day of the week. I play music all the time. That's my deal.'

There were also other internal issues within Metallica that Jason Newsted regarded with a mixture of quiet despair and bristling contempt. With the always complicated relationship between Hetfield and Ulrich entering a trough that seemed deeper than usual, Q Prime decided to call in outside help. As with so much else regarding the workings of the Metallica machine, Newsted was not consulted on this matter. When he entered room 627 of the Ritz Carlton hotel in San Francisco to inform his colleagues that from this point he would be referred to in the press as 'former Metallica bassist Jason Newsted' he was surprised discover four people were waiting for his arrival: three musicians and one 'Performance Enhancement Coach'. He was not impressed.

'I said, "Who is this and what is he doing here?" ' recalls the bass player. 'I said, "Excuse me sir, I don't know you and you don't know me and you don't know our band and you have nothing to do with any of this so I'd like you to leave. I'm not trying to be rude, but get the fuck out of here." [After this] he listened from the next room [while] I laid my shit down. We decided to have another meeting one week later and he was there again! It didn't mean shit. He hadn't been through anything, not one second of the life that we'd been through had he been through with us. He had no place being there.'

Newsted considered the reality of Metallica's surroundings and felt yet further emboldened by his decision to leave. The fact that the four men who shared each other's lives to a point of uncommon intimacy and intensity 'could not just talk to each other' without the help of a mediator 'was one of the things that pissed me off more than anything'.

'We couldn't just hang out and talk about it?' he asks, both animated and incredulous. 'I told everyone [what might be on the cards] three months before I chose to make the announcement that I was leaving the band. No one reached out to me. No one called me and said, "Dude, are you sure? Don't you think we should keep the band together?" Everybody fucking knew. No one tried to stop me.'

Eavesdropping on the proceedings unfolding in room 627, the Performance Enhancement Coach did not need letters after his name to realise that things could have been going better. On the other side of the door, the four members of Metallica were by now engaged in 'a full and frank exchange of views'. Tempers were roused and voices raised. After pacing the floor and considering his options, the behaviourist swallowed hard and swung open the hotel room door. His presence was met by complete silence and four entrenched scowls.

'Excuse me,' said the visitor. 'I respect what you're doing, but I'm here for these kind of situations.'

It was at this point that Metallica as it had existed since October 1986 made its final collective decision. Silently, the four men signalled their consent. Just to be sure, Lars Ulrich, ever the conciliator, said, 'Let him stay.'

In his chosen field, Phil Towle came highly recommended. His job was both simple and complicated: he was charged with uncovering methods by which highly skilled blue-chip organisations might learn to communicate and operate in a harmonious manner. In other words, he was paid to figure out how to make sure that multi-millionaires played nice. His work in this field took him to the fractious confines of Major League Baseball locker rooms, as well as the practice facilities of teams in America's National Football League, the world's most profitable sporting enterprise. In particular, Towle also worked with individual athletes such as former NFL defensive line man Kevin Carter, and coaches such as the Super-Bowl-winning former St Louis Rams gaffer, Dick Vermeil. The latter said of Towle that 'Phil has not only helped re-hone my leadership skills, but also helped me deal with my personal hang-ups . . . He's a winner!' In the field of popular music, Towle also attempted (and failed) to come to the aid of Stone Temple Pilots and their then acutely drug-addicted front man Scott Weiland, as well as Tom Morello, the guitarist with Rage Against the Machine and Audioslave, who described the therapist as being a man 'who as a friend [is] a great counselor, and [who] as a counselor [is] a great friend'.

In Metallica's orbit Towle cut an incongruous figure. While Hetfield, Ulrich and Hammett appeared to be fit, relatively young men dressed in biker boots and Converse Chuck Taylor hi-top trainers, Towle dressed like a man forever ill at ease with the concept of 'dress-down Friday'. A resident of Kansas City, Missouri, he carried himself with an unflappable air of professional level-headedness that stood in high-definition contrast to the sometimes infantile, but often profound, screeches of dislocation emanating from the frustrated faces of the three-man band.

For Metallica, though, Towle was their knight in a bright yellow jumper. At the time of the therapist's arrival in the Bay Area, the trio were a shambles. That neither party had any real clue as to both the intensity and the duration of the course of therapy on which they were about to embark, what *was* obvious was that this was a union that had sailed its ship into the rocks.

'I see it as my job to exist in the moment,' says Towle, recalling the state of ruin that met him in San Francisco in the opening months of 2001. 'I ask the question, "What do Metallica need today, and how can I help them achieve what it is they need today? How can I help the band today in a way that will mean that by tomorrow some progress has been made?" [But] in its complexity the situation with Metallica was unlike anything I'd ever seen, before or since. And I don't expect to see anything like it again.'

It was at this time that Hammett revealed to *Playboy* magazine, 'There are a lot of soap operas and petty dramas that come with being in this band.' It was on this same (very) public forum that Ulrich would suggest that Hetfield's quiet homophobia was due to the fact that the front man was less than sure of his own sexuality. 'I know he's homophobic,' said the drummer. 'Let there be no question about that. I think homophobia is questioning your own sexuality and not being comfortable with it.' On the state of dysfunction evident in his band, James Hetfield conceded, 'There is a little ugliness lately,' before insisting, 'And it shouldn't be discussed in the press.'

At the time Metallica sat down with *Playboy* for what was inarguably their most revealing and startling interview to date, the group was a quartet; by the time Rob Tannenbaum's piece was published, they were a trio.

'I wasn't surprised that Jason Newsted quit Metallica,' Tannenbaum later admitted. 'I'd spent a day with each of the four and I've never seen a band so quarrelsome and fractious. Most of the barbs were cloaked in humour: Newsted mocked Hetfield's singing, Hetfield mocked Ulrich's drumming, and Ulrich, whom I interviewed last, responded to several of Hetfield's quotes with scorn. But genuine tension was evident at these interviews – the last ever to be conducted with this Metallica line-up – because they shared one trait; each talked about his need for solitude. Paradoxically, this is a band of loners, and the conflict between unity and individualism was pretty clear.'

Jason Newsted announced his departure from Metallica with a typically diplomatic and gracious statement. It read, 'Due to private and personal reasons and the physical damage I have done to myself over the years while playing the music I love, I must step away from the band. This is the most difficult decision of my life, made in the best interests of my family, myself and the continued growth of Metallica. I extend my love, thanks and best wishes to my brothers James, Lars, Kirk and the rest of the Metallica family, friends and fans who have made these years so unforgettable.'

For their part, the remaining members of Metallica afforded the bassist the respect that he had always deserved. In a reciprocal statement released to the press, Lars Ulrich said, 'We part ways with Jason with more love, more mutual respect and more understanding of each other than at any point in the past.' Expression of this opinion begged the question, if this is so then why is Newsted leaving? The drummer added that 'James, Kirk and I look forward to embracing the next chapter of Metallica with a huge amount of appreciation for the last [fifteen years] with Jason . . .' In the same statement, James Hetfield told readers that 'playing with someone who has such unbridled passion for music will forever be a huge inspiration. Onstage every night, he was a driving force to us all, fans and band alike. His connection [to both] will never be broken.' For his part Kirk Hammett needed just eight well-chosen words with which to make his point. 'Jason is our brother,' he said, adding, 'he will be missed.'

Despite these kind expressions of eternal fraternity, in old-fashioned parlance Metallica were burned out. The slights and miscommunications, the jealousies and competitiveness that existed between Hetfield and Ulrich about which of them owned Metallica, the emotional inarticulacy that had for years been pushed out of sight by a sea of alcohol and bowls of cocaine were finally coming home and were ready to roost. As the three-piece found themselves at the Presidio recording facility in San Francisco, the band attempted to begin work on a new album while at the same time embarking on a course of therapy with their new Performance Enhancement Coach. As if this weren't all quite enough, the state of the band was about to be thrown into yet further chaos.

†

On the occasion of the first birthday of James and wife Francesca Hetfield's second child, Castor, the boy's father held in his hands not a birthday cake but a hunting rifle. Instead of being at home in Northern California, he had flown to Siberia on Russia's eastern front. Each morning he would rise at dawn and with a troop of fellow hunters head out into the wilderness in pursuit of the Russian bear. Having secured their kill for the day, the party would be photographed around the animal's strewn corpse before spending the rest of the day sinking shots of vodka. 'There was', Hetfield explained, 'nothing else to do.'

Back at the family home, this and numerous other examples of Hetfield's unilateral impulses meant a domestic scene that was less than blissful. Having previously given up alcohol for a year, he attempted to rationalise his situation – 'It was okay to have a few glasses of wine with dinner because that's what normal people do – which is how it all starts again' – and duly hopped off the wagon. But this was okay, anyway, he internalised, because temperance didn't cause 'the skies to part' and the only thing the front man learned from the experience was that 'it was just life, but less fun' and that 'drinking is a part of me'.

'I wouldn't say I'm an alcoholic,' was his 'I'm-glad-that's-all-sorted-then' diagnosis, albeit one coloured with a measure of self-awareness.

'But then, you know, alcoholics say they're not alcoholics.'

They do, and he was one. Francesca Hetfield certainly knew that her husband was an alcoholic, and that things could not continue. As Metallica's engines stalled in disagreement and disarray over the musical direction of their next album, Francesca threw her husband out of the house.

'My wife finally told me, "Hey! I'm not one of your yes men on the road. Get the fuck out!" ' Hetfield recalled.

As he would subsequently admit, he was a 'horrible' influence on the children. With the help of a friend, Hetfield was able to find himself an apartment in which he would reside 'for a long time'. His entreaties to return to the family home were met with a resolve from Francesca Hetfield that might as well have been made out of jade.

'My wife said, "You're not coming back until you sort this out",' he recalls. 'You get some therapy. Not just the drinking, but all the other crap that goes along with it, you know. The disrespect, doing whatever you want whenever you want." I had to grow up at some point. I had a family . . .'

So a man who it seemed had done his growing up in public decided to try a different tack. With his wife's injunction reverberating in his ears, Hetfield removed himself to an undisclosed rehabilitation clinic and let it be known that he

'The Little Engine That Could': Lars Ulrich,
shot in London, July 1, 2003.

'Papa Het': James Hetfield onstage at the Amsterdam Arena,
The Netherlands, June 21, 2004.

Above left: Metallica at the 35th annual Grammy Awards, February 24, 1993.
Above right: Kirk Hammett unplugged, at Neil Young's Bridge School Benefit, October 18, 1997.
Below: The band onstage at London's LA2 club on August 23, 1995, ahead of their 'Escape from the Studio' show at Donington Park.

Lars Ulrich and James Hetfield relaxing backstage at the Oakland Coliseum on September 24, 1992, ahead of show 21 of Metallica's co-headlining tour with Guns N' Roses.
Below: Hetfield (on drums) jamming with Kirk Hammett and John Marshall, backstage at the Oakland Coliseum on the same afternoon. Metal Church guitarist Marshall was drafted into the band to play rhythm guitar after Hetfield was injured onstage at Montreal's Olympic Stadium on August 8, 1992.

Metallica at the MTV Music Awards, September 5, 1991. The quartet performed their new single 'Enter Sandman' at the ceremony in Los Angeles.

Jason Newsted onstage at London's Wembley Stadium, at the Freddie Mercury tribute concert held on April 20, 1992. Other performers included Guns N' Roses, Def Leppard and Spinal Tap.

Trujillo, Ulrich, Hetfield and Hammett in Istanbul, Turkey, July 27, 2008.
Below: Robert Trujillo on stage at Madison Square Garden, New York, November 14, 2009.

Slayer's Kerry King, Megadeth's Dave Mustaine, Anthrax's Scott Ian and Metallica's James Hetfield at Bemowo Airport, Warsaw, Poland at the first 'Big Four' show, June 16, 2009. *Below:* Lou Reed with Kirk Hammett at the second of the Rock and Roll Hall of Fame's 25th Anniversary Concerts at Madison Square Garden, New York, October 30, 2009.

Right: Dave Mustaine and James Hetfield at the Fillmore, San Francisco, on December 10, 2011, the final night of Metallica's four thirtieth-anniversary concerts. *Below:* the band onstage at the Fillmore that same evening.

The Hetfield Family at the Rock and Roll Hall of Fame induction ceremony, at the Public Hall, Cleveland, Ohio, on April 4, 2009.
Below: The Ulrich family at the 56th annual Grammy Awards ceremony, held at the Staples Center, Los Angeles, on January 26, 2014.

would remain there for as long as it took to untangle the many knots in his psyche, as well as learn how to face each encroaching night without the aid of alcohol. The front man also revealed that this was a period during which he would be separate from Metallica in a personal, musical and organisational sense. Bob Rock, for one, appeared devastated that his papers had been stamped '*persona non grata*' until such time as Hetfield was able to once again face what he defined as 'the business side' of the band. Even closer to home, Lars Ulrich was empathetic to his friend's plight, as well as being awake to the sense of genuine fear to which Hetfield's life had succumbed (a fear which for years had been kept at bay by its twin brother, anger). But at the same time he could be forgiven for wondering what permanent damage had been caused by the shock waves emanating from Hetfield's troubled core. It was far more than self-interest that led the drummer to look around the utter wreckage that was Metallica and marvel at what had happened to them and what would happen next.

Hetfield's absence went from weeks to months, to many months. He could not, or would not, say when he might return to the flock, or indeed if at all. Bereft and bewildered, the Dane feared for the worst. He understood that Metallica 'had had a good run' but that maybe now it was time for the band to be spoken of in a different tense. A listless summer came and went, followed by a season that saw the clear Californian sky turn blotting-paper blue earlier each evening. In an attempt to shadow their front man's intensive course of therapy, Ulrich and Hammett continued their own therapy sessions with Phil Towle.

'Lars and Kirk did not just sit still while James was in rehab,' says Towle, speaking to this book's authors. 'They wanted to embark on something themselves; they wanted James to come back and see that they too had made an effort to address the problems that were facing the band.'

But while Towle says that the efforts of Metallica's drummer and lead guitarist should be applauded, it is Hetfield who, he believes, became 'the poster boy for mental health'.

'You have to remember', he says, 'that this was a time when people didn't admit to undertaking that kind of intensive therapy. There was rehab, sure, where people went to give up drinking or drugs, but that was kind of all that was admitted to. James went to rehab to learn how to become a different person. A kinder person; a more gentle person. This angry person whose public image was all about strength and immovability suddenly admitted to personal failings, frailties and weaknesses. He showed people, "Hey, if I can admit to these things and seek help for them, then why can't you?" By doing this he set a trend not just for celebrities and people in bands, but really for everyone.'

The week before Thanksgiving, Kirk Hammett celebrated his thirty-ninth birthday. To mark this occasion, on November 18, 2001, the lead guitarist hired a restaurant and bar in San Francisco. By the time the birthday man arrived at the venue, the room was already crowded with family and friends. Smiling in appreciation at the number of people that had chosen to spend their evening in his company, the man who was born and raised in the very city in which he now stood at first failed to notice that the crowd was parting to allow room for the one person he did not expect to be in attendance. There, standing directly in his line of sight, was a smiling Hetfield.

'I had never been so pleased to see him,' Hammett confessed.

†

This, though, was not the happy ending that would herald the start of a new life for the band. Almost a year on from the departure of Jason Newsted, Metallica were still without a permanent bass player, the search for which had not yet even begun. Although the three men had written a number of songs, none of them were particularly inspiring or even much liked. Days were ticking by as if seconds on a clock, and for the first time in their career the band was unable to use its collective force as a battering ram with which to obliterate any obstacle that lay in its path.

Hetfield had emerged from rehab in the autumn of 2002 a fragile and frightened man, shorn of the calloused skin that formed his armour of old. The front man described his time away from band and family as having been 'college for my soul', but now blinking into the light he was also aware that the lessons he had learned at the private clinic would have to be tested not just in Real Life but at the site of so many battles that had been lost in the past.

'I've been in Metallica since I was nineteen years old, which can be a very unusual environment for someone with my personality to be in,' he said. 'It's a very intense environment, and it's easy to find yourself not knowing how to live your life outside of that environment, which is what happened to me. I didn't know *anything* about life. I didn't know that I could live my life in a different way to how it was in the band since I was nineteen, which was very excessive and very intense. And if you have addictive behaviour then you don't always make the best choices for yourself. And I definitely didn't make the best choices for myself. Rehab definitely taught me how to live.'

With regard to his relationship with Metallica, Hetfield realised that in order to flourish in an environment one must be unafraid of being separated from it for ever. In pursuit of this he 'truly had to believe that I would survive without Metallica and that my health and well-being and my family was most important. I had to get my priorities in order, basically. I knew Metallica was my passion but I wasn't going to allow it to still rule me in my mind and my reality. It took me a while to get to that point and I couldn't come back until I had reached [it].'

In attempting to piece himself together as a better man,

Hetfield mined his life for lessons that might be learned. He would recall seemingly comically incongruous moments from his childhood to apply to the person he was trying to become. He remembered sharing a car with a father who had become so short-sighted that he would literally speed past the off-ramp of a freeway because he was unable to read the words on the signs hanging overhead. ('I'd be, like, Dad you just missed it!' he recalled.) But the son realised that now he too would soon be at the point where he would have to buy books in audio rather than print form, and that like his father he had turned his face against this encroaching reality. In finally accepting this and buying a pair of glasses, the front man was able 'to see things well, literally'.

For anyone abreast of the kind of yearning expressed in a number of the songs from *Load* and *Reload*, it was clear that Hetfield was becoming the person about whom he so often sung. He recognised that he was a flawed man with character traits both of strength and vulnerability, a figure burdened with instincts, some of which might prove fatal. For the less well-briefed, or the less imaginative, among Metallica's core constituents, however, the James Hetfield that emerged sober and sensible from rehab struck a less than reassuring figure, like God overheard placing a call to the Samaritans.

He is quick to admit that in the past it suited him to present to the world an image of indestructibility, the kind of figure whose face might appear at home on the side of Mount Rushmore. 'That's what I wanted to be,' he'll say, 'that's what I needed in my life. That's what I wanted to see. That's what I wanted to portray.

'Through all the instability of childhood I wanted something that was a rock, something stable,' he adds. 'But at the end of the day we're all human and things change for a reason. With that perception blasted out of their mind [after he left rehab] I've no doubt that it turned off a lot of fans. I'd walk in somewhere and people would expect me to be this hard-ass who gets up on the table and demands beer for everyone. When you don't do that it suddenly becomes a case of, "Wow, I thought you were different." How much that hurts [me] is so amazing but they only mean it in a nice way. They get their perception the way they get it. They build their own perception of you [that is informed by] the way they need to see you. And when it's different from that, it really shakes their world.

'But I've learned that you have to be yourself. Whatever you put out, that's what you'll attract [in response]. It's as simple as that, the law of attraction. If you're putting out the image of the hard-ass that doesn't want to bend and who would rather break [than do so], you're going to attract the kind of fans that are looking for that kind of character. I realise now that all I can do is live and survive life.'

†

James Hetfield may have been empowered with a greater and healthier sense of self-awareness, but the question of how this new-look human being might fit back into the dynamic of his old band was a pressing one, not least because not everything about the front man was new. Whether by failure or design, the rehabilitation clinic in which he had been seconded for months on end did not reset his hard drive entirely. When Hetfield finally rejoined Ulrich and Hammett (as well as Bob Rock, now the band's temporary bass player), it became obvious that the front man's instinct to control all situations remained the same as it had always been.

In the past this was something with which the group could deal, not least because in Ulrich Metallica had another member capable of playing the unstoppable force to Hetfield's immovable object. But as 2001 passed into a brand-new year, this long-enduring dynamic was further challenged by the question of how the front man might best be reintegrated into the band without jeopardising a recovery that had really only just begun.

The solution as Hetfield saw it was for Metallica to work on their now spectacularly delayed new album for just four hours each day, beginning at noon. This was a proposal to which Ulrich might have peaceably consented were it not for the fact that it came with one crippling caveat: that when their band mate was *not* at the studio, neither Ulrich, Hammett nor Bob Rock could tinker with the work in any way. In fact, Hetfield stipulated, they weren't even to listen to that day's recordings without him present in the room.

At this, a band that was already split into two camps split into two more. While not overjoyed at Hetfield's terms and conditions, Hammett nonetheless believed they were wishes which should be adhered to, if only for the greater good. But for his part, Ulrich could do nothing other than regard his band mate's condition as a wholly disheartening lack of faith in anyone but himself. 'I feel so disrespected,' he would say. Bob Rock simply could not understand what harm could be caused by listening to music when just one of the four people involved in its recording happened to be absent.

But these were Hetfield's wishes, and here was the barrel over which he ultimately had the other three men. Whereas in the past recording sessions would last for up to twenty-four hours, in 2002 Metallica and Bob Rock would convene for just 240 minutes each working day. It was in this restricted space that these old dogs somehow learned the new trick of making music in a different way. The pace may have been glacial, but inch by inch and week by week Metallica's new album began to take form.

†

After more than a year, and with only the dots and crosses missing from a collection that by now had been given the title *St Anger*, Metallica convened for their first concert since performing a private show for members of their fan club at their new group headquarters in San Rafael, California – the location at which *St Anger* was recorded – in April the previous year. For the third time, on January 19, 2003, the band's equipment trucks made their way to the Oakland Network Coliseum. It was here that tens of thousands of Oakland Raiders fans had gathered for an American football play-off game against the Tennessee Titans.

As is the case at NFL stadiums from Secaucus to Seattle, supporters arrived early to tailgate – the particularly American practice of firing up a barbecue over which steaks the size of phone directories could be cooked medium-rare and eaten with beers icy from hours in a cool box. When the team were the Los Angeles Raiders, tailgate parties outside the LA Coliseum would often end in fist-fights and virtual riots; but when the Southern Californian incarnation of the team began to post losing records, in time the crowds dwindled to the point where it seemed that more people were on the field than in the stands, a typically 'LA' phenomenon. Since returning 'home' to Oakland in 1995, the club's image may have softened somewhat – with its fans more often cited for misdemeanours rather than felonies – but the notion that the Oakland Raiders and their pirate logo represented the NFL's most rough 'n' tumble franchise remained intact. This image, of course, fitted James Hetfield like a tailored suit, and was the one outlaw quality he was able to spare from the funeral pyre of his old self set ablaze in rehab. As the ideal occasion at which to announce the fact that Metallica were back on the chain gang, a Raiders play-off game was tough to top. The group's original plan was to perform on the Coliseum field at half time (not to mention live on network television) but instead the decision was taken to play before the game on a flat-bed truck in the parking lot. Dressed in the Raiders' uniform of black shirts with silver numbers, the makeshift quarter further energised a crowd already alive with electricity with a six-song set that included 'Battery', 'Seek & Destroy' and 'Fuel'.

But if Metallica's public and private selves were finally beginning to unify, other concerns were ongoing. By this point it had been more than two years since Jason Newsted had left the band, and for those two years Bob Rock had played bass on their new album. But with *St Anger* almost a wrap, and a summer tour of the largest stadiums in North America soon to be announced, the group's need for a permanent fourth member was now a code-red matter of priority.

†

On the last Saturday of February 2003 one of this book's authors is on a British Airways flight from London Heathrow Airport to San Francisco International Airport to interview Hetfield, Ulrich and Hammett. This purpose is explained to the white-shirted representative of the US Department of Immigration & Naturalization sitting in a booth checking the passports and stories of those wishing to visit the City by the Bay. 'Really?' he says, nodding his head slightly. Asking the Englishman to place the fingers of his right hand on a green scanner that stands at shoulder height, the official asks, 'So who do you think will be the new Metallica bass player?' The visitor replies that in all honesty, he has no idea. The official nods his and says, 'I think Pepper Keenan will get the job.'

The interview for which the writer has flown 6,000 miles will be Metallica's first since the dishearteningly shambolic front presented in *Playboy* two years earlier. It is a world exclusive, an audience with one of the most popular and forensically examined bands of the day at the time of their most uncertain hour. It has been revealed to the press that the group's eighth album of original songs, *St Anger*, will meet its expectant public at the start of the summer. It is also known that the quartet will tour the world for the first time in three years. Following a four- night tune-up at the Fillmore in San Francisco, the group will fly (once again, by private jet) to Europe for a month of appearances on the bills of numerous grandly lucrative festivals. As well as this, the band will perform three concerts in one day, in Paris on June 11. Rumours have also begun to circulate that the San Franciscans will headline the Leeds and Reading festivals on the final weekend at the end of the English summer.

The docket for activities to be undertaken in the US is even more impressive. Metallica will return to the road in North America not with a series of dates at arenas, or even amphitheatres (the 'sheds'), but with a twenty-one-date tour of twenty of the largest stadiums on the continent. The 2003 Summer Sanitarium tour will see the headliners perform on the same stage as Limp Bizkit, Linkin Park, Deftones and Mudvayne, younger bands all. It is also understood by everyone that in order to undertake these live commitments Metallica will require the services of a bass player other than Bob Rock.

The identity of the man chosen as the replacement for Jason Newsted, it was explained, was as yet undecided: the writer's world exclusive would be conducted with three, not four, musicians. Despite this disappointing news, en route to HQ, Metallica's studio and business facility in San Rafael, it's difficult not to smile and think, 'Well, a scoop is still a scoop!' as the car travels over the Golden Gate Bridge and through the iconic rainbow arch of the Waldo Tunnel. As Hetfield himself once sang, this is 'a good day to be alive'.

It is an even better day to be alive when it is revealed that today's interview for *Kerrang!* magazine will be the very first to feature a contribution from Metallica's new bassist. This is the age before social media, so although the news will leak out it will not explode into the sky like a bomb in a fireworks factory. The pictures taken by *Kerrang!* photographer Paul Harries will be the first sessions for which the group have posed. The image of the four men crowding the cover of the magazine – across which is splashed the legend: 'Metallica:. New Line Up. New Album. New Danger' – will be the first image that British and Irish readers will see of Metallica 4.0.

Clearly, the group had taken their own sweet time choosing a fourth member. At HQ, throughout the autumn and winter of 2002, potential recruits such as Corrosion of Conformity's Pepper Keenan, Marilyn Manson sidekick Twiggy Ramirez (aka Jeordie White), Kyuss's Scott Reeder and Nine Inch Nails's utility man Denny Lohner were first asked to break bread with Hetfield, Ulrich and Hammett and then invited to make music. Those that most impressed as men and musicians were invited back for a second time. By this point, though, it was clear that the abilities of one applicant stood higher than those with whom he was in competition. It quickly became clear that Metallica had found their fourth bass player.

✝

Robert Agustin Trujillo was born on October 23, 1964, in Santa Monica, California. Described by his mother as being 'a really good boy' who never once 'caused any problems for me', from the youngest age the son showed an appetite for whatever music he happened to hear. At home the family stereo would bounce to the sounds of James Brown, Led Zeppelin and the infectious grooves of Tamla Motown, the beat of which would send him dancing from room to room. As an infant, on a visit to Disneyland in nearby Anaheim, Trujillo danced alone and without a care to a band playing Disney standards while every other child in the theatre watched from a sedentary position.

With the Pacific Ocean just a Frisbee throw away, Trujillo occupied his time surfing the waves of both Santa Monica and neighbouring Venice Beach, and it was from this latter location that he picked up the habit of skateboarding. These teenage years lacked either drama or danger, and by the time he was sixteen he had cut back on the hours dedicated to waves and half-pipes and instead set his sights on a career as a professional musician. Profoundly inspired by the music of jazz composer and bass player Jaco Pastorius, he soon mastered a command of this instrument to a level sufficient for him to perform with other friends at teenage backyard parties. But instead of songs by Kiss or Black Sabbath, he would lead these groups into cover versions of songs by Eric Clapton.

By now Trujillo was a student at Venice High School, one of the tougher seats of learning in an area known as 'Urban LA'. Venice – so named because one of its founding fathers, conservationist and developer Abbot Kinney, envisioned the location as being *the* Venice of the West Coast – was also the home to what was at first one of Los Angeles' most remarkable bands.

Formed in 1981 by vocalist Mike Muir, Suicidal Tendencies were a group of such unharnessed fury as to make Metallica sound like the Partridge Family. Like Metallica, the group fell between two stools. Ostensibly a hardcore punk band – and a *very* hardcore punk band at that – the appearance of lead guitar solos in many of the band's songs drew charges of heathenism and heresy from the scene's moral arbiters. Married to this was a sense of confusion regarding the group's visual image. That many among Suicidal Tendencies audiences dressed as the band did in baggy board shorts and bandanas led many to conclude that 'ST' were a band with an affiliation to gang culture, a misconception that for years hampered the group's ability to perform in and around Los Angeles. Always a man with a pronounced persecution complex, Mike Muir railed against this state of affairs in the manner of a man rather enjoying protesting so much.

At the start of the Eighties the punk scene in Los Angeles was by far America's most impressive and varied, not to mention often its most pointlessly violent and nihilistic. But despite LA having found the space for bands ranging from the stare-at-the-wall fury of Black Flag to the artful buzz of X, Suicidal Tendencies proved to be a touch too much. When the group released their self-titled debut album in 1982, readers of the underground magazine *Flipside* promptly voted it the worst record of the year. Even those who believe themselves to be on the cutting edge can sometimes be bamboozled by music that not so much defies convention as seems ignorant of its very existence in the first place. *Suicidal Tendencies* remains one of the most incendiary albums of the Eighties, as well as one of its most surprisingly successful. Powered by MTV's unlikely decision to playlist the band's alienation-*über-alles* anthem 'Institutionalized', the record found its way into the bedrooms of more than 100,000 listless teenagers in the US alone.

Robert Trujillo became a member of Suicidal Tendencies at the time of the band's third album, *Controlled by Hatred/Feel Like Shit . . . Déjà Vu*. But with their music veering towards thrash metal cliché and turbid rock mediocrity, this was not a high point in their career. With Trujillo's help, the group were able to reverse their fortunes with 1991's *Lights, Camera, Revolution* album, the point from which the quintet began to find favour with a larger and newer audience. An invitation to appear as the opening act on 1994's Shit Hit the Sheds tour provided the occasion at which Trujillo and Metallica would first meet.

†

By 2001 Robert Trujillo had swapped his gig with Suicidal Tendencies for the position of bassist in Ozzy Osbourne's band. This was a world of private jets and high-end musicianship in the form of guitarist Zakk Wylde and one-time Faith No More drummer Mike 'Puffy' Bordin. For his part Ozzy had been reinvigorated by the advent of his own summer Ozzfest tour, a shed-filling caravan that heralded a renaissance in the headliner's fortunes that was as perplexing and it was pronounced. By any measure, Trujillo had 'made it'.

By any measure, that is, except the standard set by Metallica. After receiving the blessing of Sharon Osbourne in 2002, Trujillo decided to audition for the role of bass player for the biggest name in metal. Flying north to the Bay Area, at HQ, the visiting musician was asked by Lars Ulrich which of their songs he might like to play. The bassist's shy mannerisms made him appear younger and far less established than he actually was. But the answer came back, 'I could try "Battery".' As the group smashed their way through one of Metallica's most formidable and enduring songs, Ulrich felt honour-bound to observe, 'That's a fucking pretty fuckin' mighty bass sound you've got going there.' As the three musicians shared meaningful glances, Bob Rock sounded a note of caution. 'I don't think you should [just] settle [for someone].' He added, 'I think you should get the right guy. If you don't hit it out of the park with one of these guys [that you're auditioning] then you're going to end up four years down the road in the same situation you did with Jason.'

But as auditions went on, it was Trujillo whose presence began to dominate the sessions. 'He was the [one] guy out of [all] of them who didn't look like he was struggling with [the music],' observed Ulrich, adding, 'With some of the other [candidates] it was like they were [playing at] ten per cent over their capabilities or something . . . I don't feel that with this guy.'

Robert Trujillo became Metallica's fourth bass player on February 24, 2003. Giving the appearance of a man who had just been told that he's sitting on a landmine, the Santa Monican sat in stunned silence as Hetfield told him that the second time he came back to audition was when he noticed that he made the band 'play better, man' and that this meant that he could 'make the band sound so much better . . . sound so solid'.

'How do you feel about that?' asked Hammett.

'I feel awesome, man,' came the answer from the mouth of a man who at that moment appeared to have very few words at his disposal.

Not to worry, though, because as ever Lars Ulrich was on hand.

'We want you to be a real member of the band and not just a hired hand,' he told the guest. 'Basically, to show you how serious we are about this, we'd like to offer you a million dollars.'

Hearing these words, Robert Trujillo made a strangulated sound somewhere between joy and disbelief. He was utterly astonished. Running his hands through what is now the best head of hair in Metallica, he struggled to compose himself, and failed. As if expecting to hear the sound of a bedside alarm clock at any moment, he admitted to the people with whom he would now share his life, 'I can't even talk right now.'

†

To enter HQ is to be struck with immediate force by just how wildly successful a band this is. The space is vast. On two storeys and covering thousands of square feet, the gated complex teems with trinkets and mementos from its owners' diamond-encrusted past. The walls are covered in frames holding Metallica concert posters stretching back over two decades. In one of the two large, high-ceilinged sound rooms is propped the head of 'Edna' the towering 'Lady Justice' figure that adorns the cover of . . . *And Justice for All* and which comprised part of the stage show for the band's Damaged Justice Tour of 1988 and 1989. A grand piano stands majestically in the other sound room, as do racks holding literally scores of guitars: Gibson Explorers, SGs and Les Pauls; Fender Stratocasters, Telecasters; signature ESP models; hollow-bodied acoustic instruments the value of which runs to thousands of dollars each. There are more drums than there are hairs on Lars Ulrich's head. To capture the sounds made by these and other instruments, one room is crowded with recording equipment of such sophistication that it appears to have been sourced from NASA. An anteroom is given over entirely to the kind of equipment required to undertake running repairs. In here there are boxes and boxes of guitar strings, drum heads and foot-pedals. Stacked on a shelf are boxes of plectrums (each one adorned with the band's original logo); next to this sits a box stuffed with the elbow-length sweat bands that have been part of James Hetfield's stage attire since 1988. On one of HQ's many corridor walls are hung frames of albums by other artists – Jethro Tull's *Aqualung*, Saxon's *Denim & Leather* and *Led Zeppelin IV* being three – that suggest that although it may often sound as if they did, Metallica did not parachute into the world from an otherwise empty sky.

At the top of a wooden flight of stairs are four spacious 'bedrooms'. It is here that each member of the band has his own private room. Hetfield's space is the first door on the left; the walls of it are currently being painted with cartoon images of men in speeding cars, each decorated in garish colours. Ulrich's room is at the end of the hall, and in here he will sit on a sofa that seems to be about to swallow him whole at any moment.

Robert Trujillo has his own room, too, although he still looks as if he can't quite believe it.

'Metallica called me a couple of days ago,' he explained for what is his first interview as a member of his new band. 'They said, "Can you get up here in the next twenty-four hours?" I flew up [from Los Angeles] the next morning.' Hetfield told the bassist that he wanted him to be 'a part of the Metallica family', words that left the bassist 'overwhelmed'.

Today, it is explained to the *Kerrang!* journalist who will break this story, each member of Metallica will be interviewed separately, with each subject answering questions in private rooms. After this comes another revelation, this one less routine. Each interview will be filmed, with Metallica at liberty to use any part of the footage they desire. The director asks the journalist to pose for a photograph and to sign a release form. Shaking hands, he introduces himself as Joe Berlinger.

As if this weren't all quite startling enough, a day that is already by turns exhilarating, intense, intimidating and bewildering reaches its apogee when Lars Ulrich asks if the journalist would care to hear a selection of songs from *St Anger*. The album isn't yet quite finished, he explains, but four or five rough mixes can be easily cued up. (Well, sure, why not?) In a mixing room, sitting on a high-backed leather chair at a console the size of the wingspan of a pterodactyl, with Ulrich and Bob Rock seated on a black leather sofa directly behind, the journalist realises that this is the first time anyone outside the Metallica camp has heard these songs, and that after an interminable gestation period producer and drummer are keen to see how the music they have recorded is received. A film of sweat prickles the brow. Critical faculties have not so much been suspended as extinguished.

A technician cues up the first song: 'St Anger' drops like a bouncing bomb from the speakers. Every time the journalist turns around – surreptitiously turning the chair on its castor wheels – he notices that Ulrich and Rock are looking directly at him. So the most difficult task in a music journalist's work book – knowing quite what to say when hearing recorded music for the first time in the company of the people who recorded it – is made even trickier when the pair break the silence that greets the conclusion of 'St Anger' by asking for an opinion. 'It's amazing,' the pair are told. 'It's incredible.' So certain is this opinion that just weeks later the first Metallica feature to be published since 2001 features the sentence, ' "St Anger" is the finest thing to which the band have [ever] put their name.'

As is now known, *St Anger* the album is in fact the *worst* thing to which Metallica have put their name. But with their first release of the twenty-first century this was a group in receipt of a number of fortunate breaks. One of these was the human fallibility of the rock press, and the fact that many writers (most writers, actually) were fans of the band in the first instance and as such naturally discounted the notion that the group's creative instincts could no longer be trusted. Another factor that came into play was that since their rhubarb with Napster, Metallica were a band obsessed with the fear that the music they had recorded might 'leak' on to the Internet before its official release date. Because of this, for the first time in the group's history no magazine or journalist was given an advance copy of *St Anger* that he or she could call their own. Instead, in order to hear Metallica's latest collection of songs reviewers were required to travel to the office of the band's PR person near Paddington in west London and listen to the CD through headphones in an office busy with working people. *St Anger* endures for seventy-five minutes and one second and is in many ways the musical equivalent of primal scream therapy. It is not an album designed to be heard in one sitting, and certainly not on a first date. Critics who were forced to do just this found their senses concussed by the conclusion of the third song and comatose by the end of the sixth. But rather than succumb to suspicions and fears that would soon enough be recognised as justified and correct, instead reviewers and writers erred on the side of kindness.

'Even the fact that for the first time in fifteen years Metallica actually *thrash* on several of these songs cannot disguise the fact that this is a band revived, not merely renewed,' was the opinion of *Kerrang!* writer Dom Lawson, who awarded the album a 'four out of five' rating in his review. This was just one of numerous notices whose hyperbole would prove overblown. The album, Lawson decided, was 'the work of a group rediscovering what made them special in the first place [but] rather than making some obsequious, conciliatory gesture towards their original fan-base, [instead had rebuilt] their sound from scratch. No ballads, no orchestras and no fucking country music. Somewhere up in the ether, Cliff Burton is taking a hit from a celestial bong and grinning from ear to ear. Welcome home, boys.'

In the days and weeks that followed the release of *St Anger* on June 5, the air leaked from Metallica's bubble with a determined and sinister hiss. Yes, it was noted, the band was back. But with what? This was a release of such a complex and contradictory nature that it could not be dismissed merely with a grimace and a shudder. In one sense *St Anger* is arrogant in its self-confidence, with songs that enter the room like a noisy guest at a Christmas party who insists on staying until Burns' Night. Here we are, the band seems to say, pushing our noses into an endless slurry of riffs each underpinned by a drum sound that is the musical equivalent of someone placing a tin bucket over your head and hitting it repeatedly with a trowel.

But in another sense the eleven songs Metallica deemed worthy of inclusion here are dishearteningly unsure of themselves. *St Anger* was the first of the band's albums to be released after the advent of the nu-metal movement, and the decision not to include a single lead guitar solo from Kirk Hammett – and bear in mind that the musician's often untouchable leads had featured as a part of all but one of the original compositions the group had recorded up to that point – is without doubt the worst the band has ever made.

Musically disadvantageous, worse yet was the possibility that in eschewing Hammett's squalling solos Metallica felt they were aligning themselves with a group such as the wildly inventive System of a Down (at the time the most popular of the new breed as well as the metal equivalent of Frank Zappa) and thus making themselves more 'relevant'.

But a surfeit of solos was not *St Anger*'s only lousy idea. Metallica had decided they would write their lyrics by committee, with each member of the band suggesting couplets and ideas. Whereas in the past words written by James Hetfield, and guarded with a psychotic vigilance, were the only aspect of Metallica's output that improved from album to album, here the group's 'talents' combined to offer up one of the worst lyrical excursions of the twenty-first century. 'These are the legs in circles run,' sang Hetfield, apparently not at all concerned that what he was attempting to communicate made no sense at all. With a lack of artistry that is actually appalling, he adds that 'these are the lips that taste no freedom' – mud in the eye of those who thought it was the tongue that did the tasting – and 'this is the feel that's not so safe.'

As the bloated corpse of *St Anger* lay cold on the slab, Lars Ulrich would go only so far in responding to what was by now a clamour of criticism. To the charge that this was Metallica's worst album to date he would admit that while 'some people may think [that]', he declined to 'rank [the band's releases] from best to worst'.

'That kind of simplicity just doesn't exist for me,' he obfuscated. 'If I was fourteen, I could probably do it. [But] now the way I see the world [it is] nothing but greys, mainly.'

Ulrich would go on to admit that during the recording process the musicians has consciously eschewed editing of any kind while deliberately pursuing a drum sound that was persistent to the point of being unbearable. As listeners wondered if all of this added up to an insult, the Dane happened upon the real motivation for *St Anger*. For the first time, the making of an album didn't seem to be a musical pursuit at all, but rather an exercise in catharsis. And as with all the band's recordings, the considerations of anyone other than themselves were simply irrelevant. Whether or not a character trait that in the past had been the group's greatest strength could suddenly become their gravest weakness is a point well worth considering.

'I'm the biggest Metallica fan, you've got to remember that,' said the drummer. 'Once again, as we've been known to do, once in a while these boundaries have to be fucked with and it was really important for us in the wake of all that stuff we had to deal with in '01, '02 and '03 to take everything that we knew and rip it to bits. Just throw it up in the air and see where the pieces landed. The pieces landed [where they did] so that was what we had to do for our own sanity. I'm really proud of the fact that we did that. I still think there are some pretty great songs, or near great songs, buried in there, but I understand that for a large majority of people it's difficult to get beyond the sonics of it. And I'm okay with that.'

Lars Ulrich would have to be, because the time had come for Metallica to take an album that no one liked and drag it around the arenas and stadiums of the world.

7 — SOME KIND OF MONSTER

The floor of a locker room most often occupied by members of the Dallas Cowboys American football team is strewn with balloons in the black, white and silver of the Oakland Raiders. Metallica are seventeen dates into their Summer Sanitarium tour, and today, August 3, 2003, is James Hetfield's fortieth birthday. In a three-room dressing area the size of a basketball court, the band is preparing for a set still hours ahead. From the stage, the thump and whirr of Linkin Park can be heard. On a trestle table hard by the locker room's entrance sit two Dallas Cowboys helmets. A note from the front office asks if Metallica would kindly sign these items – a Sharpie pen has been provided – for inclusion in the Cowboys' museum. This the band do, but not before Hetfield has scrawled the words 'Go Raiders!' on the piece of paper.

The Summer Sanitarium caravan costs a million dollars a day to keep on the road. The tour operates on a principle best described as 'the leap-frog method', and occupies three stadiums at any given time. The group played a Saturday-night set at the vast and at the time brand-new Reliant Stadium in Houston. With the band in Dallas on the Sunday, the platform on which Metallica performed – itself as long as an airport runway – was lifted from the scaffold that supported it and transported to Salt Lake City for a date at the USANA Amphitheatre four nights hence, the steelwork for which is already in place. While this happens, the scaffold from Houston will be dismantled and transported to Washington State in preparation for an appearance at Seahawk Stadium on the Friday night, where the stage that is being used on Sunday in Dallas will sit. As well as this, Summer

Sanitarium has two PA systems, each of which hangs above the heads of the crowd like a giant satellite. The group also owns two full lighting rigs of such incandescence that when the show begins one wonders if it is to herald the arrival of a metal band or a close encounter of the third kind.

Backstage there is a yoga room. There is a production room in which people sit at computers and respond to the crackle of two-way radios. The tour carries with it a full-time masseuse. The size of the backstage compound is such that for all it matters the dressing room occupied by the support acts might as well be on Mars. In the less exclusive 'guest area' you will find 'the rubber room', a place where those with the required wristbands are able to drink beer. Patrons enter at their own risk; to tell the people standing at the bar that you've flown in from London is to be stared at with eyes reminiscent of those of a heavily tranquillised cat.

In Metallica's dressing area there sits a large orange birthday cake, its top decorated with a picture of Hetfield smiling wildly while leaning out of the window of a high-performance car. Following this evening's show, Metallica will leave the Texas Stadium while fans front of house are still cheering the night's final song. The band will then fly home to San Francisco where they will ride go-karts until dawn in celebration of the first day of their front man's fifth decade alive.

As afternoon creeps towards evening, Hetfield sits alone in a Cowboys' treatment room. He speaks on a mobile phone to one of his three children at home in Northern California. Kirk Hammett enters the room and with the kind of gentle intimacy that can only come from twenty years of friendship asks, 'Are we bothering you?' With a graceful shake of the head, Hetfield quietly says, 'No, not at all.' Moments earlier Hammett revealed that after a show Metallica 'always' shower together, but has declined to reveal which of the group's members boasts the most enhanced manhood ('No, I would not care to share that,' he says). As Hetfield speaks in a kind and melodious voice to the child on the other end of the phone, Hammett begins idly kicking at the balloons that litter the floor. These items are here, he explains, for the purpose of 'balloon therapy'. Attempting to keep check on a grin that is threatening to break loose across his face, the lead guitarist tells the English journalist that each day the four members of Metallica 'swim' through a sea of balloons in order to 'find peace' with themselves. As soon as he has said this, Hammett is on his belly, front-crawling his way through an event that might one day comprise a popular draw in the Very Special Olympics. His actions cause the stretched rubber to squeak loudly. 'It's therapy!' he explains, his expensive teeth grinning in total delight, his expensive hair falling over his face. 'Metallica is into therapy!'

An hour later, the member of the band that is 'into therapy' even more than the others sits answering questions. In order to help ease Hetfield's passage back into the regimented yet often chaotic routine that is life on the road, Metallica's live commitments in 2003 are undertaken at a pace that is more relaxed than has been the norm, certainly for them. For the duration of the Summer Sanitarium tour, the band will perform on a Friday, Saturday and Sunday evening (occasionally on a Thursday) and fly back to the Bay Area in time to meet the dawn of a Monday morning. This way Hetfield is able to spend the lion's share of the working week not working. Immersing himself first into the shallow end of life as a touring musician, the argument went, would mean the front man would have a better chance of continuing his recovery even in a setting of endless and easy temptation.

'I could so easily fall back [into the habit of] hanging out with the boys in the strip club,' he admits, adding that in 2003 he views such carnal pursuits as being 'a waste of time'. Instead his energies are focused on attempting to repair relationships that had been allowed to wither on the vine, friends who in the past the front man would call 'every eight months or so' and whose resentment in the face of such inattention would be far from mollified by the singer's defence of 'Don't you see how big [Metallica] has become? Do you not see how important I think I am?'

'You know,' he says, 'I spent far too long believing I was God. And, really, I didn't do a particularly good job, did I?'

Outside in the fetid summer air of the Texan summer, at the gates of the stadium turnstiles click to the sound of entry. Ticket-holders have each paid $125 to see the Summer Sanitarium tour's date in Dallas. But here, as in other North American cities, audiences have not flown to Metallica's flame in quite the numbers either band or concert promoter expected. Today in the Dallas suburb of Irving, somewhere in the region of 40,000 people will convene on this shabby thirty-two-year-old park, 25,000 fewer than attended Metallica's last appearance here three summers previously.

At the time of the Summer Sanitarium tour's announcement, rumours circulated Live Nation had paid Metallica $28 million to promote the tour, but the numbers were not adding up as the summer of 2003 approached. For the most part, the gigs attracted audiences in numbers between 35,000 and 50,000 people per night. There were exceptions. In Los Angeles the LA Coliseum reverberated to the roar of 60,000 ticket-holders, while a home-town concert at San Francisco's Candlestick Park on August 10 attracted the attention of a further 10,000 fans.

But one should be wary of regarding the 25,000 vacant seats at the Texas Stadium on August 3 as a sign that Metallica were in rapid decline. *St Anger* might have attained 'only' double platinum status on the *Billboard* Hot 200, but the quartet's previous two releases – an album of cover versions and a live CD recorded with an orchestra, remember – each sold more than five million copies in the US alone. With regard to the Summer Sanitarium tour, it is wise to consider the numbers that came rather than the capacity of the stadiums in which these people gathered. In order to accommodate Hetfield's desire to be broken in slowly, Metallica were faced with a choice: either play multiple nights in arenas or sheds – and on a tour featuring more nights off than on, this would have taken months – or else book themselves into the most enormous of enormodomes.

'We haven't done a tour like this for three fucking years,' says Lars Ulrich, as ever a mixture of hyperactivity and Tourette's. 'And with the greatest respect to a tour like the Ozzfest, this isn't something we view as a franchise. I don't think this is something we will do again for maybe four or five years, or until we feel the time is right.' He agrees that in order to undertake this tour in a relatively truncated twenty-city form Metallica were forced to hit not the sheds but the stadiums. 'That's the thing,' he says. 'There's a big leap between 18,000 in a pavilion and a 60,000-capacity stadium. We'd sell out the pavilion two nights over, at least, so this tour is going great.'

As one would expect, Ulrich will neither confirm or deny the fee supposedly paid to them by Live Nation for promoting the tour. He does, though, explain the simple economics of this vast undertaking.

'Here's how it works,' he says, as if speaking to a child. 'We pay for *everything*: the other bands, the crew, the stage, everything. So we have a big pile of money coming in and a big pile of money coming out. And at the end, we'll see what's left.' The obvious question, then, is will Metallica's balance from the tour be written in black ink or in red? Ulrich considers the question. 'It's gonna be close,' is his answer.

An hour later the drummer is up and about on the balls of his feet. The man who happily undressed before the disbelieving eyes of Hammett the very first time the two men met is today gambolling about dressed only in black football shorts and trainers though a dressing room busy with band mates, employees and a journalist. Stage time will soon be upon Metallica, and with a momentum as inevitable as it is purposeful the group are turning their minds to the elevated platform that lies just a short walk up a concrete ramp to the left of their dressing-room door. At the opposite end of the room there is an area that has been curtained off, inside which stand a drum kit, two amplifiers, a bass amp, two guitars and one bass. It is here, away from prying eyes, that the band will play one song in preparation for the two hours' worth of music on which they will then embark in front of tonight's paying audience.

Lars enters the space, and immediately exits it. 'There's a fucking photographer in there,' he exclaims, pulling on a black T-shirt and muttering how, anyway, his pooch always looks bigger when he's sitting down (this despite the fact that were one to offer a description of the drummer to the police one of the words employed would be 'thin'). With a tap on the shoulder and a nod of the head, the journalist learns that he will be permitted to watch Metallica as they prepare privately for their appearance. Ulrich is the first inside, clattering out a beat on his Tama drum kit. Over the course of the next minute, he is joined by his three band mates. At a sign invisible to the naked eye, the quartet begins to play in unison. It is to Hetfield's throttled riff that Metallica prepare to lash up the action in Dallas by tearing through 'Battery', a song they will repeat for the benefit of 40,000 people in just five minutes' time. As the dressing-room door is held open and Metallica are escorted the hundred yards to the stage, already the familiar, elegant strains of 'The Ecstasy of Gold' are under threat from the collective roar emanating from 40,000 faces.

Two hours later Hetfield stands onstage smeared with the detritus of what seems like several cans' worth of crazy-string and the dripping deposits of many custard pies. As he smiles and rubs matter from his eyes, the people he can see in the glare of the Texas Stadium spotlights are wishing him a happy birthday in song. Tonight Metallica have completed fifteen songs, and all that is required is for the band to resume 'Enter Sandman' – paused at the point of Hetfield's diaphragm-busting 'oh!' that follows the song's final chorus – before being transported home to California. As he picks out the notes of the main riff, the band join in before Ulrich stops the song again. Waiting just a moment, the drummer counts the band back into 'Enter Sandman', and as he does so the black sky overhead is fractured by the sight of exploding pyrotechnics.

Earlier that day Hetfield had commented, 'I think at the moment the band is playing as good as we've ever played: the guitars sound great and everything has just come together in a big way.' It is, he said, 'really something to be a part of this'. The journalist had listened politely to these words, thinking 'no danger of that quote ever being used'. But onstage that evening the vibrancy and energy of the group onstage – not to mention the affirmation of health and security that the quartet once more represented both to themselves and those who looked to them for some kind of reassurance – bestowed upon his words a greater resonance. In short: 'Really. Metallica are back.'

It is only in the back of a taxi cab an hour later that a thought causes a smile of contentment to be compromised by a frown. You realise that aside from 'Frantic' and 'St Anger' from Metallica's misfiring new album, each of the fourteen other songs that comprise the set are at least twelve years old. The band had decided not to trouble their audience with anything from *Load* or *Reload*.

It is aboard a flight back to London the next day that another, more troubling thought begins to slide into view: the notion that Metallica are becoming a physically impacting, emotionally stirring, musically astounding antique.

✝

Joe Berlinger is an adherent of what he calls the 'fifteen-minute rule'. In order not to squander time precious or otherwise, he refuses to wait for more than a quarter of an hour for anything, whether it be a film, a table at a restaurant or, indeed, a person. After this, he is off into the long grass. There is, though, an exception to every rule, and on the occasion of a business meeting with Metallica he broke his golden fifteen-minute stipulation sixteen times over.

That day, Berlinger was joined by his working partner Bruce Sinofsky. The pair, documentary film-makers, at the time were justly celebrated for their first feature, *Paradise Lost: The Child Murders at Robin Hood Hills*. The film tells the story of the West Memphis Three, a trio of teenagers who were convicted of the murders of three people in the US state of Arkansas. As the guilty verdicts were returned following a trial that alleged practices of Satanism as well as the testimony of 'expert witnesses', the qualifications of whom were deeply irregular, Damian Echols was sentenced to death while Jesse Misskelley and Jason Baldwin each received a tariff of life in prison. Convinced that the West Memphis Three were innocent of the crimes for which they had been convicted – as would prove to be the case, when the three men were finally granted release from prison in 2011 – Berlinger and Sinofsky set about committing to film a most compelling story of injustice, horror and institutionalised ineptitude that soon became a cause célèbre. Despite their reputation as a band that would only do something for a buck, Metallica permitted Berlinger and Sinofsky to use their music in the film free of charge. This was also the case for the pair's second documentary on the subject, *Paradise Lost 2: Revelations*, released in 2000.

Prior to the release of this second instalment, in the summer of 1999 the two film-makers were summoned to New York's Four Seasons hotel on Manhattan's West 57th Street. Seated in the hushed opulence of the lobby, the pair waited, and then waited some more. Every so often the doors of one of the elevators would disgorge Peter Mensch, Metallica's co-manager, who would explain that their audience with his charges was imminent. But as time slouched by, Berlinger began to wonder if he was waiting for the world's most popular metal band, or Godot. He was, he says, 'seething'.

The meeting was Q Prime's idea, and was thus concerned more with commerce than creativity. Metallica were about to take the next year off and the band's management desired a stop-gap 'product' that would keep the quartet in the public eye even though its members were devoting time to their private lives. (The fact that 2000 was the year that Napster blew up in their faces like a package from ACME addressed to Wile E. Coyote was of course not yet known.) It was Cliff Burnstein who suggested to Berlinger that he and Sinofsky might direct what was essentially an 'infomercial', a film that could be distributed as 'pay to play' on late-night television as a means of shifting old albums via a toll-free number. As the authors of a widely acclaimed documentary feature film that ticked the box of 'serious journalism', this was not an idea of which either man was wildly enamoured.

Instead Berlinger and Sinofsky's idea was to suggest to Q Prime and Metallica that, along with footage compiled from Ulrich's predictably compendious collection of Metallica video footage, the band might consent to being filmed in their private environment in order to show what Berlinger described as their more 'personal' side. When this idea was put to the group in Ulrich's penthouse suite, the group looked at Berlinger as if he'd suggested they might fancy performing in drag. As Hammett muttered about how he viewed his private time as being just that, Hetfield simply glowered. As the film-makers took the lift back down, Berlinger said to his partner that he didn't think their collaboration with Metallica would come to pass.

'No shit,' was Sinofsky's response.

Just eighteen months later Metallica decided that, actually, they were willing to unveil their more 'personal' side to anyone who cared to look. Armed with cameras and boom mics, Berlinger and Sinofsky flew from New York to San Francisco to embark on an adventure that would swallow the next two years of their lives (as well as a further twelve months entangled in post-production work). Their brief may at first have been only vaguely defined – as late as February 2003 the notion of editing the footage into six half-hour television programmes was still under consideration – but as the cameras rolled, it quickly became obvious that the two men were flies on the wall who could scarcely believe their luck.

Generally speaking, the worse things are for a subject, the better this is for a journalist or documentary-maker. So while in 2001 and 2002 Metallica wondered if the bell now tolled for them, all Berlinger and Sinofsky could hear (at least in a creative sense) was the sound of trumpets parping in their ears. As was the case with Phil Towle, the two men became part of Metallica's inner circle to the point where the band appeared to forget that they were being filmed at all (which is not uncommon among people who get used to the presence of a camera in their lives).

But Metallica *were* being filmed, and at extraordinary length. Over the two years cameras were trained on the band for 180 days. When the film-makers finally said, 'That's a wrap,' they had shot 1,602 hours of footage. The group's voices could be heard on seven miles of DAT tape. A total of 428 people had posed for Polaroids and signed release forms permitting the use of their likeness on film. One of this book's authors signed such a form and then watched in dismay as his face failed to grace anything but the cutting-room floor.

Metallica may have personally bankrolled Berlinger and Sinofsky's work – and at a cost of millions of dollars – but when it came to compiling the footage the film-makers were left to their own instincts. As the group reviewed the rushes it became increasingly obvious that this was a story that would be best served as a feature film rather than a 'reality' television series in the style of then popular *The Osbournes*, not least because on US television commercial breaks arrive with a frequency that is as disruptive as it is irritating. Ulrich in particular recognised that, handled with care, the footage might be edited into the kind of film watched by people who didn't buy popcorn when they went to the cinema (as fanciful as this idea might have sounded at the time). Ever true to his own instincts Ulrich lobbied for the format of a feature film.

The result was *Some Kind of Monster*, a documentary, the clarity and naked authority of which obliterates the story of disunity as told by literally hundreds of journalists in magazine articles published the previous year. For their part, once the band had held open their door to the cameras, they did not flinch at the prospect of allowing the world to see the mess they were in. Metallica had spoken of *everything* on the film, from Hetfield's endless stories of his spell in rehab to Lars's frank admission that he feared that the band he loved as much as anything in life had run its natural course. But somehow the words written when Metallica were on the hustings for *St Anger* did not come close to framing the disintegration and decay that had seeped into the band's immune system. Following a series of screenings at the world's most prestigious film festivals (including a rapturous response from the opinion-formers at the Sundance film festival in Utah in January of 2004) *Some Kind of Monster* was released on July 31. Metallica fans across the world duly made their way to independent cinemas to watch it: they would emerge two hours and twenty minutes later asking one question. *How* did it come to *this*?

Some Kind of Monster is a film that groans with the weight of collective despair, acute anxieties, unchecked resentment and, sometimes, grandly amusing examples of personal folly and human fallibility. Equally remarkable, however, is the fact that the film had arrived as if from nowhere. The default setting of all groups is to present to their public a united front, a facade that their audience often complicitly accepts as the entire truth, hearing what they want to hear and disregarding the rest. But in private all bands have their cliques and squabbles, their simmering grievances and often distasteful politics. The only difference is that Metallica were the first to edit theirs into a feature film that went on limited release in cinema theatres.

The results adhered to the strictest laws of unintended consequences. *Some Kind of Monster* did for Metallica what innumerable expensive press and marketing campaigns had failed to manage: it brought the band the attention and respect of people who not only did not like them – or did not believe that they liked them – but who also suspected that the genre the group represented was the least valid of all musical subcultures. Overnight *Some Kind of Monster* changed the perception of its subjects in the eyes of strangers. That Metallica represented not just entertainment but also art was finally accepted by some people who had previously considered the band – if they had considered them at all – only with condescension.

There were, of course, some who viewed Metallica's very public blood-letting as being not only unnecessary but actually somehow axiomatically 'un-metal'. Predictably this point of view was best encapsulated by Slayer guitarist Kerry King, who after viewing the film derided its protagonists for being 'fragile old men'. The overwhelming majority of people who saw *Some Kind of Monster*, though, recognised the scale of both the human and the creative achievement it represented.

The piece pivots on an extraordinary scene that sees Ulrich attempting to make sense of the shifting sands on which Metallica now stands. As he is speaking, Hetfield sits and listens. He is discussing their work on *St Anger*; the drummer is hurt and bewildered by Hetfield's insistence that work on the album must stop the moment the front man leaves HQ each day at 4 p.m. Seated at the same kitchen table as Hetfield are Kirk Hammett, Bob Rock and Phil Towle. Ulrich, however, is not seated; instead he paces the floor in the manner of a caged and unhappy animal.

'I just think you're fucking self-obsessed,' says the drummer. 'And what makes it worse is that when you talk about me you always talk about control and manipulation. But I think you use control on purpose and I think you control inadvertently. I think you control by the rules you always set. I think you control by how you always judge people. I think you control by your absence. You control all of this even when you're not here.'

As he listens to the man with whom he formed Metallica twenty years earlier, Hetfield sits impassively. His eyes do not track the drummer's constant movements. The only indication that Hetfield is even listening to what is being said comes with the slow and deliberate exhalation of air through his nose. Perhaps a technique learned in rehab, nonetheless the effect is reminiscent of a gun's safety-catch clicking to its off setting.

'I don't understand who you are,' the drummer continues. 'I don't understand the programme. I don't understand all this stuff.' Ulrich regards the man with whom he used to share hotel rooms, with whom he shared a house, not to mention one of the people with whom he showers after concerts. He utters a sentence so quietly devastating that it appears to slip by almost unnoticed. 'I realise now that I barely knew you before,' he says. 'All these rules and shit, man. This is a fucking rock 'n' roll band. I don't want fucking rules. I understand that you need to leave at four. I respect it. [But] don't tell me that I can't sit and listen to something with Bob at four fifteen if I want to. What the fuck is that?' But, as quickly as it had reared into view, the frustration and anger that is coursing through Ulrich's veins suddenly gives way to the thing that informed those emotions in the first place:

fear. 'I don't want to end up like Jason [Newsted],' he confesses, as if this were even possible. Here it sounds as if Ulrich is almost pleading. 'Okay? I don't want to be pushed away. I don't want it to happen twice.' But the moment this fear of being marginalised to the point of extinction has been articulated, it is gone. In its place there is a gas-guzzling charge to the precipice of the vertiginous cliff that stands at the end of the band's world.

'If we're going to do it then let's do it full on or [let's] not do it at all,' he says.

In the gravid silence that follows, the very existence of Metallica is suddenly no more secure than a secret in a soap opera. Ulrich continues to pace like an accused man waiting the verdict of a jury of his peers. He can't think of anything more to say, or perhaps there's just too much to say.

'Fuck,' he says, almost in a whisper.

'Fuck,' this time louder.

'Fuck,' louder still.

By now Ulrich is leaning over the table and has his face just inches from that of Hetfield. With a sense of frustration that might be about to overwhelm him, the drummer once more says, 'Fuck!' As this happens, the front man does not move, or react in any way. It is a remarkable show of restraint.

'I think my calmness had a lot to do with me just having come out of therapy,' Hetfield will say of his response to an outburst he admits 'had to come out'.

'I also think that being filmed had a lot to do with it too. Afterwards I said [to Lars], "That happens once and I'll accept it. But I don't want you invading my space like that again." It's as simple as that.'

By this point Phil Towle's full-time place of work was the setting where Hetfield held down his own part-time job, HQ in San Rafael. Now resident in San Francisco – the city in which he and his wife still live – the Pasadena-born Performance Enhancement

Coach sits stoically while the volcano that is Lars Ulrich volleys lava all over the shop. But if Towle is as silent as everyone else in the room bar the Dane, his eyes are far from still. They dart from place to place, measuring the response of each combatant to the words spewing forth from a man whose reserve is now shattered.

'I was scared because without question that was a pivotal moment,' says Towle, looking back. 'That could so easily have been the point where James said, "That's it, it's all over . . ." Here he was, back with a band that he loved deeply, but at a time when he was fractured and was trying to put himself back together. And the band was a constant reminder of the things that had caused him to fall apart. So he's trying to adjust, and he's back with his mates that he hasn't seen for a long time. But since then he now has a different agenda, and it is an agenda that is colliding with the agenda of the guys who have been waiting patiently for him to come back. So they're feeling resentful about this, as well as about a lot of other things as well.

'When this collision in the kitchen occurs it does so in a very, very dramatic way. But you have to remember that this was Lars's first opportunity to share with James directly just how angry he was, about this and other things too. While James was away in a secure place, he and Kirk had put their professional work on hold for him. They didn't know even if they had a band any more. So you have a tremendous amount of anxiety being channelled through Lars. And his point of view was, "We waited for you and now you're dictating terms to us. You were the one who had to go to rehab. You are the one who fucked up." Kirk's not really the kind of person to confront James like that, and Bob [Rock]'s relationship with the band is slightly different, so it's not really his place to address the issue. So it's down to Lars. But it was scary to him, and to them, and to me as well, actually. "What is going to become of us?" Watching all of this unfold, I realised that my strategy had to be to let it all play out. Because had I tried to

intervene before the feelings had been expressed then they would
have gone underground again, and then who knows how long it
would be before they returned to the surface? What happened
that day was both a breaking point *and* a breaking-*through* point.
It was one of those moments that come along in life when you
just have to, as I say, trust the process. And out of that came some
really good stuff. It didn't come all out once, but that was the
catalyst. It was definitely their "Come to Jesus" moment.'

Towle understands that while the viewer sees *a* story of the
techniques used to bring Metallica back together as one, he or
she does not witness *the* story in anything like its entirety. 'There
is so much work that we did that just isn't in there,' he says, in a
tone of voice that suggests that he understands why. The mind
boggles at the scenes of collective lunacy and corrective therapy
that are now gathering dust on shelves and in film canisters at
locations unknown. Scenes like the occasion of Kirk Hammett's
birthday, where the his friends and colleagues celebrated the start
of the lead guitarist's fifth decade by arriving at HQ dressed in
Hawaiian shirts. All, that is, except Lars Ulrich, who had not
been told about this. As a civilised but happy gathering cut a
cake on which can be seen a likeness of Hammett on a surfboard,
outside sits a drummer, sulking.

'No one ever does anything for me,' he pouts. At first it is
Rock who attempts to mollify the Dane – 'Your birthday is the
day after Christmas!' he reasons – before, inevitably, Phil Towle
steps once more into the breach.

'I'm the only one who didn't know!' exclaims the drummer.

Towle, himself dressed in a Hawaiian shirt, regards Lars with
silence, knowing that this is a field of play on to which he can
only enter once the storm clouds overhead have dispersed.

'I wish someone would have fucking let me know,' he says.
'How do you think it feels showing up here and being the only
one who doesn't have a Hawaiian shirt on? People go, "Oh it's

because he's so rebellious" . . . [but] I'm permanently ambushed with this fucking shit . . .'

In a mellifluous and measured voice, Towle points out to Ulrich that 'the moment you got here you could have joined the festivities but you chose not to. And as you distanced yourself you felt worse.' These words are spoken as if Towle is Ulrich's father.

Ulrich knows this to be true. But as trifling as the matter may appear – thirty-nine-year-old man sulks over party dress code – at its core his irritation and feelings of exclusion are justified. This, too, he knows, and for the time being this is propelling his anger onward. 'Life is an eternal birthday party for somebody else, with an occasional five-minute work spurt,' he observes, his annoyance dispersing into other areas of discontent.

'You have to understand Lars's role in the band,' says Towle today. 'The musical creator is James. [In relation] to that, Lars is the baseline. He can organise. He can co-produce. He's great with Pro Tools, and he was in the studio for everything that needed doing. Lars was the grounding force for everything that Metallica have ever done. He was the outside promoter, the guy who risked himself [taking on] Napster. And to Lars that role of grounding is very natural; from a young age he's learned to be independent. Lars is very careful, he anticipates things and manages expectations. But when he is blind-sided by something, – and it doesn't matter what it is, it wasn't about the shirts at all – at that point he feels threatened and insecure. He came in that day and discovered that it was Hawaiian shirt day and [said], "I didn't know!" And this is a big problem for Lars. Suddenly he's thinking, I didn't know about this and because I didn't know about it then bad things can happen! I've been blind-sided and this freaks me out.'

In one sense *Some Kind of Monster* can be viewed as an exercise in taking a side: Team Ulrich or Team Hetfield. But this battle royal of common human struggle takes place in an environment different from that in which almost every member of the audience lives their lives. This is a donnybrook on Multi-Millionaires' Row. Peace breaks out only after the soothing balm of therapy has been applied. While the viewers themselves are not part of this therapy, nonetheless they are bombarded with its terminology. The temptation is to dismiss this as being nothing more than the kind of mumbo jumbo one might find inside a fortune cookie. That all of this makes sense to a band now two years into their process of reparation is exactly as it should be. But that audiences should view this transition with a measure of mockery is also understandable.

Inevitably it was Towle who found himself in the barrel. Even to moderate and conciliatory eyes, the notion that Towle is *Some Kind of Monster*'s oddest component is a difficult one to shift. More than a decade after his time with Metallica, being interviewed for this book, the Performance Enhancement Coach comes across as an immediately likeable, approachable and generous figure; a stranger on the end of a phone line who is uncommonly helpful and quietly charismatic. It should also be remembered that of all the people that appear on screen in Berlinger and Sinofsky's masterpiece, Towle is the only one not used to having a camera trained upon him. Neither was his cause aided by the band clambering aboard their repaired juggernaut and deciding unilaterally that his presence was no longer required. The trio's mutterings about their fears of how the man who has nursed them back to health seems now to believe himself to be an actual member of Metallica are disrespectful. The decision to present him with his redundancy papers not as part of a negotiation but as a fait accompli is, at best, unkind. Suddenly it is Phil Towle's turn to be blind-sided, and the finality of Metallica's news causes him to shed a tear on camera, the memory of which tugs at his sleeve to this day.

'I was wounded, legitimately wounded, by my own expectations,' he says. 'That's not [the group's] problem, that's my problem. But I would love to redo that part of our work . . .

My expectation was that my work was going to continue on for a little longer than it did. This was predicated by an agreement I had with at least one member of the band who asked me to continue. But then they had a meeting on their own, which they're certainly entitled to do, and decided differently. But the person I had the agreement with was pretty solid that there was work still to be done, which was something I concurred with. So I was disappointed and I was trying to figure out on the spot how to handle that. And I handled it poorly. The group came to an agreement that was the decision of the three of them. I would have liked to have been a part of that, but I wasn't. But I didn't want to expose these differences on camera. So I did a good job of taking the hit but I did a bad job of processing what I was hearing. So I did not like that that became the centrepiece of how I left, and that people who were watching the movie might think that I was just trying to selfishly hang on for my own reasons.'

Either way, as Metallica prepared to begin the hard sell of their new album, the musicians slowed their juggernaut long enough only to drop off Towle at the next slip road. The therapist did accompany the band on a number of early dates of their 2003 tour, and he had personal contact with the group in the intervening years, as well as a professional association with one unnamed member for a further year. But in terms of working with Metallica as a band, 2003 was the end of the line.

Yet while this exit may have been less than seamless, Phil Towle can, and should, be consoled by the fact that more than anyone else he is the one person that can take credit for allowing this strangest of monsters to live.

†

Just one month prior to the release of *Some Kind of Monster*, however, Metallica threw doubt on the notion that this was a band stronger and wiser than ever before. The occasion was the final night of the three-day Download festival at Donington Park – the successor to the Monsters of Rock happening of previous summers – where, on June 6, 2004, 60,000 people watched the Sunday evening sets while gathered in front of a stage that awaited the arrival of just one more band. The hour, though, is getting late. Metallica should have been onstage at least sixty minutes ago, but no word of the cause of this delay has been relayed to the patrons at Castle Donington.

In the guest area behind the stage the conversation centres on just one topic: the rumour that Lars Ulrich is not 'on site'. It is said that the drummer has been flown to hospital, and that although Metallica will honour their commitments this evening they will do so with a series of guest drummers. As jokes abound about how at least on this Sunday evening people will get to see the band play with musicians capable of keeping time, this strange whisper becomes more credible with each passing minute. This is the one weekend of the year when *Kerrang!* magazine sends pages to printers just two days before the magazine can be bought in shops – usually the weekly publication goes to press the previous Friday – and the potential non-appearance of Metallica's most redoubtable member frays the nerves of a team of editors, journalists and photographers that are already in a state of high alert. But while the rumours fly like bullets, facts are harder to come by.

At ninety minutes past their allotted stage time, James Hetfield, Kirk Hammett and Robert Trujillo walk out onto the stage. Their presence is met by a cheer that is tinged with uncertainty. The musicians have made themselves seen prior to their intro tape. More than this, though, they are a drummer short (and not just any drummer). In a voice, the resonance of which cannot entirely obscure its uncertainty, Hetfield announces to scores of thousands of people that Lars Ulrich will not be performing with Metallica this evening. He explains that a medical matter has meant that his band mate of twenty-three years will be spending the night in hospital, but that this is merely a precautionary measure. The 'Metallica family' has no cause to worry unduly as the drummer will be fine. Later in the evening, however, Hetfield will make a rather cryptic reference to how he hopes that Ulrich is able to work through the issues that he is presently facing. For their audience at Donington Park that evening, Metallica muscle on with the help of Slayer's Dave Lombardo, Slipknot's Joey Jordison and Ulrich's own drum technician Fleming Larsen. The set, Hetfield informs his audience, will 'either be one of the best or one of the worst things you've ever seen'. Curiously, it is neither.

The band, though, can count themselves lucky that it is their songs that every metal musician since 1985 has learned to play before any others. As Joey Jordison is quick to admit, 'Metallica is *the* fucking band.' The group that inspired the then-Slipknot drummer to spend hours playing drums in his parents' basement with the stereo behind him, 'just *cranking* those records' and learning Lars's drums beat for beat. 'I did that for years and I know those first four records front to back.'

On site at the festival the message came through to Jordison that Metallica were in keen need of assistance. The task may have been akin to jumping into fire, but the drummer did not need to be asked twice.

'Honestly, it was like, "They need help, there's 70,000 people waiting on them out there, and they're asking me?" Getting to play with Metallica? Come on, it was amazing man! It's one of my most treasured memories. I said [to them] I know all of your stuff, whatever you throw out at me I'll know it. Of course I was going to help them out.'

Two days later Ulrich attempted to quell the by now boisterous rumours regarding the first Metallica concert not to feature his presence on the drum stool. Posted as a video message on the band's website, his words do not exactly sift mud from the waters. Speaking from the group's dressing room backstage at the Südweststadium in the German city of Ludwigshafen, the Dane is keen to tell his viewers that he has arrived on site early so he has time to head out for a run. He makes a show of drinking fresh orange juice and eating a banana. In his efforts to address his absence from the Download stage forty-eight hours earlier, however, Ulrich sounds not a great deal more convincing than does the mayor of Amity in *Jaws*, when he describes a man-eating shark as a 'predator that allegedly injured some bathers'.

'It must be a slow news day,' he says, sort of addressing the clamour of conversation his absence has inspired. 'Drummer misses rock show.' Ulrich then alludes to Metallica's increased workload in 2004 – a year that saw the group undertake a tour of three continents and perform 116 shows – and admits that 'at my age' the schedule 'kind of caught up with me the other day and I had to chill out. But there's no need to bore people with the details, but I had a little episode on the plane en route to Donington the other day.'

While viewers to a man and woman thought, 'We wouldn't be at all bored with the details, actually,' in the place of hard evidence stood hyperbolic rumour. By the end of the week, it was being said that the cause of Ulrich's absence was the fact that his wife had caught him in bed with two female fans. The result of this, it was said, at least by some, was that the drummer pushed his face into a pile of cocaine of a size sufficient to land him in hospital. So fantastically otherworldly was this claim that it seemed only fair to one of this book's authors that this charge be put to Ulrich directly and at the earliest convenience.

'For the record,' was his still good-natured reply, 'my wife did not catch me in bed with two women and I did not end up in hospital because I'd taken too much cocaine.'

As with all the rumours, this particular doozy attained some kind of currency because its roots were planted in the reality of Lars Ulrich's public image. As has been seen, this was the decade that saw James Hetfield shed almost all of the habits that once occupied his time. Stage left, Kirk Hammett also confessed to giving up cocaine, a drug he had grown to hate even while loving the smell. Had he continued inhaling sharply while bent double, 'I would have gone under' he said. So by default, as well as by a little bit more than default, Lars Ulrich remained Metallica's most unreconstructed member, someone who still enjoyed 'a bump [of cocaine] every now and again'.

The logical conclusion of this is the deduction that while Metallica are a band as ever united by music, away from the recording studio and stage they are a group populated by disparate individuals who share little common ground on which to stand. With one of the best questions that has ever been asked of Hetfield, the English journalist Ben Mitchell addressed this notion in 2007 when he asked him if he loved the drummer with whom he had shared the entirety of his adult life.

'I do,' came his answer, without pause or equivocation. 'There is no doubt that we were put together on this journey for a reason. We hooked up and, as is the case with my wife and I, opposites do attract [although] it is a never-ending battle. But we've got this chemistry that works even though resentments get in the way and sometimes we can't see that it works. There's an agitation, a friction, a spark that just happens. [These days] we're better at listening to each other and maybe at listening to feedback about each other, or perceptions of each other, but it's still tough.'

But while love remains the most fundamental emotion of the human condition, it is something over which one rarely has much control. To love someone is not, necessarily, to like them. And while through thick and very, very thin Hetfield and Ulrich have managed to keep their bubbling volcano of occasional enmity from spewing forth with terminal force, with each passing year it seems as if the two men have drifted further and further apart to the point where now they are united by what they have created together, rather than by being the people they are today. Asked if there were any activities other than Metallica that front man and drummer might enjoy together, Hetfield answers, 'No,' before considering his options once more and offering, 'Movies, maybe.' With his arm extended in search of straws he then says, 'Besides children and family life, we're both very into art.' But unfortunately the pair's tastes run to 'completely different kinds of art'. This is a little bit like suggesting that Wolfgang Amadeus Mozart and Captain Sensible share common ground because they were both 'into' music.

Mitchell also asked Lars Ulrich if he felt a commonality with James Hetfield outside the confines of the now mended Metallica. The question summoned forth from the drummer that most rare of responses: silence. The Dane was forced to admit that this was 'a good question', but one to which he was able to furnish an answer only after a pause.

'We're both pretty passionate about movies,' came the reply finally. 'And we're very passionate about [ice] hockey. We're both big Sharks supporters – the San Jose Sharks are our local hockey team. We both like fine food. We both put our shoes on in the morning.' But . . .

'When we're in there playing I really enjoy it,' he says, 'much more than I have in years. We come and go when we have to. The priorities are the kids and families. The main thing we have in common other than Metallica is that we both prioritise our families over [the band] and that's a new thing. The fact that we've had kids at the same time and [they are thus] of the same age is probably literally, directly responsible for the band still being together. [Without having that in common] we probably couldn't sustain the relationship.'

While James Hetfield is Metallica's most respected member, Lars Ulrich is the most well liked. Nowhere is he held in higher regard than among the press corps. The manner in which this status has been attained is simple: Ulrich charms and engages everyone who comes into his orbit. This he does with an innate capacity for sincerity that seems entirely natural. In this sense, he is the rock musician's equivalent of Bill Clinton. But if this is all a grand calculation, a schmooze that has lasted for more than thirty years, it doesn't seem to be so. Writers and photographers the world over rarely, if ever, feel glad-handed by the Dane, despite the fact that at certain points in his band's career the number of interviews given by him on any given day exceeded the number of hot meals he had ingested by a factor of two to one.

His eye for detail and his memory are extraordinary. Backstage at the O2 Arena in 2009, he told one of this book's authors how that evening's set would include a song the writer would like – 'The Outlaw Torn' – a reference to a live review written after the band's concert at Earl's Court some *six years* previously. Furthermore, his manners can be beguiling. Asked in the summer of 2003 by one of the present writers whether or not the rumour that Metallica were to play a surprise set at that summer's Download festival was true, the drummer answered that it was not. He explained that their headline slot at the Leeds and Reading festivals in August meant this would mean a contractual conflict of interest. But Metallica *did* undertake an unannounced set in the East Midlands that weekend. Shortly after the band had bid a surprised and delighted audience a good day, in London a music journalist's mobile phone began to ring. It was Ulrich, apologising for lying about his group's plans for the weekend.

Best of all, following a dispute (with one of the authors of this book again) about whether 'anticipatory' was a genuine word – Ulrich said it was, the writer said it wasn't (and to this day cites Lars's Danish accent as his defence case) – the next time the pair met, the drummer produced from his pocket a photocopied page from the dictionary with the word under discussion circled by the ink from a Sharpie pen.

The result of such attention to detail is a press that adores him. Even fun is made affectionately, such as the period when *Kerrang!* insisted on referring to the drummer as 'the tubby tub-thumper'. But in London in June 2008 Ulrich behaved in a manner so at odds with what people who believe they know him but really don't would expect that it beggars belief. This is the first time the incident has been described in print.

Foo Fighters had flown from Los Angeles to England in good time for what remains the quartet's most prestigious and well-attended brace of concerts at Wembley Stadium. An 'in-the-round' stage was being prepared on which Dave Grohl's band would perform on the following Friday and Saturday nights. The group were staying at the Metropolitan Hotel, a lodging of choice for high-end rock stars, situated at the southernmost point of London's lovely Park Lane. Boasting the always over-subscribed sushi restaurant, Nobu, and a then impossibly fashionable and celebrity-strewn bar (the 'Met Bar'), the Metropolitan Hotel's sumptuous beds have supported the weight of, among others, Slash and Duff McKagan from Guns N' Roses and Nine Inch Nails' musical director Trent Reznor.

That evening, a Wednesday, June 4, the Met Bar and the hotel lobby were the site of an informal gathering called by the Foo Fighters. In attendance were a number of the band's friends, as well as representatives of the group's management company and others who worked the band's cause. Drummer Taylor Hawkins had invited along Queen guitarist Brian May. The other famous person in attendance that evening was Lars Ulrich.

'Everybody was just in really high spirits, drinking and having a laugh,' says one participant, who has asked to remain anonymous. 'It was so different from the usual kind of music industry gathering. Dave [Grohl] was there, of course, and everyone knows that he's quite affable anyway and so he was making everyone feel welcome, giving some of the girls there a friendly kiss as a greeting – that kind of thing. I can't remember at what point Lars came over to Dave, but when he did they hugged and were really giving it the "bro" act. Dave was saying that were it not for Lars he would have never taken up the drums, and Lars was saying, "No it's this guy, he's the best drummer." It really was gushing stuff, boys being boys.'

As the hours passed the crowd at the gathering thinned. But this was a night that would not end early. At 4 a.m. about seven people were still seated around a table in the hotel lobby. It was at this point that Ulrich emphatically broke the convivial atmosphere.

'I don't remember seeing anything of Lars for ages after [his exchanges with Dave Grohl],' recalls the eyewitness. 'I was just hanging out with my friends until about four, four thirty in the morning. It was super late . . . There was a guy to my right, and I remember Lars just coming out of nowhere and going to kick him. But he missed him. And I just thought this was high jinks, you know, like a joke. But he got up, turned round and knocked this guy out of his chair, and started shouting at him. At this point he picked up the chair and threw the chair *on* him. Then he started laying into this guy, who was just laid in the foetal position, not moving at all. He made no effort to defend himself at all. And Lars was shouting, "Don't you fucking do that again when I'm around . . ." or words to that effect.

'Although all this must have lasted for only six or seven seconds, for me watching it kind of took place in a state of suspended disbelief with a whole different perception of time. No one got up to do anything [about what was happening], everyone just sat there staring. But I do remember everyone looking to Dave to do something because, you know, he was the one other famous person in the room. It was as if somehow because of this he was the only person capable of stopping what Lars was doing. I don't know if that makes sense? But Dave wasn't doing anything, he just stared back. Finally someone thought to say to [Ulrich] "What the fuck are you doing?" When he heard this he turned to the person who had spoken and . . . I really wish I could remember exactly what he said, but I do remember it being really aggressive. Obviously this signalled the end of the night for me, and me and my friends marched out of the hotel. But thinking about it afterward it seemed like somehow you were supposed to let people [as famous as Ulrich] get away with this kind of thing and not intervene. I mean, apart from one person no one else said *anything*.'

Just weeks after what the eyewitness described as a 'really quite upsetting' moment of unpleasantness, Ulrich is once again interviewed by one of this book's authors. The subject of what occurred at the Metropolitan Hotel is broached, but for once the drummer is unwilling to speak on or off the record. Instead he mumbles, 'No . . . that's not important.' As if realising that 'not important' is not the right phrase, he then says, 'It's private.'

Unwilling to let the issue drop, the journalist says that on hearing about the incident he was disappointed with Lars Ulrich. 'Yeah,' is his answer. 'I was disappointed in myself.'

8 — BROKEN, BEAT & SCARRED

As the sun sets over Istanbul, the four members of Metallica take in the evening air. With twilight embracing the oval banks of the tastefully decrepit Ali Sami Yen Stadium in the centre of this exhilarating and utterly chaotic city, twenty-five carefully selected members of the band's fan club wait to meet men whose feet have not trodden on Turkish soil for sixteen years. When it comes to 'meet 'n' greets' normally, the more popular the act, the less keen they are to meet their public. In recent years an odious practice has begun to infiltrate the higher echelons of the music industry, meaning that only those that have purchased 'golden circle' tickets to an arena or stadium show will be permitted to shake hands and exchange the smallest of talk with the artist whose name appears on increasingly over-priced tickets. It is not uncommon for entry to the 'golden circle' to cost £1,000, face value. No longer a game for young men, rock music *is* becoming a sport for the rich.

But here, as is the case with so much they do, Metallica buck the trend. The band not only offer this service free of charge – asking fans to pay only for the pleasure of seeing them perform – but James Hetfield, Lars Ulrich, Kirk Hammett and Robert Trujillo appear to quietly savour their interactions with people for whom their presence is a matter of the utmost importance. As at all venues they will play in 2008 and 2009, Metallica greet the small gathering of fans for nothing.

The quartet arrive at tonight's venue having flown in from Milan. They are due onstage in less than an hour. Already the concrete bowl that stands behind them reverberates to the sound of 42,000 people chanting the band's name over and over again. The three Americans and one Dane seem not to notice the collective commotion caused by their scheduled appearance in Istanbul, and if they do it is not something that is remarked upon. This might be because the intensity of the adoration surging through the air on this glorious Sunday evening is not untypical of the clamour that still attracts itself to the band. As one of the writers of this book surveys the scene, he thinks of the unfortunate incident earlier in the decade when three of these four people went mad and considers whether, really, it was that much of a surprise.

Galatasaray FC would later relocate to a brand-new stadium, but in 2008 the Ali Sami Yen Stadium is home to the team, and is a notorious location. On match days the club's supporters hang banners in the stands that read 'Welcome to Hell', but tonight the crowd that packs the park is in the seventh heaven. Backstage the organisation is time-efficient to a militaristic degree. Every minute that Metallica are on site is accounted for. The moment time is called on tonight's set, the group will be doing what they describe as 'a runner' with each musician seated in a limousine en route to the airport before the first wave of fans exits the ground. (The opposite to a 'runner', incidentally, is 'a jogger', where the band unwind for an hour or so at the venue.) Since entering the compound, each member has sat for an interview with a visiting English music journalist. They have gurned wildly for photographs taken by *Kerrang!*'s Ashley Maile. They will find time to jam through 'Creeping Death' as well as '. . . And Justice for All' minutes before heading to the stage, performing this time not in an American football team's locker room but in the back of an equipment truck. They will find time for a massage. Most importantly for the twenty-five people waiting hesitantly in the open air behind the stadium, Metallica will find time for them.

Today members of Metallica's fan club have travelled to this crossroads between East and West from troubled regions such as

Iran, Lebanon and even Palestine. One guest is a thirty-something Iraqi Kurd. Standing as tall as an NBA forward, the man is nervous and uncertain. As the band shake hands, sign albums and posters, and pose for photographs in a manner far more effortlessly convivial than any other meet 'n' greet the journalist has previously witnessed, James Hetfield finally stands before the Kurdish supporter. In a voice as serious as it is alive with wonder, Hetfield is informed, 'You are my idol.' *Idol*, not hero. The front man has long since learned to accept such staggering statements in a manner that prohibits absorption. But while his response of 'Thanks, man' is non-committal, it is delivered in a tone that seems to say that although he hesitates to accept the accolade, he understands that the man whose hand he is shaking really means it.

Metallica's extraordinarily intense relationship with their most dedicated fans – the true fanatics – pulses with the same energy and instinct as it did twenty-five years ago. That the band was better than its peers was a given, but then as now this is a love affair grounded not in competency but in conviction. In that sense, it doesn't *really* matter, at least for the moment, that it has now been five years since the band last released a studio album, nor that the latest album was the much-derided *St Anger*. It is as if its creators and its audience are pretending that the whole misadventure never actually happened, and it is all but unheard of for the band to play anything from their most recent release – in fact tonight in Turkey the most recent songs aired are from 'The Black Album'. On the rare occasions when Metallica decide to play a song from *St Anger* – as the band does with 'Frantic' at a fan-club only concert at London's O2 Arena in September – James Hetfield acknowledges the bemusement of the crowd by saying of the song's parent album, 'It's okay [not to like it]; we all have our favourites.' Because of this, Metallica's public profile has not taken a hit. Following the somewhat underwhelming Summer Sanitarium tour of North American stadiums in 2003, in 2004 the band moved their operation indoors for a tour of US and Canadian hockey arenas that saw 'sold out' signs appear wherever it roamed, in some cases for multiple nights.

At this point Metallica appeared equipped once again to do whatever they desired, and what they desired to do most was to take a nap. Heading off to bed at the end of 2004, the group decided they didn't really fancy getting up again for three whole years. In the intervening period they performed live a mere thirty-two times, and did little in the way of conventional work. Instead in 2005 the band opened for the Rolling Stones over two nights at SBC Park in San Francisco; and the following year they appeared in an episode of *The Simpsons* as well as performing two acoustic sets at the Mountain View Shoreline Amphitheatre in support of Neil Young's Bridge School Benefit charity. That was the event that saw the quartet perform a version of the Dire Straits song 'Brothers in Arms' that was as close to being sublime as makes no difference.

A total absence of recorded music and a paucity of personal appearances did nothing to dim Metallica's flame. Defying the laws of commercial gravity, their profile refused to meet the horizon. An apropos-of-nothing headline performance on July 8, 2007, at Wembley Stadium (featuring a commercially underwhelming under card of HIM, Mastodon and Machine Head) still managed to draw more than 60,000 faces to England's national stadium. The band also allowed the stage on which they played to be used for a Live Earth concert on July 7, featuring contributions from Madonna, Foo Fighters, Beastie Boys and many others, and staged to raise awareness of the issue of climate change. Metallica proved once again that they weren't always a good mix at the party by playing exactly the same stiff three-song set that they'd chosen for the Freddie Mercury Tribute Concert at the old Wembley Stadium fifteen years earlier.

By rights, of course, so much treading of water and idling of

engines should have signalled to others that this was a band fast
asleep on the job and whose crown as the Kings of Metal was going
cheap. But almost a quarter of a century after Metallica had made
Iron Maiden – a band whose members were not appreciably older
than themselves – seem moth-balled and toothless *overnight*, here
they were being permitted to idly kick a can on the road for three
years. As the four musicians whistled down the wind, not one
band emerged with the kind of moxy required to stride into their
light. Once again Metallica were able to count themselves lucky.

'I don't know why no one has emerged to steal our thunder,'
says Kirk Hammett, griping ever so slightly at what he regards as
being 'a provocative question'. He says, 'I really have no idea why
that hasn't happened. But I hope someone *does* rise up, because
we'd like to rise to their challenge . . . We need young bands.
Young bands are the role models for the even younger people
who will form the bands that come after them.'

'There is an earthquake going on in the music industry,' says
Hetfield. As if this isn't quite descriptive enough, the front man
then holds out his hands before him and allows them to shake
violently. Like a child playing a trumpet, his cheeks fill with air as
he forces a guttural earth-shifting sound from his throat.

'But this band is relevant,' he says.

This is exactly what Metallica fans want to hear, and precisely
what they want to believe. On the hustings for a new album that
is soon to hover into view, Lars Ulrich lets it be known that Phil
Towle told the band in 2003 that the musical rewards of their two
years together would be heard not on *St Anger* but on the album
that followed.

'With *St Anger* it became so open-minded that it became
unfocused,' was Hetfield's bald admission. 'We went from tearing
each other's throats with sarcasm and anger, and not speaking,
to the polar opposite. Suddenly we were embracing every stupid
idea so as not to hurt anyone's feelings. We thought *St Anger* was

going to be amazing, but it turned out to be more of a statement than [the] Metallica music we enjoy playing live. It was more of a purge, just getting that shit out of me as a catalyst for the next chapter.'

All around the world fans of the band, concerned that musically at least Metallica were beginning to slide into the past tense, began to rub their hands in anticipation. Suddenly all the right things were being said. The follies of the recent past had been purged. A group that had over-compensated for their failure to communicate had finally righted their course by realising that a now fundamental love and respect for one another would not be blown apart by the odd 'full and frank' exchange of views. From this it was deduced that once more Metallica were a band that could be trusted. This, though, was an illusion worthy of any member of the Magic Circle. For, when it came to decisions fundamental to the group's identity, sounds made by the voices of strangers were still music to their ears.

Turner Duckworth is a firm of brand consultants and designers based in London and San Francisco. The company has as its clients such blue-chip favourites as Coca-Cola, Google, Amazon and the upmarket British supermarket chain Waitrose. Inevitably the catalyst for Metallica's entry into the world of creative industry gobbledygook was Lars Ulrich. In 2008 Ulrich's son attended the same school as one of co-founder David Turner's sons. Over the course of weeks spent idly chatting at the school gates, the drummer learned what Turner did for a living. Ulrich's interest was piqued, and he was soon telling his fellow parent about how when it came time to release Metallica's next album the group (by which he meant, its drummer) 'didn't want to take the usual approach'. Seeing that Turner believed himself to be 'the closest thing they had to another arty person', discussions were soon in train as to how Turner Duckworth might help Metallica achieve this new approach. In time the results of the collaboration were seen as being sufficiently 'root and branch' that the trade magazine *Creative Review* would observe that 'it's fair to say that TD have re-branded the band', an undertaking that constituted 'a complete overhaul of the [group's] identity'.

David Turner and Bruce Duckworth were invited to discuss these ideas with the band at a meeting convened at HQ in San Rafael. On arrival, the two executives were greeted by Ulrich and led into the compound's spacious kitchen area. Waiting for them were James Hetfield, Kirk Hammett and Robert Trujillo. Each of the three faces stared at the visitors with expressions of perfect indifference.

'I didn't know if they were into this or not,' recalls Turner. 'I thought, if we're going to bring anything to this, it's the principle of branding to make everything coherent.'

Rather than showing David Turner their own principles of branding and placing a hot fork on his skin, instead Metallica engaged their guests. The executives were told that the songs for the band's next album had been written, but the album title had yet to be decided. Turner was informed that four working titles were under consideration and that he 'should tell them which one was the good one'. Turner explained that in order to do this he would first need to learn more about the lyrical nature of the songs intended for inclusion. All eyes turned to Hetfield. Since the head-in-hands horror that was the lyric sheet that accompanied *St Anger*, Hetfield had once more installed himself as the band's sole lyricist. Because of this Metallica's latest litter of songs were again drawn from the front man's now tamed but still beating heart of darkness. Well, it was explained, really, you know, the songs are about, well, they're about a lot of things. Stuff like, well, erm . . . for example . . . uh . . . all right, the songs are about death.

'It was clear that all the songs [linked to] death,' says Turner. '[They were about] facing up to the nature of death and the fear and attraction that surrounds death. And then, from the four titles, they had their answer: *Death Magnetic*. And if we were going to come up with a graphic representation of that, people would see how everything was all linked together. So from a show of hands, that became the title.'

Turner and Duckworth had already been busy. The pair had attended numerous Metallica concerts in order to learn, as Bruce Duckworth put it, 'about the people [we] were targeting'.

'With branding there comes an awareness of what consumers like and don't like,' Duckworth explained, adding, 'There's a world they're comfortable with – they have expectations and this influences the communication you need to create.'

Despite the abundance of shop-talk, here Duckworth was on to something. Many Metallica fans were uncomfortable with the band's decision to jettison their original, Hetfield-designed logo for the occasion of the *Load* album. It was understood as if by instinct that not only could that work not be bettered – it remains one of the rock music's most striking and iconic images – but also that in placing this design into storage the quartet were turning their backs on their old selves in a manner that was somehow more unsettling than the new sounds with which they were then experimenting. The band *did* use variations on their original logo on both *Garage Inc.* and *S&M*, but employed different icons for *Load, Reload* and *St Anger*, none of which were particularly impressive. Worse still, on the band's European tour at the end of 2003, not one piece of apparel on sale at Earl's Court had featured the logo.

Turner Duckworth's first act in their efforts to re-brand Metallica was to take the band name as it appears on *Kill 'Em All* and to reposition it in ways so subtle as to be invisible to the naked eye.

'The logo itself was a big deal and it convinced me that we were a good fit with Metallica,' explains Duckworth. 'It runs parallel to the Coke identity work we did where people had designed the soul out of it. Lars said that he would love it if we would look at the old logo and see if there was something in it; an authentic quality to it. The interesting thing was, once we put the logo on the web, the response from fans was great. And there's an iconic M that works with the title of the new album. It all fits together.

'Of all the band members, Lars is probably the [one] most into design and is very brand-aware,' Duckworth noted. 'While the word "branding" is abused these days, they do see themselves as a brand.'

The next task facing Turner and Duckworth was to compile a booklet for the CD with images that would echo and accentuate the sentiments expressed on the album itself. Here the pair were given the space they needed to operate. Despite a repertoire of songs often brazen in their brilliance, in terms of album artwork Metallica's visual sense has sometimes been deficient. The front covers of the group's first four albums are no better than functional, and even the near-nothingness that comprises the sleeve of 'The Black Album' seems to have come about because its creators could not be bothered wasting any more time attempting to find a sufficiently striking image they might marry to their striking music. When it came to *St Anger*, the quartet even managed to entice a picture from long-time collaborator Pushead – one of the most distinctive pop-artists of the day – that is no more than adequate. (The exception to this rule is the beautiful booklet that accompanies the *S&M* set, which features as its cover a wide-screen shot of Hetfield's midriff, guitar in hand, with the San Francisco Symphony framed behind him.)

The artwork for *Death Magnetic* is by some distance the most lavish and carefully designed extension to any of Metallica's studio albums. The white and grey cover shows a coffin-shaped hole, with motion marks that suggest a terrible magnetic pull. That the title of the album is only really implied by the artwork is a nice touch, as is the fact that the hole is real, and has been cut not just into the front cover but also into nine other right-hand pages. Hetfield believes this coffin-shaped hole represents a portal to another world – 'the next room', if you will – but the other three members, not to mention the rest of the world, saw a series of graves. Photographed around these final resting places are a series of unsettling images, each one drained of colour. Here death is casting its eye not just on the wreckage of a smashed automobile, but also on a young man curled up in bed, on the tanned and athletic bodies of sun-seekers on a busy beach and on a crowd at a public event. This final picture is striking. That one silhouetted figure has his left hand fashioned into the devil-horn sign suggests that this audience is Metallica's own. Such a carefully considered composition of *Death Magnetic's* outer layers is evocative and artful. Within a genre often presented with the most garish and ill-judged artwork imaginable, it is masterful.

'There's now this atmosphere [in which] budgets have really narrowed over the last twenty years,' says Turner. 'In the US there are only about three stores most people buy their music from – like Walmart – where it's so consolidated, so conformist in terms of size [and the use of] shrink-wrap, that the label were excited to do something different. And Metallica have an interesting arrangement. They share the costs of packaging with the record company. It's an unusual deal, but it means that they call the shots and can make something more elaborate. That's how much they believe in the package.' As for the decision to invite Turner and Duckworth to join the band on the other side of the stage curtain, Turner infers that 'Lars was actually keen to involve people who weren't from the music industry, who weren't jaded. '[He wanted] people who wouldn't [just] stick to a jewel case.'

✝

Death Magnetic was released in a jewel case on September 12, 2008. Given that James Hetfield announced that work would begin on Metallica's new album in 2004, it's fair to say that its gestation period was not so much elephantine as it was glacial, as a result of the process once again beginning with band archivist and borderline obsessive-compulsive Lars Ulrich sifting through hundreds of riff tapes to identify its key building blocks. This process of meticulous preparation stood in marked contrast to the work on *St Anger*, where no member of Metallica arrived at HQ with any material prepared in advance. Kirk Hammett – who himself became a father for the first time in 2006 – admitted that in the twenty-first century 'the band's schedule has to fit around things such as school holidays'.

It took an age. As early as 2006 the quartet were printing the words 'Escape from the Studio' on the back of T-shirts that were piled chest-high at the merchandise stalls of the European festivals at which they were stuffing their pockets. But when the studio did finally manage to recapture Metallica, a project that for the longest time lacked shape or focus began to take on its own inevitable momentum. This, though, did not happen without its creators first ringing the most fundamental of changes to their inner circle. As it had for producer Fleming Rasmussen a generation earlier, this time the bell tolled for Bob Rock.

But although the outcome was the same as it had been following the completion of . . . *And Justice for All*, the reasons were different. While Rasmussen was dispatched because his charges desired a different sound for their music, Rock's place in the band's story shifted from present to past tense simply because they had learned everything the Canadian had to teach them. The days when Metallica required a producer 'who would yell at us' were years gone. They no longer needed constant supervision and someone to mediate between Hetfield and Ulrich, two men who would only unite in order to bare their fangs in the direction of their producer. All things must come to an end, and so did this most fruitful creative alliance, one which began with album that would exit the *Billboard* 200 only six months before its successor was released, *five years later*.

In appointing Rock's successor, however, Metallica did not display the kind of imaginative derring-do they did in 1990.

Rick Rubin is without question the most influential and revered record producer of the past thirty years, a man whose name is known by listeners who would not normally think to check the credits printed on the back of an album. The native of Long Beach, New York, first placed his foot in the door of a music industry that he would soon blow to smithereens when as a twenty-year-old he formed the Def Jam record label from his one-room dormitory in New York University's Weinstein Hall. Four years later Def Jam would have on its roster no fewer than three multi-platinum artists in the shape of Run DMC, the Beastie Boys and LL Cool J, the combined sounds of which would bring the then entirely revolutionary early-day hip hop to the suburbs and to the mainstream. But the notion that Rubin and his partner Russell Simmons were concerned only with turning hip hop into hit pop was disproved by the presence on the roster of Public Enemy. At precisely the hour at which his label had been straitjacketed and pigeon-holed as a rap imprint, Rubin signed Slayer, and in the autumn of 1986 unleashed upon the world the gnashing, foaming, swivel-eyed fury of *Reign in Blood*, arguably the finest metal album ever released. It was *Reign in Blood* that killed thrash metal dead for all but the band that had created it, a fact that Lars Ulrich understood as an instinct and about which he could not have been happier.

By way of Neil Diamond, Red Hot Chili Peppers, Johnny Cash, Tom Petty and System of a Down – to mention only a few – by 2006 Rick Rubin had produced what seems like everyone from AC/DC to ZZ Top. Almost a quarter of a century after founding Def Jam, his CV did not require the addition of the name Metallica in order to impress. As well as being the most in-demand technician in the history of recorded music, he was also by then the co-chairman of Columbia Records. Although intrigued by the invitation to collaborate with a group he describes as being 'one of the biggest and most important . . . in the world', the New Yorker was at the same time troubled by a question tugging persistently at his sleeve: 'Do they have it in them to make another great record?'

The producer admitted to feeling 'a sense of fear' informed by 'the fact that I didn't like [*St Anger*] and I haven't liked the last few albums.' The problem as he saw it was that the band had ceased to trust their instincts and were instead relying on the crutches of ever-expanding technology. At the recording studio at HQ there stood a large LCD screen on which the frequencies and sound waves of the music the band was making were displayed. According to Rubin, 'the music was being looked at as much as being listened to.' The producer suggested that the best way for Metallica to go about rediscovering their mojo would be for its members to stop listening with their eyes and instead to make music together, to jam in one room and to look each other in the eye instead of looking at the screen. He told the four men that in his opinion the best approach was not to record anything in earnest until the writing process had been completed. This would ensure a greater sense of focus, he reasoned, and avoid such nebulous concerns as seeking out 'vibes' that were 'greasy' or 'loose', or whatever other buzzwords might happen to be buzzing around the head of their drummer. Right you are, nodded Metallica, and, waving goodbye, watched as their new, very expensive, producer left their lives for weeks, and sometimes months at a time.

As far back as 1994 Slayer guitarist Kerry King had joked that during the recording sessions for *Divine Intervention* – the last of the band's albums on which Rick Rubin would work in anything other than an 'executive' capacity – the producer's presence in the recording studio was most noticeable by its absence. Weezer front man Rivers Cuomo would reveal that his band ended their working relationship with Rubin for much the same reason. Metallica, though, seemed happy with their new producer's unusual working methods. As the band's latest collection of riffs and titles began to coalesce into songs, Rubin would visit HQ and make suggestions as to how the material might be tightened and improved.

The recording sessions for *Death Magnetic* would yield fourteen original songs and one cover version. The latter was Metallica's take on Iron Maiden's 'Remember Tomorrow' recorded for inclusion on a *Kerrang!* tribute CD in honour of the east London band (on which the San Franciscans *asked* to be featured and did so free of charge). Of the fourteen songs on which Hetfield, Ulrich, Hammett and Trujillo were credited as composers – the group shared writing credits on each track – ten were selected for inclusion on *Death Magnetic*. In an effort to recapture the spirit heard on what were now widely seen as Metallica's 'classic' albums, producer and artist would sit and listen to *Master of Puppets*. Meanwhile Rubin would urge Hetfield to write 'direct' lyrics that didn't try to be unnecessarily 'clever'. When it came to recording these words, the producer argued that this directness be best served by a performance propelled by anger and brute force.

'If ever [Hetfield] sounded like a guy who was trying to technically sing, I would steer him away from that,' he explains. 'It was more about somebody being as close to spilling their guts as possible.'

On May 22, 2008, Metallica called time on the recording sessions for *Death Magnetic*. In their pursuit of excellence, the band had considered every note of the hour and a quarter's worth of songs that would feature on the album. They compared every take with those that they had tracked earlier, and were willing, as

Rubin explains, 'to know that if you spend 300 hours working on a part, be ready to throw those 300 hours away if [the results are] not better than what we did in five minutes.' With the producer focused on Hetfield's vocal performance, Ulrich was free to coax from Hammett the kind of lead guitar work for which he was justly celebrated. With the component parts now finally ready to be pieced together, Metallica's faith in Rubin was sufficient for them to create an album that, in terms of sound, bore less of a resemblance to the sumptuous and aerated expanse of Bob Rock and more to a naked insistence reminiscent of Steve Albini.

'This album is some of the best music we've made in the past fifteen years,' says Hammett of a release that features his first collection of guitar solos *this century*. When the musician speaks of this, his hands begin to play an imaginary guitar. 'Some of the albums we made [after] 'The Black Album' were us trying to get away from a perceived Metallica sound. That was the right thing for us at the time. But we don't feel that we have to do that any more. And to be truthful, it's fun to play fast, to be heavy. We're all on the same page with regards to that. I'd even go so far as to say that we even *missed* playing that way.'

'I can honestly say that this is the best album that we could possibly have made,' is Ulrich's opinion. 'Can I guarantee that people will like it as much as they like our older albums? No, I can't; I can't offer any guarantees. But I can promise you that we could not have made a better album.'

Just seven days after its release *Death Magnetic* had stage-dived its way to the top of the charts in no fewer than thirty-four countries. In the US a CD that Metallica insist on referring to as their ninth studio album – it is actually their tenth – became the sixth consecutive release by the group to debut at the summit of the *Billboard* Hot 200, the first band to achieve this feat. Once again reviewers were required to listen to the album away from the safety of their own homes. In the UK individual listening sessions were convened in a wooden-floored boardroom on the fifth floor of the London office of Universal Records, at the west end of Kensington High Street. Before the band's English PR would press play on an unmarked CD, journalists were first required to surrender their mobile phones, coats and bags. As with *St Anger* five years earlier, once again the critics threw caution to the winds.

'It's easily their best work in 17 years,' NME boldly stated. 'No band will ever again come to equal their success,' was the opinion of *Kerrang!*

Initial reactions to *Death Magnetic* can be said to have been made by people drunk on a cocktail of nostalgia and relief. No discussion of the album was complete without the use of the phrase 'gone back'. Metallica had 'gone back' to what they do best, had 'gone back' to their roots. James Hetfield's annoyance expressed aboard a private jet en route to Ghent thirteen years previously at those who longed for the band to put their music into reverse was no longer a pressing concern.

In many ways *Death Magnetic does* hark back to what were by now safer times. Listeners could hardly fail to notice that Metallica's 'ninth' studio album featured snippets lifted wholesale from both 'Blackened' and 'One', songs written almost half a lifetime ago. Neither could they fail to spot the album's structural template – growling monster-ballad at track four, elongated instrumental in the penultimate slot, followed by unreconstructed thrash anthem – that recalled the sequencing of both *Master of Puppets* and . . . *And Justice for All*. As if this trail of breadcrumbs wasn't quite enough, the front of the album was, of course, adorned with Turner Duckworth's new version of the band's old logo.

Metallica's hurried dash back to their younger selves carries with it a faint aroma of career-panic, even flop-sweat. While in the Eighties the band's music was seen as trailblazing, not so much foreign as alien, by the twenty-first century it was viewed as being a warm and luxurious duvet under which all might seek shelter. It is for this reason that, despite its sonic similarities, *Death Magnetic* is *not* the same as *Master of Puppets*; and to believe that it was ever likely to be is folly. The band had already changed the shape of the mainstream, and in doing so had already made their point. How on earth could anyone expect them to make it again?

But while this blast into the past can be viewed as the work of musicians exhaling heavily while attempting to slide their legs into long-discarded drainpipe jeans, in other ways the album is less easy to dismiss. Measured on its musical rather than contextual merits, *Death Magnetic* has much to recommend it. The very first sound the listener hears is that of a human heart beating quietly, a pulse that is superseded by a guitar motif that at best lives no further than next-door-but-one from 'Enter Sandman'. But there is energy here, and plenty of it. Rather than re-imagining their most redoubtable radio staple, instead 'That Was Just Your Life' sees Metallica floor the pedal and surge screaming into the distance. Propelled by Hetfield's unerring right hand and Kirk Hammett's squalling guitar solo, *Death Magnetic*'s opening track finds Metallica once again indulging their curiosity with regard to tempos and structure without succumbing to its worst excesses. This is also the case in the well-titled 'All Nightmare Long', a composition that once again proves how much can be achieved with just a few flicks of the wrist. This, though, is as nothing when compared to the speed at which Hetfield's rhythm guitar greets the conclusion of Hammett's guitar solo on 'My Apocalypse', *Death Magnetic*'s relentless closing song. By this point in the proceedings, Metallica's brakes are truly shot; the listener can only marvel at the manner in which Hetfield accompanies Ulrich's manic drumbeat with guitar notes that fly loose like sharp stones from a council gritter. Equally exhilarating is the sound of Hetfield's voice swelling with anger as he tells the listener of one who is 'split apart' and who must 'spit it out!'

Following the rock-bottom awfulness of its predecessor, on *Death Magnetic* Hetfield manages to relocate his lyrical mojo. Or at least, by and large he does. Clearly a line such as 'What don't kill ya makes you more strong' from 'Broken, Beat & Scarred' is some way below par. In other places, though, the listener is spared from things that go clunk in the night, and instead is free to marvel at the often sensational manner in which Hetfield is able to combine the personal with the poetic. With the front man by now having been involved in more fender-benders than Dick Dastardly, 'My Apocalypse' once more sees the narrator return to the 'desolating hail of fire' that can be found on any freeway. As was the case on 'Fuel', the final destination is not pretty, with the singer describing a scene of 'crushing metal ripping skin, tossing body mannequin, spilling blood [and] bleeding gas' and of lovers who each become a 'dripping bloody valentine'. Elsewhere this resonant sketch of roadside ruin is replaced by the feelings of dislocation with which Hetfield has wrestled since the days of his traumatic childhood. On 'That Was Just Your Life' it is difficult to know whether the narrator is pleased that he has found a way to 'disconnect somehow' or whether he is at all alarmed that he will 'never stop the bleeding now'. Not that it matters anyway, not really, seeing how the time is now upon us when present and past tense change shifts. 'And there it went,' he says, a state of troubled consciousness that was 'almost like your life'. On 'The Day That Never Comes' Hetfield once more harvests the bitter fruits of 'The Unforgiven' and 'Low Man's Lyric', but this time does so with a good deal more defiance, as well as a measure of hope. Once again the song is sung from a position of oppression, and once more Hetfield's allegiance is with the oppressed. Here he is 'waiting for the one, the day that never comes', the point at which he can 'stand up and feel the warmth,' were it not for the fact that 'the sunshine never comes'. Unlike in 1991 and then in 1997, however, in 2008 this is simply not good enough. The narrator is now sufficiently self-possessed as to be able to review his dismal surroundings and promise to 'splatter colour on this grey'. The song's final words are a pledge. 'This I swear. This I swear! This. I. Swear!'

But if *Death Magnetic* heralds a lyrical return to form, for Kirk Hammett it is nothing less than a new high-water mark of consistent excellence. The lead guitarist's sense of hurt at Hetfield and Ulrich's bewildering decision not to showcase his towering talents on *St Anger* is one of the least-considered aspects of Metallica's 2003 *folie à trois*. To his credit, while Hetfield and Ulrich fought like two cats in a pillowcase, Hammett met endless questions about why it was that his talents had suddenly been overlooked with a level of diplomacy worthy of the UN. This decision not to purge himself publicly paid dividends – as Phil Towle said it would – on *Death Magnetic*. It is here that a dam that has been full to bursting for a decade finally breaks its banks. That it does so with a range that arcs from the imperiously tasteful to the impossibly frenetic shows not only the skill of Hammett as a musician but also just how damned stupid his band mates were to overlook this point in the first place. The lead guitarist's contribution to an album that did much to repair Metallica's public image is significant. And while it is the case that *Death Magnetic* is over-long by two songs ('Cyanide' and 'The Judas Kiss' being merely functional), its arrival was nonetheless greeted with a clamour sufficient to drag its creators' creative identity back into the present tense. When the inevitable world tour in support of their latest album began in earnest at San Francisco's Cow Palace on October 17, 2008, no fewer than five of *Death Magnetic's* ten songs were included as part of the set. This number would remain constant until 2010, when the excursion finally cooled its jets.

'We understand the importance of staying relevant,' said James Hetfield on this very subject. 'We understand the importance of playing new songs. We understand how important it is not to become a nostalgia act. No one in the band wants us to be that. Metallica still has something to offer. But no matter what the public thinks, as a band we will do what we have to do.

'We always have.'

✝

More than any other band, Metallica's story of success is one that has relied upon the kindness of strangers to an uncommon degree. As has been seen, in 1982 the hardcore heavy metal underground in the US was a small but fertile community scattered across a vast land mass. With a total absence of mainstream media coverage, and not a chance of radio airplay, this network would keep the fires burning in a manner of a web powered not with technology but by willpower alone. Obscure albums were bought by mail order from Europe. Magazines such as *Kerrang!* and *Aardschok* were sourced. Concerts were bootlegged on tape and traded all over the nation. Most crucially of all, in lieu of any kind of unifying voice or domestic infrastructure, many were the young men and women who understood that if this kind of music was to achieve any momentum it was they who must build the tracks on which the train could be set in motion.

In Los Angeles Brian Slagel founded Metal Blade Records and in 1982 issued the compilation album on which appears Metallica's first bona fide public appearance. One state north, in rural Oregon, a fanzine editor named K. J. Doughton was so stunned by the band's *No Life Til Leather* demo that he phoned Lars Ulrich and ask for an interview. In turn, Ulrich was sufficiently flattered that in response he asked Doughton if he would like to run Metallica's fan club. The following March, upon hearing the band on tape New Jersey metal hustler Johnny

Zazula called Doughton and set in motion a course of events that would see Metallica drive to the east coast and 'Johnny Z' and wife Marsha remortgage their home in order to finance and release the band's debut album, *Kill 'Em All*, as well as to manage the young and at the time *very* unruly quartet.

Although Metallica's career is littered with examples of the band turning their backs on relationships that no longer served them well, it would be wrong to say that the San Franciscans ever forgot an act of kindness or support undertaken in their name. On the weekend of April 3 and 4, 2009, the band had the chance to prove this, and to put their money where their gratitude was. This they did by paying for the flights, hotels and all other expenses for 150 people ferried from numerous points in North America and Europe to Cleveland, Ohio. And while the decaying rust-belt city might not have been anyone's destination of choice for a getaway weekend, the occasion to which the invitees were summoned could hardly have been more prestigious

The Rock and Roll Hall of Fame Foundation was created in 2003 by the Turkish music industry impresario and Atlantic Records founder Ahmet Ertegun. Three years later the organisation had begun to induct artists into its Hall of Fame in a manner similar to the practices of the National Hockey League in Toronto and the Major League Baseball in Cooperstown, New York. But unlike them, Ahmet's creation as yet had no home. Despite obvious candidates such as Detroit and Memphis – the respective birthplaces of Tamla Motown and Sun Records – the nod went to Cleveland, a city with no real musical heritage of which to speak. Apart, that is, from just one thing: it was here that DJ Alan Freed coined the phrase 'rock 'n' roll' as a means of describing a movement the power of which was sufficient to create a whole new international demographic, the teenager.

The list of artists allowed into the Rock and Roll Hall of Fame since 1986 reads like a compendium of the very finest writers and musicians in the history of popular music. At a ceremony staged each spring the Hall of Fame has officially honoured Chuck Berry and B. B. King, the Rolling Stones and The Beatles, The Who and Simon & Garfunkel, the Sex Pistols and the Ramones, Bruce Springsteen and Elvis Costello & The Attractions, and Guns N' Roses and Nirvana, to name only a few.

When it was announced that the Rock and Roll Hall of Fame Class of 2009 was to feature Metallica, the band was quick to realise that this achievement came about only in part because of the music for which it had become universally known. As soon as it had been decided that the San Franciscan quartet would personally attend the induction ceremony, it was also decided that they would not be doing so alone. Working at speed Q Prime secured 150 four-star hotel rooms for use by such long-time-no-see faces as Brian Slagel, Ron Quintana (the man who unwittingly provided Lars Ulrich with the name 'Metallica' some twenty-seven years earlier), Phil Towle and, of course, Jason Newsted. In lieu of Cliff Burton Metallica invited the bassist's father, Ray. (Both Jason Newsted and Cliff Burton would also be inducted into 'The Hall'.) The only person to decline Metallica's invitation was, naturally, Dave Mustaine, with the guitarist (actually rather graciously) explaining that as a former member of the band he felt he should be honoured in the same way as its current members as well as Cliff Burton and Jason Newsted. But the fact that Mustaine did not record any albums with Metallica provided the reason his name could not feature on the proposed Roll of Honour.

'After nearly three decades of tenacious, uncompromising world domination, the band has scoured the globe for all the key players, and invited each to this historical, unprecedented event,' was how K. J. Doughton described the Cleveland pilgrimage. 'Forget *Some Kind of Monster*, this is some kind of miracle. This is not about marketing. This is not about money. This is testament to the fact that the nurturing umbilical cord between band and supporters is still intact. The bonds of brotherhood remain in place. Metallica have assembled their own history, person by person, to reunite and link together.'

It is difficult to overestimate the level of pride that greeted each of Metallica's monumental achievements in the years that preceded the period at which they were deemed worthy of cover-star status by *Rolling Stone*. The band did not just break down doors, smash through brick walls and shatter glass ceilings. They proved to the people who believed in them, and to those who had helped them, that success could be achieved without compromise. More than this, the nature of this success was intensified not in spite of a refusal to compromise but *because* of such a rebuttal. This point was made explicit by Red Hot Chili Peppers bass player Flea, the man charged with delivering the speech that inducted Metallica into the Rock and Roll Hall of Fame.

'In the world of three-minute-long catchy pop songs that dominated the radio [in the Eighties], these Metallica guys were writing and playing ten-minute-long songs that blasted your face off,' he said. 'I don't think they were sitting around wondering how they could [become] a bunch of fancy rock stars; I think they just wanted to do some rocking. Their motivation was, and is, pure. The fact that they have connected with the world in the way that they have is phenomenal. They have become a household name, with music that is anything but mainstream. This is outsider music. And for it to do what it has done is truly mind-blowing.'

The manner in which Flea's own career mirrors the trajectory set by Metallica is uncanny. After departing the ranks of the thrillingly unpleasant Hollywood punk band Fear, Michael Peter 'Flea' Balzary set his course with the Red Hot Chili Peppers. As with the band he eulogised onstage in Cleveland, 'the Chilis' were alarmingly out of step with popular trends. But as did the San Franciscan quartet, so too did Flea's own group crack the mainstream, with the blockbusting *Blood Sugar Sex Magik* album released just a month after 'The Black Album'. As Metallica and 150 of their supporters smiled affectionately at the words being spoken onstage at the Rock and Roll Hall of Fame, Flea shared with them the memory of the first time he heard Metallica's music. He was in the Red Hot Chili Peppers' tour van, somewhere in the middle of America, listening to the radio. God knows what radio station it was, but on to the air was unleashed the song 'Fight Fire With Fire'. As the bass player listened to *Ride the Lightning*'s most abrasive track, Flea found himself 'riveted to the radio'. As this story is recalled for the audience in Cleveland, the bassist is quick to point out that this animal magnetism is a quality that has survived each and every one of the band's numerous changes of mood.

'[Metallica's music] is as intense and as inventive as ever,' he says. 'If you're going to have a Rock and Roll Hall of Fame, and if you're going to be really disciplined and strict about only ever allowing bands in it that have been true originals, and that [have] without question single-handedly furthered the evolution of the art form of rock 'n' roll music, that push envelope of what rock music is, and [have] inspired countless others to try and follow their footsteps on the new trail they blaze, then by that strictest criteria you [have] got to have Metallica in it.'

His final words are these: 'James Hetfield, Lars Ulrich, Kirk Hammett, Jason Newsted and Cliff Burton – it is my sincere honour to induct you all into the Rock and Roll Hall of Fame.'

There is, of course, the matter as to whether the members of a rock band should consent to being lionised in such a formal manner as is the tradition of the 'R&R' Hall of Fame. But on April 4 a band who not so long ago appeared live on MTV and sang two grandly offensive songs for no reason whatsoever seemed to regard their circumstances that evening as an honour sufficient to overwhelm whatever quiet qualms they may or may not have harboured regarding the threat to art posed by well-mannered domesticity.

In opening his own induction speech Ulrich is gracious enough to point to the members of the public seated far away from the stage. 'You know,' he says, 'remember one thing, this is really about you people up on the balcony. Just remember that, all right? The real reason we are here [is] for all the people on the balcony.' As ever Ulrich's speech is loose and likeable in an energetically shambolic kind of a way. He has no qualms about admitting to his audience that 'I didn't write anything down.' Hetfield, on the other hand, is by 2009 a commanding and charismatic public speaker. When the front man takes time to thank the band's fans, what is a fairly boilerplate remark somehow manages to bring down the house. It is Hetfield who addresses the crowd in Cleveland last, and who says that he would 'like to dedicate this, my part of this, to young musicians out there who are the next generations of music and [who are] expressing their passions. I would also like to dedicate it to quite the opposite: the people who are stuck, the people who are stuck in an image, the people who are stuck and afraid to be honest, and [afraid to] dream a big dream. [To them I say] dream big and dare to fail. I dare you to do that, because [Metallica are] living proof that it is possible to make a dream come true.'

With these words Hetfield turns to Ulrich and says 'Right?' The drummer nods his head in agreement. Hetfield then says, 'And lastly and greatestly [sic] here, I want to thank Lars for calling me [in 1981] so we can include each other in our dreams of being in the greatest heavy metal band in the world.' With these words, Hetfield walks over to the man with whom he shares a most complicated yet durable relationship and embraces his friend for more than half a minute.

'I remember seeing James embracing Lars and thinking that he, and they, were recreating their formation of the band,' says

Phil Towle, who at the time watched the pair unite from the floor of the Rock and Roll Hall of Fame. 'They were reconnecting with that memorable, appreciative level a love and respect for one another and what they had jointly given birth to. It was a beautiful, healing moment as well. Theirs was a marriage that had gone bad that was now resolving itself, and this was further affirmation of that.'

If at this point there were any remaining doubts that Metallica had 'made it' in the grandest sense of the term, and in a manner acknowledged on the most prestigious of platforms, they were cast aside when Metallica gathered onstage to play a short set. Following renditions of 'Master of Puppets' and 'Enter Sandman', Hetfield, Ulrich, Hammett, Trujillo and Newsted were joined by guitarists Jimmy Page, Jeff Beck, Ronnie Wood and Aerosmith's Joe Perry for a diamond-encrusted run through 'Train Kept a Rollin''. It is at this very point that Metallica's coronation into the ranks of 'rock royalty' is marked on the statute books.

But even at home onstage with some of the most famous and celebrated rock musicians in the world, still Metallica are an unusual fit. As heard on the Aerosmith's 1974 *Get Your Wings* album, 'Train Kept A Rollin'' is a song equipped with a sense of street-smart hustle, of a desperate energy that suggests steam rising forth from the sidewalks of a sexually charged city. But from the mouth of James Hetfield, these qualities are chased from the song as if pursued by a tank. Instead, the lyric is delivered with the same kind of coiled annoyance as can be heard on tracks such 'Holier Than Thou' or 'Wasting My Hate'. Given the sheer wholesale weight of world-class talent gathered onstage at the Rock and Roll Hall of Fame, it is a curious and curiously stilted performance. It is as if Hetfield will forever be able to access the anger that propelled his band into public view almost thirty years ago, but despite having seen far more than his fair share of 'action' he is unable to convincingly convey what is really rock 'n' roll's key ingredient – sex. It is because of this that Metallica will forever remain a very heavy metal band, a presence that while *in* the mainstream is not quite *of* the mainstream.

As it so happens, this suits one member of Metallica just fine. Over the course of the first weekend of April, the band hired out Cleveland's House of Blues venue, just one in a nationwide chain of balconied rooms that look as if they were all ordered from the same catalogue. It was here that people who truly can claim to be a part of the 'Metallica family' gallivanted and reminisced until the time when the sun prepared to begin its work for the day. This being an occasion staged by Metallica, of course, Lars Ulrich was in attendance; this being a party, of course, he was drunk. He sat talking with two of his invited guests, Scott Ian and Charlie Benante, rhythm guitarist and drummer of Anthrax respectively. Twenty-six years ago, when Metallica arrived in New York City penniless and freezing, it was Ian and Benante (along with original Anthrax bassist Danny Lilker) that would arrive at the practice facility, where the Californian band was sleeping, armed with sandwich toasters, hot plates and provisions. This act of kindness did not go unnoticed, and three years later Anthrax were invited to tour Europe as Metallica's support act on the excursion that would claim the life of Cliff Burton. Although the two parties remained friends, in 2009 it had been twenty-two years since they had appeared on the same concert stage. But despite wildly differing fortunes in the careers of both groups – it would have to be a very slow year indeed for Anthrax to be inducted into the Rock and Roll Hall of Fame – the New York quintet were one of the acts that for a few years at least were spoken of in the same sentence as Metallica as being trailblazers in the then nascent and feared 'thrash metal' movement.

For the longest time Metallica did everything in their power to escape the straitjacket into which they'd been fastened by unimaginative music journalists, a manoeuvre they executed successfully and with spectacular results. But a generation removed from this epic struggle, Lars Ulrich appeared to regard these times with a kinder eye. Drunk but serious, that evening he presented Scott Ian and Charlie Benante with a startling proposition.

9 — THAT WAS JUST YOUR LIFE

As cheers reverberate around Bemowo Airport, a disused military facility in Warsaw's western district, James Hetfield extends his arms before him and motions for the 88,000 people in his line of sight to be quiet. Metallica have been onstage for almost two hours: seventeen of the eighteen songs whose titles are printed in bold black type upon the sheet of white paper at Hetfield's feet have been presented for the appreciation of the Polish audience, and according to that list, 'Seek & Destroy' will close the show. As the crowd falls silent, Hetfield asks his band's lighting director Rob Koenig to switch on the house lights that he might better see his band's 'Warsaw family'.

'We would love to take a good look at history right here,' he says quietly.

As the audience is illuminated in brilliant white light, Lars Ulrich rises to his feet behind his drum kit and joins in the applause. Hetfield then approaches his microphone stand once more.

'I can hopefully speak for all the bands here tonight,' he says, 'for Anthrax, Megadeth, Slayer and Metallica: we thank you so much for your support in flying the flag for heavy, live music. Together this is ". . . Seek. And. Destroy"!'

The first-ever show to feature thrash metal's 'Big Four' is almost at an end.

†

The genesis of the most talked-about Metallica tour of the decade lay, officially at least, with Ulrich. Holding court at the bar of

Cleveland's House of Blues on the opening weekend of April 2009, the Dane was in typically voluble mood, and Anthrax's Scott Ian and Charlie Benante were content to let their old friend run his mouth. As talk turned, as it was bound to do, to memories of days gone by, Ulrich was struck by an idea which nagged and nagged even as the conversation swirled around him. 'Imagine if we all got together again,' he said. 'Imagine . . . you guys, us, Slayer, Megadeth, the four of us, on tour.'

'The Big Four!' he exclaimed, gesturing as if to present the words on a concert poster. 'Live! For One Night Only!'

'That would be fucking amazing,' Ian said. 'But really, it's never going to happen, is it?'

'Well,' said the drummer, with a meaningful look, 'we're kicking around ideas.'

In the months that followed Ian found himself drawn into conversations about Metallica more often that he would have wished. That July Dave Mustaine inadvertently ratted out the Anthrax guitarist as being the source of a long-standing rumour that Metallica were on the verge of kicking Lars Ulrich out of his own band in 1986, before the death of Cliff Burton threw all the group's plans into disarray. Asked if there was any truth in the twenty-year-old rumour Mustaine said, 'That's what Scott told me. He said that when Metallica got home, that James, Cliff and Kirk were going to fire Lars.'

Within hours of the story appearing on metal news site *Blabbermouth*, Scott Ian tweeted his response from Anthrax's Twitter account.

'Story's not true,' he wrote. 'Little does anyone know but Lars actually owns the name, good luck ever kicking him out.'

In the weeks that followed, with Anthrax in some disarray following the unanticipated departure of their vocalist Dan Nelson, Ian would be forced to deny his part in the story to a sceptical metal media time and time again. But when the New

Yorkers arrived in Europe to play a one-off date at the Sonisphere festival at Knebworth (with former vocalist John Bush temporarily reinstated as front man) the guitarist discovered that this over-ripe rumour had been usurped by new whispers circulating backstage among industry folk. The talk of the field was that Metallica were sounding out Sonisphere's promoters about the idea of bringing a Metallica/Slayer/Megadeth/Anthrax package to Europe the following summer. When he returned home to Los Angeles, Ian placed a call to his long-time friend Kirk Hammett and asked 'Is this happening? Is it really happening?' As much as he pretended to be above this off-the-peg industry tittle-tattle, Ian's heart sank a little when his friend said, 'No, no, no.'

Hammett addressed the rumours himself in an interview in October.

'That tour is not going to happen,' he told Atlanta rock station DJs Shaffee and El Jefe. 'I've been hearing that. We've all been hearing that for a while. I get asked [about] it regularly. And as far as a tour going on, it's not going to happen. Conflicting schedules, conflicting personalities, [a lot of] conflicting things.' This said, and surely not inadvertently, Hammett permitted a chink of light to pierce the dark sky.

'It's a good idea though,' he conceded. 'And, personally, I can see the significance of playing a tour like that, but it's not going to happen.'

And yet, in the face of such stonewall denial, the story would not die. In fact the rumours grew stronger, prompting Scott Ian to place a second call to Hammett as the year drew to a close. And on this occasion, when Hammett was asked, 'Is this really happening?' Metallica's guitarist laughed and said 'Yes'.

†

The bracketing of Metallica, Slayer, Megadeth and Anthrax as thrash metal's Big Four was somewhat arbitrary. Journalists at the London office of *Kerrang!* magazine were still adjusting to the rise in popularity of the movement in 1986 when they coined the term, seeking to differentiate the first wave of thrash bands from the second-wave acts – Nuclear Assault, Flotsam and Jetsam, Sepultura, Kreator, Destruction and such – that were by then flooding the magazine's glossy pages with a relentless frequency. It is difficult now to comprehend the sheer speed and volume with which bands inspired by Metallica and Slayer stormed the palaces of mainstream metal in the mid-Eighties. Exhilarating the young and horrifying the old, 'thrash' was the first sub-genre to catch the nascent metal press flat-footed. Journalists who had appeared young and credible just two years earlier were left bewildered by the noises now emanating from the US, Germany and Brazil; and in print, it showed. In Don Kaye and Paul Miller *Kerrang!* had two writers who *were* genuine fans of thrash metal – and who covered the field particularly well – but this was the vocal minority. Many were the writers who lavished praise upon bands they did not like while secretly living in hope that this whole noisy business would quietly go away.

As such the term 'Big Four' was as much a security blanket for the press as it was a statement of fact for the reader. Had Exodus released their second album *Pleasures of the Flesh* in the same year that *Master of Puppets, Reign in Blood* and *Peace Sells . . . But Who's Buying?* emerged, it surely would have been they, and not Anthrax, who would have been nominated as the fourth component of the quartet. (In fact as late as 1990 Dave Mustaine was lobbying for the term to be expanded to 'The Big Five' in order to accommodate the San Franciscan quintet.) But they didn't; and they weren't; and by such small margins, history is defined.

In truth the concept of the Big Four existed only from 1986 to 1991 when the phenomenal success of 'The Black Album' re-defined the four bands as 'The Big One plus Three'. But the romance of the term endured. During a period when the audience for heavy metal exploded, all four bands hit creative and commercial peaks: for a generation of metal fans going through adolescence, this was a golden era that saw the music to which they listened dovetail perfectly with the discovering of sex, drugs, alcohol and a growing sense of self-definition. The standard of albums the four groups released during this five-year period – *Reign in Blood* and *Seasons in the Abyss* from Slayer, *Rust in Peace* from Megadeth and *Among the Living* by Anthrax – was startlingly high, ensuring that two decades later, fans could look back on this period as being modern metal's halcyon days. And rightly so.

The news that the four bands were to share a stage for the first time ever broke via Metallica's website on December 14, 2009, with the announcement of Sonisphere festival dates in Poland (June 16) and Czech Republic (June 19). Further dates would subsequently be added in Switzerland, Bulgaria, Greece, Romania and Turkey.

'Who would have thought that more than twenty-five years after its inception, thrash metal's Big Four would not only still be around and more popular than ever, but will now play together for the first time,' Ulrich declared in a statement on the website. 'What a mindfuck! Bring it on!'

'People have been talking about these four bands playing together since 1984,' said Scott Ian. 'That's twenty-six years of expectation! And the thing is, I believe, not only will we live up to the expectations, we will shatter them! No other four bands as influential as the four of us have ever done this. Imagine if The Beatles, Stones, The Who and Zeppelin had done shows? Or Sabbath, Priest, Maiden, Motörhead? Well, I may be getting into some rarefied air here but as a fan, that's how big I feel this is.'

Not to be outdone on the hype front Dave Mustaine commented that the dates represented a 'once-in-a-lifetime opportunity' for metal fans to see 'the four greatest heavy metal bands in American history'.

'If there are any heads left at the end of this festival that haven't banged, they don't belong there,' Megadeth's front man added.

Amid such stirring calls to arms, a more detached observer might have looked beyond the heat and light that accompanied the announcement and noted a certain expediency in the timing of this touching family reunion. Since the close of the Madly in Anger with the World tour in the winter of 2004, Metallica had proved adept at finding new cover stories for taking their production on the road with no new 'product' to promote. 2006's Escape from the Studio '06 excursion was convened under the auspices of the group celebrating the twentieth anniversary of the *Master of Puppets* album, a return to Europe the following summer was billed as a 'Sick of the Studio' tour, and a third lucrative European trek in three years was branded as a 'European Vacation' for the quartet. 'We're a US export the way Coca-Cola is,' Q Prime's Cliff Burnstein subsequently told the *Wall Street Journal*, using words that were not just true but actually a little too much so. 'We look for the best markets to go to.' Looking to return to Europe for a seventh leg of the World Magnetic Tour – at a time when economists were gravely concerned about the financial stability of the region, and just twelve months after they had helped launch the Sonisphere franchise in Europe for their long-term agent John Jackson's K2 Agency – would require a certain amount of creative marketing and strategic planning. The idea of getting the old gang back together, then, was a canny master stroke from an organisation that – by sheer coincidence, obviously – last clasped Megadeth to its bosom in the spring of 1993, when the world's biggest metal band faced the prospect of playing to a half-empty Milton Keynes Bowl.

On June 15, 2010, at Metallica's invitation, the members of all four bands assembled at a small Italian restaurant in Warsaw to break bread together for the first time. Metallica had requested that the groups' managers, agents, security guards and wives stay away for the evening: this was to be an occasion for the seventeen musicians alone, an opportunity for old friends to reconnect and for decades-old feuds to be laid aside. There was much to discuss.

Metallica's most recent attempt to lay old ghosts to rest had ended badly. The band had reached out to Dave Mustaine in 2001, explaining that they were undertaking group therapy, and suggesting that this might be an appropriate opportunity to address the question of Mustaine's dismissal from the band eighteen years previously. Megadeth's front man accepted the invitation – 'I figured I'd endured enough counselling because of Metallica, I might as well go through counselling with Metallica', he later commented – but was surprised to find a film crew present when he arrived to meet Lars Ulrich at the Ritz Carlton hotel in San Francisco on September 13, 2001, the occasion of his fortieth birthday. In his 2010 autobiography, Mustaine recalled feeling 'ambushed' by the presence of Joe Berlinger and Bruce Sinofsky's cameras, but he consented, nonetheless, to being filmed. The encounter became one of the key scenes in *Some Kind of Monster*, one crackling with raw emotion. While acknowledging that he had been the architect of his own downfall within the band – 'I fucked up' he admitted – Mustaine spoke of the sadness and betrayal he felt on being ejected from a unit he considered to be his family, and of the resentment and bitterness he had nurtured since that day. 'Maybe for some people eighteen years is a long time,' he said. 'To me it seems like yesterday.'

'All I had was you and James,' he said quietly. 'We had dreams.'

Months later Mustaine was shown Berlinger and Sinofsky's edit of the thirty-minute conversation. At this point, Mustaine maintains, he withdrew his permission for the segment to be included in the film, arguing that the cut was 'manipulative' and misleading. Because Mustaine had signed Metallica's release form on the day of his conversation with Ulrich, however, the film-makers were within their legal rights to use the footage regardless of Mustaine's change of heart.

'He was not super-receptive to it,' Ulrich admitted. 'We were kind of debating what we should do with that. We're past the point of pissing people off, at least on purpose. [But] we couldn't figure out if it was his managers or him; it was just odd.'

'I had aspirations at one point of becoming friends with James [Hetfield] and Lars [Ulrich] and doing something again some day in my career, but that door is shut now,' Mustaine stated in 2004. 'That was the final betrayal . . . He told me that this was supposed to be about healing. And it was more furthering his career at my expense. I'm done with Lars Ulrich. I'm done with them.'

Five years on, when the notion of a Big Four tour was first mooted, a wary Mustaine initially turned down Metallica's overtures, mindful that his former band mates would be calling the shots. 'As much as this would be great for the fans, it's not good for us,' he told his manager.

'That was the businessman in me talking,' he admitted. 'But the little kid who played guitar, and whose life was saved by music? That kid wanted it in the worst way.'

On the evening of June 15, 2010, Mustaine once more made peace with his old friends.

'The things I got upset about back then don't bother me any more,' he reflected the following morning. 'At one point I was so bitter about everything, but then one day I thought, "Dave, you're one of the greatest guitar players in the world and you've been in the two biggest heavy metal bands in existence on the planet." And that's when I realised how fortunate I am.

'Last night Lars and I were telling jokes, and James and I were talking about the old times and Kirk and I were talking about our horses because we have the same kind of horses . . .' he continued. 'We were rivals once, but it doesn't feel like there's any rivalry now; we're all on the same team, for heavy metal. This is like a class reunion. All we wanted to do was to matter. We were young kids, we were hungry, and we wanted to play guitar and have people say, "You mean something in this world. You are going to make a difference." I made a difference. And I love that. That's all I needed.'

✝

On the morning of June 16, approximately 5,000 UK rock fans descended on Warsaw in anticipation of witnessing a piece of musical history. Among this number were a gaggle of UK journalists who had accepted an invitation from the Sonisphere festival's PR team to document the day. The party included Geoff Barton, the former editor of *Sounds* and *Kerrang!* whose writings on the New Wave of British Heavy Metal had fuelled Lars Ulrich's rock star dreams, Metallica biographer Joel McIver, BBC Radio 1's *Rock Show* presenter Daniel P. Carter, and one of the writers of this book.

The skies above the airport in Bemowo were dishwater grey that afternoon, and the backstage area sparse and utilitarian. The dressing rooms were basic, just white marquees erected specifically for the occasion. Nearby there was a stall, staffed by unfeasibly pretty Polish girls dressed in air stewardess uniforms, that offered complimentary vodka. Over the course of the afternoon a succession of black SUVs with tinted windows deposited band members on site, and as the American musicians exchanged high fives and bear hugs it was evident that any lingering awkwardness or unease between men who'd traded barbed insults so often in the past had been resolved.

'Those West Coast bands and their dramas!' laughed New York's Scott Ian when questioned backstage. 'I'm totally kidding, but really, whatever dramas there have been over the past twenty-five years, what does it matter? It's so stupid. I was sitting last night with James, looking at another table where Lars and Dave were talking and I was saying to James, "The last time I saw the two of them talking was when Dave was in Metallica." Last night was amazing, there was a real energy and vibe in the room from every band, just like, "Can you fucking believe this?" Everyone is really pumped about this.'

Smoothly working the backstage area, with hugs and handshakes for all, Lars Ulrich was in an equally positive frame of mind. Having spent the previous twelve months soothing egos and re-building bridges between the camps, swapping emails and text messages with old friends across time zones, the Dane's ebullience was as justified as it was understandable.

'Obviously as we get older we don't take any of this stuff for granted,' he insisted. 'The mad ego, "Look how big our dicks are", type of thing was probably left behind in our thirties for most of us and I think we're all – well, I can't speak for the other bands – but for Metallica, we're obviously much more appreciative and much more humbled and, "Oh wow, look at all the people that still give a shit." It's pretty amazing. When you put this type of thing together, we could all sit around and drool over the old days, but the question is whether anyone else really gives a shit. And it's been pretty endearing and heart-warming to see how many people are actually really into this. My dear friend Brian Slagel had a theory that with so many of the younger kids now so much of what happened in the Nineties – with grunge and rap-rock stuff and whatever – doesn't show up on their radar. And it seems like a lot of the younger kids reference the Eighties more when they want something hard and heavy.

'But for us, this isn't about looking back on the old days and thinking, "Wow, look how much more fun we had back then . . ." There was a different energy then, a lot of naive energy, a lot of innocence, a lot of spunk and a lot of chest-pumping and a lot of "live fast . . ." bravado. And I think that we're not sitting around thinking we miss the better old days; it's more like, "Holy fuck, we actually all survived it!" It was more like we all made it through. Here are four bands that are still functioning and in many people's opinions are still as relevant as we all were back in the day, four bands that are continuing to put out albums, that is as vital as it ever was. It's cool, because Metallica is kinda the secondary thing in all our lives now that we have kids and families, and in the wake of that I think Metallica has become more fun, because we don't take it all quite as seriously as we did ten or twenty years ago. I think there's more of a celebratory energy now. Obviously there were some nostalgic elements in the wake of that whole Rock and Roll Hall of Fame thing and that's what made us want to look back and kinda celebrate the past as much as we celebrate the present and future. But it's not, "I wish the grand old days were still here."'

Asked if there was still a competitive streak in his make-up which made him want to blow his old friends off the stage, the drummer snorted with laughter and spoke as if addressing a particularly slow-witted child.

'Er, I don't feel that coming up much,' he responded. 'It's not so much about blowing everyone else offstage as about blowing our own minds these days. It's more about being the best that we can be each night. A couple of years ago when we started the whole *Death Magnetic* thing we invited a lot of our younger new friends – like Lamb of God and Machine Head – out on tour with us and what's happened is that it's not so much a competitive thing as that we're all inspiring one another. When you take the stage after Machine Head, Lamb of God or Mastodon you better be on your game and firing on all cylinders. So it's more a big circle of inspiration.'

Of all the musicians milling around the backstage compound, Slayer guitarist Kerry King arguably had the most justified reputation as a plain speaker. With an honesty as bald as his cranium, for much of his career King appeared to be at war with the entire industry just as much as he seemed to regard himself as the conscience of modern metal. Forever bruising egos and repositioning noses, to King the notion of kept counsel was anathema. Of Dave Mustaine, alongside whom he actually played as part of the original Megadeth line-up, he once said, 'Ask anybody in the biz about Dave Mustaine, and if they have an opinion, [it will be that] he's a cocksucker . . . ' Backstage at Bemowo the guitarist was diplomatic enough to acknowledge that the initiative for the Big Four tour lay squarely with Metallica. 'It's all down to Metallica wanting to do it because they're so much bigger than everyone else,' he stated, correctly – but even at his most house-trained, there was a touch of mischief to his response when asked how Slayer had continued to remain relevant.

'We never made any horrible moves, and we never changed to become popular,' he replied. 'We're the thrash version of AC/DC: you know what you're going to get when you come to see us. We've basically done the same thing for twenty-five years, so it's like we come with a guarantee: we've always delivered.'

The fact that King views this statement as being something of which he can be proud is obvious. But it is also true that this sense of familiarity has meant that increasingly the quartet are seen as what *Kerrang!* writer Nick Ruskell described as a 'pipe-and-slippers' act. This means that, ironically, of any band of the Big Four, it is Slayer that have in their own way travelled the furthest distance from what they once were. Still possessed of a live fury – in fact the Angelinos are even more furious in concert than ever before – long gone are the days when Slayer were capable of surprise, let alone shock.

'The gigs are going to be awesome,' King insisted. 'I'm just going to enjoy the hell out of them. I think it should be a worldwide event. I said to James [Hetfield] at dinner last night, "Dude, this is awesome, *everybody* should see it." I'm hoping

James will keep it in mind and we can go more places.'

Sitting on Slayer's tour bus, Tom Araya echoed his guitarist's sentiments.

'I heard that Metallica were going to wait to see how this goes before committing to anything else,' he said. 'And I'm like, "You have to wait and see?" I *know* this would be awesome everywhere!'

Asked if he could imagine the heavy metal world existing without the Big Four, Araya's answer was thoughtful.

'Metal would still exist,' he said slowly, 'but I don't think metal would *mean* as much as it means now without these four bands.'

As Slayer clambered aboard golf carts to transport them the 400 metres between the backstage area and the Bemowo stage, James Hetfield was there to wave them off. 'Kick ass!' were his considered words of advice. When the LA quartet returned to the backstage compound, Kerry King was literally punching the air with happiness. Dave Mustaine was in equally emotional mood after his band's early evening set. Playing in front of a *Rust in Peace* backdrop, and performing that album in its entirety to mark twenty years since its release, his band nonetheless managed to avoid sounding like an exercise in fusty nostalgia. Even the fact that his band's name was listed as 'Megadeath' on production notices around the backstage area didn't dampen the singer's mood.

'This is so fantastic,' he beamed. 'I was one of the guys that helped build this whole scene and I'm just so honoured to be here. Fuck man, it's like one of the best days of my life. I feel like I've been born again,' said the born-again Christian.

There would be no doubt, however, as to the band of the day.

'Warsaw, do you know what's happening?' Hetfield asked at the outset of Metallica's headline set. 'This is like a dream for every metalhead. You're a part of it and we're a part of it.'

A cursory glance at the eighteen-song set performed by Metallica in Warsaw on June 16, 2010 offers few surprises. The show opened with 'Creeping Death', closed with 'Seek & Destroy' and featured just four songs written in the years following 'The Black Album'. But here Metallica's adherence to formula could be seen as a mark of respect both for the occasion and their tour mates alike. There was no grandstanding, no posturing, no indulgence to signify that the San Franciscans believed themselves to be either bigger or better than the event itself. On the surface, it was just another Metallica show. But if ever a Metallica show merited the term 'dignified' this was the occasion.

On June 22, an invitation to the party was extended to the wider Metallica family, when a (delayed) cinecast of the tour's appearance in Bulgaria was replayed to picture houses worldwide, playing in seventy-nine cinemas in the UK and 450 theatres in the US.

'Obviously nothing is ever going to replace the thrill of being in the front row at a gig,' Lars Ulrich acknowledged, 'but with surround sound and high-definition pictures this is as close as you're going to get to that experience. If I were a twelve-year-old kid in Copenhagen again, I'd be sitting in the cinema with my denim jacket and my unwashed hair ready to throw down.'

The occasion was marked by the tour's most talked-about moment, a set-closing jam featuring members of all four bands performing Diamond Head's 'Am I Evil?' Though Slayer's Kerry King, Jeff Hanneman and Tom Araya were conspicuous by their absence onstage – the trio having to sit elsewhere in Sofia's Lebski Stadium to approve edited footage of their set ahead of its transmission in cinemas from London to Leipzig – Hetfield, Joey Belladonna and Dave Mustaine traded vocals on a surprisingly disciplined and respectful version of the New Wave of British Heavy Metal classic, prompting cinema audiences worldwide to rise from their seats and stage impromptu circle pits in front of IMAX screens, a fittingly spontaneous outbreak of good-natured anarchism of which the original Bay Area 'Trues' would doubtless have approved.

The World Magnetic tour reached its conclusion in Australia, with a three-night stand on November 18, 20 and 21 at Melbourne's Rod Laver Arena. *So What!* magazine editor Steffan Chirazi was on hand to file an end-of-term report.

'143 arena shows, 34 festivals, 29 stadium shows, 4 club/theater shows, 3 TV/radio shows, 2 Rock And Roll Hall of Fame shows . . . two natural disasters with the Icelandic volcano and the Christchurch, NZ earthquake but no shows lost,' he wrote. 'Seven new babies were born to Metallica crew members, there was an engagement . . . and a marriage . . . there have been approximately 180 crew members for whom this has been a life taking up varying degrees of 24-7 time; 14 have made it from the first show to the last.

'It's the first time I've seen a tour end where everyone in the band hadn't grown tired of each other,' Chirazi noted. 'No fights. No major grumbles. No passive–aggressive games. Just four men who were genuinely enjoying every night they brought this music to you, and furthermore, genuinely enjoying their own beautiful, harmonious chemistry.'

†

To no one's surprise, the Big Four concept was resurrected in 2011. On January 16 Metallica announced that they'd be 'bringing the love to our home turf', with an appearance at the Empire Polo Club in Indio, California, the traditional home of the annual Coachella festival on April 23.

'We don't want to cram this down people's throats,' said Ulrich, fingering his wallet. 'If there is enough demand for it, obviously there's a very strong possibility that there'll be more shows, but we don't want to over-extend the welcome and we also don't want to turn it into something that becomes just this whole nostalgia trip.'

Rather brilliantly, when the day came, Ulrich almost missed

his own party. That afternoon the drummer was turned away from the gates of the Empire Polo Club by a security guard who spotted that Ulrich's vehicle did not have a parking pass for the festival's production area.

'Is this ID enough?' Ulrich pouted, pointing at his face.

'I don't know who you are,' the female security guard shrugged, waving the Dane away.

When he finally made it on site with the appropriate accreditation, Ulrich was greeted by familiar faces – Brian Slagel, Brian Lew, K. J. Doughton and Doug Goodman among them. Also present was Doug Marrs, Metallica's first 'roadie' worthy of the name. Marrs's association with the headliners actually pre-dated their origins, as he'd helped set up James Hetfield's equipment in a garage on LA's Eastbrook Avenue back when the teenager was man-handling Black Sabbath and Led Zeppelin songs as a member of high-school band Obsession.

It was always going to be an emotional night.

As in Europe the previous summer, the billing saw Anthrax open the show, with Megadeth following. Slayer's Special Guest set provided one of the night's powerful and poignant moments. Guitarist Jeff Hanneman had been forced into a leave of absence from the band after being bitten by a venomous spider while luxuriating in a Jacuzzi. Incredibly the result of this was that he contracted the rare flesh-eating disease, necrotising fasciitis, a condition that, while sounding like a title typical of many Slayer songs, actually jeopardised the musician's life. But in California Hanneman was able to re-join his band mates and replacement guitarist Gary Holt (of Exodus) for a surge through the classic songs 'South of Heaven' and 'Angel of Death'. In typically gruesome fashion, Hanneman removed the right sleeve of his T-shirt in order to show the audience his noticeably disfigured arm.

But the night, inevitably, would belong to Metallica.

'This was a defining performance,' wrote *Rolling Stone* reporter Matt Diehl, 'demonstrating why Metallica remains one of the tightest, most powerful bands ever, metal or otherwise. Throughout, they clearly showed how they dragged thrash sounds to the mainstream through sheer musical charisma and commitment.'

Asked about the possibility of further US dates, Ulrich proved to be a slippery interviewee.

'I don't think it will turn into a forty-date arena tour,' he insisted. 'That would make it less special. I like the fact that there's an element of chaos to the whole thing. It shouldn't be sterile, streamlined and perfect: it needs an edgy underbelly to remain authentic.'

The following week, a September 14 Big Four date at New York's Yankee Stadium was added to the docket. The caravan descended on the new billion-dollar stadium in the Bronx following a summer of Sonisphere dates in Europe, which rather undermined Ulrich's contention that the format should remain 'edgy'. That sense that this was now a 'Special Occasion' was also undone by the sheer volume of wobbly phone footage that had been deposited on YouTube since the first date in Poland. But in New York's northernmost borough the quartet did manage to stage one further surprise. As a stadium full of people began to turn their minds to the fresh hell of a post-gig subway station, the members of Slayer, Megadeth and Anthrax joined Metallica onstage for a rumble through Motörhead's eternal 'Overkill'.

With this the Big Four reunion came to an end, precisely at the point before the title of its final song would become a fitting description of the entire venture.

Bigger surprises, however, lay just ahead.

10 — PUMPING BLOOD

In White City a man in black is making things difficult. It is the final Thursday afternoon of October, 2011, and Lou Reed and Metallica are standing on the shining floor of a large studio at BBC Television Centre. Outside the descending gloom is accompanied by a dismal mist of rain. Inside the sound battering the walls of this dimly lit space is equally oppressive. It is a song taken from the forthcoming album *Lulu*, a ten-song set jointly recorded by the New York *provocateur* and the juggernaut from San Francisco.

In just a few hours' time Reed and Metallica will play the song 'The View' for a recording of the programme *Later . . . With Jools Holland*. This is not just the BBC's flagship music programme but in fact the last remaining programme of its type on network television, and tonight will be Metallica's third appearance on the show, a feat unheard of for a metal band.

Lou Reed and Metallica's practice run through 'The View' is the first time they have performed the song outside a rehearsal or recording studio. The sound is good, the playing strong. But there is a problem. After completing a song so implausibly heavy as to make 'Sad But True' sound like 'How Much Is That Doggy in the Window?', Reed and Metallica are approached by a young woman with a clipboard. She introduces herself as being the programme's floor manager. In a well-spoken voice that could not be more apologetic, it is explained to the five musicians that owing a unforeseen hitch the technicians at work on *Later . . .* have neglected to time the duration of the song that has just been played. This information, they are told, is required in order to establish the running time of the programme on which they will later appear. The floor manager asks the men if they can play the song for a second time.

These words are delivered to Lars Ulrich. Seated behind an orange Tama drum kit, the Dane considers the question before saying, 'I think this is the guy to speak to.' He nods in the direction of Lou Reed.

'No,' is Reed's answer.

'Right. But, you see, we really can't work out how long the show will be if we don't time the . . .'

'No,' says Reed for a second time. He tells the floor manager that she 'should have done it right the first time'. As he speaks, Lou Reed doesn't sound angry or even at all irritated. But he's not playing the song again; simple as that. It's just the way it is.

Two years prior to this outburst, Lou Reed and Metallica stepped out together in public for the first time. The occasion was the second of two Rock and Roll Hall of Fame 25th Anniversary Concerts staged at Madison Square Garden on October 29 and 30, 2009. Featuring performances from Bruce Springsteen & The E Street Band, U2, Simon & Garfunkel, Mick Jagger, Patti Smith and Jerry Lee Lewis, to name only a few, the first night's performance was bursting at the seams to such an extent that the gig endured for six hours. Come the second night, it was Metallica's turn to bring their own sprinkling of stardust to the Garden's stage. That evening the band played just three original songs, 'For Whom the Bell Tolls', 'One' and, of course, 'Enter Sandman', and used the space from this clear-out to invite on to the stage no fewer than three special guests. In between these Metallica standards, Ozzy Osbourne joined the San Franciscans for a run though the Black Sabbath classics 'Iron Man' and 'Paranoid'. The Kinks' kingpin Ray Davies – the man who deserves some credit as the inventor of heavy metal – was also on hand to perform 'You Really Got Me' and 'All Day and All of the Night' with the band.

But it was the introduction of Metallica's first guest of the evening that truly threatened to blow the Garden's circular wooden roof from its moorings and send it clattering into the Roman columns of the 8th Avenue post office building opposite.

'Please, New York, welcome your own Lou Reed,' announced James Hetfield as 17,000 people found their voices but lost their minds.

Twenty years earlier Reed had released *New York*, an album so relentlessly unflattering that it's a wonder that the citizens of Gotham ever forgave him. But New Yorkers like nothing so much as celebrating their own, so Reed's description of a 'Statue of Bigotry' the motto of which is 'Give me your hungry, your tired, your poor [and] I'll piss on them' was by now so much water under the 59th Street Bridge. Such was the clamour that greeted his arrival on the stage at Madison Square Garden that even Lou Reed himself could not resist a smile. As Metallica led their guest into 'Sweet Jane' and then 'White Light/White Heat', the union between the night's loudest band and the world's most contrary man seemed like an unusually comfortable fit. After the performance Reed bid Metallica good night and turned towards the limousine that would drive him down a circular ramp to the street five storeys below. Suddenly, though, he paused and turned around. Shouting in the direction of Ulrich, Reed announced that he and Metallica 'should do this again . . .', adding, 'Let's make a record together one day.'

Eighteen months later Lou Reed and Metallica were doing just that. Work began on the album that would quickly become *Lulu* in the spring of 2011, perfect timing for those who heard of the collaboration and assumed it to be an April Fool's joke. But as Reed himself would point out, it wasn't as if he was making a record with Cher. There was, he insisted, common ground between the two camps, even if a sceptical press corps and a twittering public lacked the wit to recognise that this might be so.

In principle at least, though, the decision by Lou Reed and Metallica to marry their fortunes together in this way served both performer and band well. The most insidious threat to artists whose music once invited unease and discomfort from the listener is that over time they will eventually be seen as just another part of the cultural furniture. While in 1986 Metallica inspired a journalist to write that the band was 'dirty, obnoxious, noisy, ugly and I hate them' (before conceding that 'you can't deny their success'), a quarter of a century later the 'return' of the group's music to this era was viewed as being a matter of great reassurance. Similarly once an amphetamined lunatic that foisted *Metal Machine Music* on the world, by 2011 Lou Reed was widely regarded as a loveable old grouch. But by joining forces over three months at HQ, both parties would emerge with a collection of songs that would remind everyone that it was still unwise to take either artist for granted.

The genesis of the album that would become *Lulu* lay in two plays penned by the German dramatist Frank Wederkind. *Earth Spirit* (1895) and *Pandora's Box* (1904) tell the story of Lulu, a sexually compelling young woman whose life sees her adopt the roles of revue dancer, circus performer, prostitute and murderer. In another life Lulu might well have been Holly from Miami, FLA, the girl who hitch-hiked all the way across the USA before landing amid the rats and ruin of the Lower East Side. It's little wonder, then, that such a character would appeal to Lou Reed's lyrical aesthetic. The New Yorker sent his musical ideas, not to mention reams of lyrics, to San Rafael; Hetfield and Ulrich convened at HQ to lend an ear. Reed sent the drummer an email that asked, simply, 'So?', to which the reply came, 'When are you getting out here?' Within an hour of their guest's arrival, the two parties were writing material. Within ten days almost ninety minutes' worth of music had been compiled and divided into ten songs. A month after this the double album was recorded.

'Lou likes being as spontaneous as possible to keep the song in its purest form,' revealed Kirk Hammett. 'We very quickly cobbled the songs together and recorded them. And then Lou says, "That's great! Let's move on." And that's just so diametrically opposed to the way we work.'

'There's no question that when you bring thought into music, it changes,' says Ulrich. 'Maybe there are times when it changes for the better, but for us it was an incredible opportunity to [say] – for close to the first time in our career – "Just leave it." '

When the ladies and gentlemen of the press heard *Lulu*, most among their number wished that Lou Reed and Metallica had done just that. As ever, journalists were expected to listen to the album at the San Franciscans' convenience. In England listening sessions were convened at Q Prime's west London office, with reviewers required to listen to the two-CD set in one sitting. The effect of this was to emerge blinking into the light as if rescued from a terrible potholing accident.

Although opinions on *Lulu* quickly soured, at the time of its release this was not an album that received universally negative reviews. In the UK the *NME*, *Kerrang!* and the BBC responded to 'Loutallica's' efforts with a measure of praise. *Uncut* magazine went further still, describing *Lulu* as 'the most extraordinary, passionate and just plain brilliant record either participant has made for a long while'.

But while those gathered in support of the year's most striking collaboration could be viewed as a fan club, those gathered in opposition constituted an army. The increasingly influential website *Pitchfork* described the release as constituting an 'exhaustingly tedious' collection, the ideas of which 'are stretched out beyond the point of utility and pounded into submission'. The American essayist Chuck Klosterman – author of *Sex, Drugs and Cocoa Puffs: A Low Culture Manifesto* – opined that 'If the Red Hot Chili Peppers acoustically covered the twelve worst Primus songs for Starbucks, it would be (slightly) better than this.' Meanwhile on foreign shores the usually thoughtful *Quietus* website believed that the overall effect of Lulu 'is that of Lou Reed ranting over some Metallica demos that were never intended for human consumption' and concluded that the ten songs amounted to nothing more artistically valid than 'wanking into a sock'.

The effect of this kind of naked hostility appeared to exhaust Ulrich. Interviewed by one of this book's authors at BBC Television Centre, the drummer went so far as to decline to talk about his band's latest studio effort. With no tour to support the album, and just a handful of television appearances undertaken at the time, it is probable that for Ulrich *Lulu* was at this point already a project waiting to be put on the shelf. But critics and constituents weren't quite so willing to let the matter lie. Twenty-eight years after Metallica predicted they would, it seemed to some as if the four horseman of the apocalypse had finally arrived. One of the band's earliest and noisiest supporters, the writer Don Kaye damned *Lulu* as being 'a catastrophic failure on almost every level . . .', a misadventure 'that could quite possibly do irreparable harm to Metallica's career'. The language here might have been shrill, but there could be no denying that the album's vital signs did not look promising.

Lulu limped onto the US *Billboard* Hot 200 at no. 36, Metallica's lowest entry for more than twenty-seven years and their first album since 1988's . . . *And Justice for All* not to debut at no. 1. Thirty-six was also the position at which it entered the UK album chart. It was as if by this point Metallica's audience understood that effectively this was now two separate groups: the one that played the family favourites at European festivals and the one that indulged in flights of fancy that were entirely berserk.

As with *St Anger* today virtually no one will admit to liking *Lulu*. But this is an album that deserves its day in court. For a start, one should wonder what exactly is expected from such a collaboration. At no point in their career have Metallica attempted to make things easy for their audience. Married to this are the creative instincts of a man who in 1992 introduced the world to the *Magic and Loss* album, one of the gloomiest releases in the history of modern music. As such, bringing the two parties together was unlikely to result in an album that was anything less than arduous.

But to state that *Lulu* triumphs simply as an example of artistic obduracy is to do the album a disservice. This is a release that is by turns oppressive, compelling, evocative and, at times, moving. On the 'speak now, think later' forums of social media, the initial chatter might have likened the ten songs to *St Anger* – the claim being that San Franciscans had 'done it again' – but, really, the truth is that Metallica have never before been showcased in quite the manner they are on *Lulu*. Particularly impressive is the performance laid down by Ulrich, whose beats range from those reminiscent of the kind of jazz players beloved of his father, Torben, to a thrash metal fury the likes of which even Metallica had not previously explored. The music to the fabulously exhausting and superbly titled 'Mistress Dread' is equal in ferocity to anything recorded by Slayer. 'The View' resonates with a rhythm so deeply embedded that one can only presume that it was recorded on an expedition to the centre of the earth.

On early encounters with *Lulu* the listener may conclude that, vocally, Lou Reed most closely resembles a mad cousin of Leonard Cohen recorded while he was out shouting at pigeons in Herald Square. But the notion that this is music that one was intended to 'get' on anything like a first listen is absurd. Any album that begins with the words 'I would cut my legs and tits off when I think of Boris Karloff and Kinski in the dark of the moon' (from 'The Brandenburg Gate') and which requests that one 'put a bloody gag to my teeth [because] I beg you to degrade me, is there waste that I could eat?' ('Mistress Dread') is clearly not aiming for mainstream acceptance. But *Lulu* is more than a rewarding exercise in depravity and perversion, is more than a bid for the title of 'Presidents of the Artistic Awkward Squad'.

But after the listener has spent seventy minutes being led on a leash through a world of sexual intensity and interpersonal unease, the album's final song is resplendent with notes of graceful release. Naturally the nineteen-minute-twenty-eight-second 'Junior Dad' features no hint of lyrical redemption – the collection's final words reveal that 'age withered him and changed him into Junior Dad', a case of 'psychic savagery' – but the music on which such sentiments are carried aloft is stirring and even profound. Built upon a beat that switches from 4/4 to 5/6 time in each bar, the track combines the kind of instrumental melody heard on songs such as 'One' and the 'The Unforgiven' with the swaggering groove of 'The Outlaw Torn' and carries all to their logical conclusions. The careful and deceptively uncomplicated refrain builds with the kind of atmospheric pressure that is usually the preserve of Tornado Alley – and in almost twenty minutes this refrain darkens into a full-blown riff only twice – yet despite the song's overwhelming gravitas, manages somehow to be one of the most accessible pieces of music to which Metallica have placed their name.

The mesmerising impact of 'Junior Dad' was not one reserved only for listeners that happened to be paying attention. At the time of recording *Lulu*'s closing song, Kirk Hammett was in the early stages of grief following the death of his father, Dennis, a man whose violent temper had been the cause of abuse both physical and emotional. The first time the lead guitarist heard the track in its completed form, just 'three or four weeks' after he died, the effect was so overwhelming as to send him running from HQ's control room to its kitchen area, his face warm with tears. Seconds later, James Hetfield walked into the room; he too was blinking back tears.

'It was insane,' recalls Hammett. '[Lou Reed] managed to take out both guitar players in Metallica in one fell swoop, with his amazingly poetic lyrics. And [then] he came into the kitchen and he was laughing. He looked at James and I and said, "That's a good one, huh?"'

†

But if Metallica were pushing themselves into the future with *Lulu*, the band also had one eye trained on the past. In 2011 it had been thirty years since Lars Ulrich and James Hetfield met for the first time. Back then Hetfield was a boy so shy that the only thing in his line of sight were his own feet, while Ulrich was a drummer so inept that each time he hit a crash cymbal the stand to which it was attached would be sent clattering to the floor. Even at that time the pair tended to regard matters from wildly differing points of view. The Dane believed that this initial jam session had gone well and was something upon which the pair could build. The American thought the drummer was beyond hope and smelled funny. As a beaming Ulrich drove away that day, had he looked in his rear-view mirror he would have seen an American teenager bent double with laughter.

But Ulrich isn't a man predisposed to looking in rear-view mirrors. And so it was from this deeply unpromising start that the two metalheads began a relationship of complicated co-dependency and conditional love of such potency that it would provide the fuel for a band that would dominate their lives. More than this, it would come to dominate the lives of millions of others, too. Of all the groups still in existence, it is not unreasonable to suggest that Metallica occupies the position of 'favourite' for more people than any other.

Given this, it seemed obvious that a party was in order. Actually, this being Metallica, it was decided that *four* parties were in order. The events would be the kind of occasions about which those who were present would speak for the rest of their lives. To share in this glory Metallica would invite musical guests from all points in North America and Europe and, as at the Rock and Roll Hall of Fame induction ceremony, they would pick up the tab for flights, hotels and every morsel of food and drink that passed anyone's lips. And as had been the case in Cleveland, it would cost a bundle.

'It feels great for Metallica to be approaching our thirtieth birthday,' says Ulrich, seated in one of his band's two dressing rooms a short walk from the *Later . . . With Jools Holland* studio. Always one to juggle time, as he speaks the drummer picks at a plate of fish that looks as if it had been caught in a lake somewhere near Chernobyl. 'If you'd have told me in 1981 that me and that guy over there, James Hetfield, would still be doing this in 2011 I would have thought you were crazy. For one thing, we were too drunk to think that far ahead. But for reasons that would take a little too much time to get into here, me and James are at the moment at least in a place in our relationship that is better than at any time in the past. You know, the truth is that with the exception of my father, James is the person in the world that I've had the longest intimate relationship with. And that's got to count for something. We're not really [going to make] too much of a big deal of being thirty, aside from one detail,' he says. 'In San Francisco in December we are playing four club shows at the Fillmore. That's gonna be great; we've got a lot of stuff planned for it. But I can't tell you what those things are right now, 'cos it would spoil the surprise.'

Metallica's four-night adopted-home-town stand began on December 5 in a venue almost as famous as the band themselves. Situated on the corner of Fillmore Street and Geary Boulevard, the Fillmore is to San Francisco's musical heritage what the Whisky a Go Go is to Los Angeles and CBGB was to New York. With space for 1,150 faces the balconied room began life as the

Majestic Hall, but became celebrated when concert promoter Bill Graham began staging concerts in the room in the Sixties. By this point the club was known as 'The Fillmore Auditorium', and on any given night audiences in the Bay Area could witness in compact and bijou quarters performances from (among others) the Grateful Dead, Jefferson Airplane, The Byrds, Cream, Miles Davis and The Doors. Such was the venue's standing in the city that even the great San Francisco earthquake of 1989 that caused panic at a World Series game in Candlestick Park could inflict only structural damage on the hall.

While for many bands an appearance at the Fillmore might feel like standing on the shoulders of giants, in the case of Metallica the intention was to stage a series of concerts that stood equal to even the venue's most historic of occasions. But Metallica's brace of thirtieth-anniversary concerts were not just a celebration studded with contributions from the great and the good, but also occasions that recognised the efforts of the obscure and even the forgotten. As in Cleveland two years earlier, here the band once again proved that they had not forgotten a single significant moment from the past thirty years. As architects of a series of events that were designed to be as comprehensive as they could possibly be, Metallica cast their net far and wide. And, as ever, they reaped a bountiful harvest.

'We think we can do anything,' said Hetfield. 'You know how selfish we are. Between Lars and me, it's like, "If we call [people and invite them to San Francisco], it can happen." As simple as that. If we put it out . . . why would it *not* happen? There were certain people who couldn't show up because of physical reasons, whether health or tour obligations, which was unfortunate. But most of the people we asked did show up.'

Those invited came in droves. In 1981 the English band Diamond Head were so beloved of Lars Ulrich that as a sixteen-year-old he had flew from Los Angeles to California to see the band perform at the Woolwich Odeon in south London. He arrived at the venue straight from Heathrow Airport. At the end of the night, the Dane hustled his way backstage and one hour later was on his way back to the band's home town of Stourbridge, where he stayed as their guest for a week. Given this, it was hardly a surprise that an invitation to San Francisco was extended to guitarist Brian Tatler and erstwhile front man Sean Harris.

The following year it was a case of the New Wave of British Heavy Metal heading to Los Angeles. In 1982 Barnsley rockers Saxon were on the road promoting their defiantly dodgy *Denim & Leather* album, an excursion which on March 27 saw the quintet perform two sets at the Whisky a Go Go: Metallica were their support band. Between their sets that night, the sound man at the Whisky told a friend that the opening act had played so fast that he believed them to be out of their minds on cocaine. It might have looked that way, too, what with the quartet drenched in sweat. This, though, was due to the fact that Saxon would not allow their local support band use of the fan that was positioned at the side of the stage. Despite this act of unkindness, twenty-nine years later an invitation to appear onstage at the Fillmore was extended to Biff Byford, the band's flaxen-haired front man.

Over the four-night stand, backstage the Fillmore's corridors were packed with faces from the past. In 1988 after a show in Dublin, Hetfield and Glenn Danzig – titular head of Danzig as well as the kingpin in the Misfits – together tipped a car onto its roof. Twenty-three years later the two men would be reunited onstage for a raucous run through 'Last Caress' and 'Green Hell', the two Misfits songs covered by Metallica on the *Garage Days Re-Revisited* EP of 1987. Other persons of influence included Danish theatrical metal god King Diamond, Judas Priest front man Rob Halford and half of Black Sabbath in the shape of Ozzy Osbourne and bassist Geezer Butler. Then there was the band from whom Metallica had twice attempted to plunder personnel.

In 1982 Ulrich had written in a notebook that Armored Saint front man John Bush would soon be his own band's new singer. For once the drummer did not get his own way. In 1986, following the death of Cliff Burton, the first person Ulrich called as a potential replacement was Armored Saint bassist Joey Vera, with whom Metallica had toured in 1984. As with Bush, Vera declined. Despite this affront to the natural order of things, the San Franciscans still dispatched plane tickets and paid hotel reservations for both men. On another front Bob Rock revived the thankless task of being Metallica's temporary bass player – albeit for fifteen months – by playing two of their least loved songs, 'Frantic' and 'Dirty Window' from *St Anger*.

'It's difficult to describe just what an amazing undertaking those four shows would have been,' is the opinion of Doug Goodman. One of the Bay Area's 'Trues' – the name given to those who helped build thrash metal's original bandwagon – Goodman saw Metallica perform at a time when Dave Mustaine was still the group's lead guitarist. Today Doug works at the higher end of the music industry and knows a logistical nightmare when he sees one. Of Metallica's 30th Anniversary Event Goodman says that 'it was a vast enterprise. It wasn't just a case of them saying, "Here's a list of the people we want to appear with us, go and invite them." Some of these people haven't been heard from in years. You have to find them, and then you have sort out their travel arrangements. Do they need visas? Are they still able to play? Are they willing to potentially travel halfway across the world just to play one or two songs? I work in this industry and I know what it takes sometimes even to get the simplest things done. It can be hard enough getting one special guest onstage on the night that you would like him to be there. But dozens of them? It's just incredible what they achieved.'

Fittingly, special attention was afforded to the people who had once been members of Metallica, even if only briefly. As was the case at the Rock and Roll Hall of Fame, this was an occasion where musicians that had been turfed onto the roadside, or else who had stepped away when things were falling apart, came together once more. Preferential treatment was bestowed upon Jason Newsted in the form of an invitation to appear at all four concerts. Such was the grace with which Metallica extended the hand of friendship to their erstwhile bass player that it seems churlish to observe that it would have been even more gracious had he been treated with this kind of respect eight, or even twenty-five, years earlier. For his part, despite an exit in 2001 that was nothing if not dignified, in the intervening years Newsted's observations about the band had taken on a tinge of bitterness, even anger. In the aftermath of his departure, the group's longest-serving bass player accused Q Prime of being complicit in his exit after it was calculated that a new face in the band would mean that 'now we can get ten more years' [worth of] money out of them'.

'That's the people that are handling this band and that's what they really think,' was his damning conclusion. This verdict may well have been correct, just as it could also be the paranoid interpretation of a now embittered man. But what is certain is that this kind of talk doesn't suit Newsted. Yet to see him onstage at the Fillmore is once more to sense the unconditional love the bass player feels for songs such as 'Battery' and 'Creeping Death'. The look of utter absorption is compelling enough to remind one of all that was good about his tenure with the band rather than the departure of a man who could simply stand no more.

Newsted, though, was not the first bass player Metallica treated like dirt. In 1982 it was Ron McGovney who was the whipping boy who could do no right. It was McGovney who would drive Metallica north from Los Angeles to San Francisco while the other members would sit in the trailer drinking raw vodka and banging on the wall whenever they needed to urinate (on one occasion an astonished McGovney watched as Lars Ulrich lay passed out on the yellow lines of Interstate 95). Shortly afterwards Ulrich announced at a party that McGovney would soon be an ex member of Metallica. As the loose-lipped Dane spoke these words, the bassist was standing just eight feet away.

But McGovney, too, accepted Metallica's invitation to join the band onstage for the first time in twenty-nine years. As he coursed his way through 'Hit the Lights', bassist and band were joined by two other musicians. One was Lloyd Grant, the guitarist whose sole contribution to Metallica was to lay down one of the guitar solos heard on an early recording of 'Hit the Lights'.

It is, though, towards the third musician onstage at the Fillmore on December 10, 2011, that 1,150 pairs of eyes are cast. Since being dispatched from the group in 1983 – and dispatched home via a four-day bus ride with not a cent to his name – it is fair to say that Dave Mustaine has not always regarded his one-time band mates with undue equilibrium. Twenty-eight years after this galling and hurtful day, Mustaine refers to the countless magazine articles in which he has poured corrosive contempt on his former colleagues as being nothing more than 'fodder', rancid examples of 'horrible garbage journalism'. To put it generously, this is choice. But while for Mustaine the spectre of Metallica is a ghost that never rests, the shadow he himself casts over the band is not something that can be easily dismissed either (even if he himself has never once noticed this). Despite contributions from musicians and artists all of whom have in some way helped shape the band that Metallica have become, the credibility of the four-night home stand at the Fillmore would have been badly dented had their original guitarist failed to appear.

There is a case to be heard that in terms of influence on the embryonic thrash metal scene, Dave Mustaine is the genre's true Founding Father. When Metallica began, James Hetfield did not play guitar, leaving Mustaine free to set the template for the group's six-string section. When Mustaine formed Megadeth in Los Angeles, he enlisted the help of Kerry King as temporary guitarist for half a dozen shows (it was then suggested to King that he jettison Slayer and join Megadeth as a full-time partner, thus beginning the first of innumerable tiffs between the two). Following this brief busman's holiday, King's own guitar style hardened from the woolly sound of early Slayer to the glass 'n' gravel spit that would follow. For his own part, as innately erratic as Mustaine's songwriting can be, his musicality is never less than sensational. Described by Slash as being 'a riff machine', his talents are such that for more thirty years anything to which he puts his name is worth a listen.

But despite the scale of his talent and the sometimes magnificent music that he has written – and written alone, at that – the most significant moment in Dave Mustaine's life remains the day he was dishonourably discharged from a band who at that the time had yet to record an album.

'It's kind of like an "inside the park" home run,' is how he describes his achievements with Megadeth, themselves one of America's most successful metal bands. 'I had to run the entire way. And while I may have scored, it would have been a lot easier to just hit it out of the park like I think we were destined to do [as Metallica] had I been able to see my alcohol problems manifesting like they were.' Of course, the fact that Mustaine could only stand and stare as Metallica 'hit it out of the park' without him served as an ongoing reminder not just of what had happened to him, but also of what might have been had it not. And while the events of April 1983 may no longer be a cause for the lead guitarist to lie awake at night screaming – indeed these days he speaks of this subject in a gracious and considered manner – the fact that his opinion is still that he 'would much rather have never gotten kicked out of Metallica than having gotten kicked out and [having to go through] all that starting over stuff' more or less negates every note of music he has played since recording demo tapes with his first band more than half a lifetime earlier.

Onstage at the Fillmore, thankfully, Hetfield contradicts his one-time band mate's words. With just half an hour to go until Metallica's four-night stand is in the history books, Hetfield starts to describe Mustaine as being someone that has 'since gone on to do amazing things in another band called Megadeth'. The crowd cheers; Hetfield smiles at the clamour and exclaims 'That's right, baby!' He adds that the musician now waiting in the wings has 'in his own right carved his own way with his own attitude, his own sound [and] his amazing songwriting . . . What happened yesterday is long gone; what happens right now is what matters. So please give a warm [fan club] welcome to Mr Dave Mustaine!'

The oddly shambolic figure that walks onto Metallica's stage is a lifetime removed from the coiled and angular presence that in 1982 looked less like a musician than a cornered rattlesnake. Mustaine embraces each member of Metallica, and with Kirk Hammett now long positioned to Hetfield's left instead joins Robert Trujillo on the other side of the stage. Tonight there is no sneer, no stare of piercing inquisitiveness. Instead Mustaine merely looks old.

By now, the five musicians are hurtling into 'Phantom Lord', a track from *Kill 'Em All* that proves that once upon a time this was a band capable of giving even the most stupid of metal acts pause for thought. But as Hetfield sings of 'crushing metal strikes on this frightening night', to his right Mustaine summons forth a guitar solo that is nothing less than the sound of electricity out on the loose and looking for trouble. The sound is not necessarily *better* than the kind of solos performed by Hammett, but it is appreciably different. As the Fillmore listens to the band that could not be, for a brief but glorious moment Metallica as they once sounded are alive in a space other than the memory of Dave Mustaine.

✝

The four nights at the Fillmore also gave the audience the opportunity to hear what a Metallica concert sounds like when the band pay attention to parts of their past it seems they would otherwise rather forget.

Since 2003 Lars Ulrich at least (who each day when on tour compiles the band's set list) seems intent on deleting all but the most tokenistic nods to music recorded during Metallica's 'middle period'. This is odd, not least because the drummer's response to a review in the *New York Times* from Giants Stadium in 2003 that enthused that the San Franciscans were playing with such an energy that it was like being transported back to the Eighties was to wonder, 'Hang on, what was wrong with us in the Nineties?' Eight years later it remains a good question. But by their thirtieth birthday this is a band that seems to care most for music made when its members wore the clothes of much younger men. In 2011 Metallica were still airing selections from *Death Magnetic*, but rarely at a rate of more than one song per evening. As for *Load* and *Reload*, ticket-holders might expect to hear 'Fuel', 'The Memory Remains' or (perhaps) 'The Outlaw Torn' – and once in a flood, *S&M*'s 'No Leaf Clover' sans orchestra – but more than one or two of these on any given night was rare.

In a famous room in an ugly quarter of a beautiful city the band revisited songs such as the brilliant 'Bleeding Me', 'The God That Failed', 'I Disappear', 'King Nothing' as well as 'The Outlaw Torn' and 'The Memory Remains'. On top of this they might reasonably have added at least another half a dozen songs from this period to the set without incurring any noticeable drop in compositional quality. This, though, is not the band that Metallica are, at least, not any more; at least, not onstage. But with time now ticking on, the hardly trifling matter as to whether the group is as equipped as it once was to deliver such material is fast becoming a pressing concern.

In 2013 Metallica put their name to what was in many ways their most ambitious project to date. Recorded at the Rogers Arena in Vancouver, *Metallica Through the Never* is a concert film the likes of which had never before been seen. Designed for release in IMAX cinemas and to be viewed in 3D, such was the spare-no-expense nature of the project that its budget was reported to be a cool $18 million. In truth, however, *Metallica Through the Never*'s journey from mad idea to cinematic reality actually cost the band $32 million.

Not for the first time, the germ of Metallica's frankly hare-brained scheme stretched years into the past.

'At some point there was talk of an IMAX project, which got pushed aside and is something we still might pick up,' said Ulrich in 2000, then unaware that the proposal would be 'pushed aside' by group therapy, a singer in rehab, internecine warfare and an album that no one liked. '[The idea] just went away because of scheduling difficulties. We met with the IMAX people a couple of times and we were looking at the *Load* tour set-up, with the collapsing stage and the guy on fire and all that crap, [all of which] would've made a great IMAX experience. But the clock stepped in. It is a timeless idea, though, so we can always come back to it . . . if we get really bored.'

The only thing that can be said in response to this is that, come 2013, Metallica must have been very bored indeed. *Through the Never* is a film so askew with pointless magical realism and so out-of-focus in its execution that it beggars belief. Directed by Nimrod Antal – whose past credits include the horror film *Vacancy* and the franchise romp *Predators* – and the now prominent actor Dane DeHaan, the production is an utterly bewildering excursion into narrative folly and visual excess. The plot, such as it is, sees a skateboarding local stagehand, Trip (played by DeHaan), transport a leather bag belonging to Metallica across a city that goes from being deserted one minute to having its streets teeming with rioters the next. Quite what has ignited the riot is not made clear. Even more mystifying is why a doll that is hanging from the van in which Trip is transporting the leather bag should suddenly come to life.

Aside from the fact that world-famous bands to not entrust personal property to local stagehands (that the character is a stranger to the three Americans and one Dane is made clear by the theatrical stare he receives from Ulrich early in the film), there is much else in *Through the Never* that makes no sense at all. Moments before Metallica are due onstage in the arena's parking lot a car comes to a halt. Out of the vehicle steps an overweight fan who proceeds to clamber onto the bonnet in order to shout the band's name. There are no other cars around, which means that the 18,000 people inside the Rogers Arena either came by bus or else, perhaps, by magic carpet. Away from the venue itself, at first the streets are similarly deserted. This, though, is not enough to prevent Trip from having a crash with the one other car that does have its motor running. As the narrative jerks towards some kind of conclusion, it becomes clear that the question the film intends its audience to ask is 'What is in the bag?' Discerning viewers, however, will have a different question. 'What on earth is in Metallica's head that they would commit to a folly such as this? What's more, how big must the singed holes in their pockets have been for them to throw more than thirty million bucks of their own money onto the screen in this manner?'

'We sat down [as a band] and took the decision not to take any money from anybody,' explains Ulrich. Anyone left wondering why this might be has clearly not been paying attention. '[The reason for this] is because we wanted to control it ourselves. We wanted to be autonomous. The size of this thing is so ridiculous when compared to making and launching a record. So you basically just make a decision, do you want to have financial partners or not? And so we sat down, looked at it, and we were, like, "Fuck it, let's just do it ourselves."'

The most frustrating aspect of *Through the Never* is that at times it appears as if it will deliver its promise successfully and on a scale not before seen even from Metallica. With the band performing from an in-the-round stage positioned in the space normally occupied by the Vancouver Canucks ice hockey team, and which at various points comprises stage sets ranging from that seen on the *Master of Puppets* tour of 1986 through to the *Death Magnetic* spectacle of recent memory, at first the onstage footage suggests that at least the concert sections of this film are set to rock with maximum force. This they occasionally do, but only for minutes a time before the director and editor decide that the audience has had quite enough of the band they came to see and cuts instead to the 'story' taking place on the streets outside.

In terms of live footage *Through the Never* occasionally frames Metallica in a sensational manner. The trouble is that just as often – more often, actually – it frames the band in a manner no more organic than cinema food. It is the shots that feature extras as fans that jar the most. Just as it is impossible to recreate on screen the sight of a crowd at a football match, so too is it beyond the ken of Nimrod Antal to portray people who are being paid for their time at the Rogers Arena in the same way as he captures the image of ticket-holders who have *paid* to be there. Sometimes it seems as if he isn't even trying. The sight of two attractive young women in the front row pulling 'stripper moves' is so obviously staged that it recalls the kind of fare beloved of the hair metal bands of the Eighties that Metallica made it their business to destroy. In subsequent scene in which James Hetfield theatrically throws a 'broken' microphone and its stand to the floor while glaring at the sound desk is about as convincing as the throes of apparent ecstasy to which he succumbs when the camera closes in on his face. So gobsmacked were the two authors of this book that during a preview screening at the Soho Screening Rooms, one turned to the other and said, 'This is so bad it could sink every word we've written.'

Not everyone felt the same way, however, and on its release on September 27, 2013 – the twenty-seventh anniversary of the death of Cliff Burton – *Through the Never* found itself making fast friends in serious quarters. Writing in *Rolling Stone*, Peter Travers assertion that the film represented 'a full throttle expression of rock & roll anarchy' suggested that the only other music film the reviewer had seen was *Summer Holiday*. On the eastern seaboard, the *Village Voice* believed Metallica's grandest gesture to be 'the most immersive concert film ever'.

Bracketed by an armful of reviews that were curiously kind-hearted, not to mention a bells-and-whistles promotional campaign that included adverts on national television, *Metallica Through the Never* prepared to make its acquaintance with anyone who desired to go to the pictures to watch a gig. If there was a point when the band might have been wondering exactly what they had got themselves into, this would have been it. As Hetfield himself confessed, Metallica 'had to borrow lots of money [to get the picture made]', that Q Prime 'chipped in', and that many involved had 'houses mortgaged and stuff . . .' Not to worry, though, as the front man was 'pretty sure' that the band would emerge from the experience without having to surrender the shirts on their backs.

'For now we're pretty sure we'll be able to at least break even and still be able to continue as people and as a band,' he said, the sweat glistening on his top lip 'But it is a lot of money, and, again, we've learned a lot.'

One would hope so, as no private school in the world charges the kind of fees Metallica paid for this lesson. When *Metallica*

Through the Never ended its theatrical run its worldwide box office tally stood at $8 million (with at least thirty per cent of this figure comprising the cut taken by the cinemas that showed the film). The picture will, of course, recoup more of its costs through sales of Blu-Ray and DVD, but with this market in the same kind of irreversible slump as that of CDs the figure will do little to nudge the film into the black. The band did release *Metallica Through the Never* as a live album, but this too met with a shrug of relative indifference. Of all the countries in which the two-CD set was released only one, Poland, was sufficiently impressed to award the set a gold disc (for sales in excess of 10,000 copies).

It is the one hour and forty minutes' worth of music as heard on *Metallica's Through the Never* that is the least interesting aspect of the band's grandest folly. Of its fifteen songs only 'Fuel', 'The Memory Remains' and 'Cyanide' had yet to reach the age of majority, while elsewhere the set list is given over to 'Master of Puppets', 'Battery', 'One', 'For Whom the Bell Tolls' and '. . . And Justice for All'. Of course, it is understandable that a band should play for its audience its most popular and best-known songs, and thus an evening without 'Enter Sandman' and 'Nothing Else Matters' would be most irregular indeed. But the trouble Metallica face is that in eschewing almost all of the songs from what might be called their 'mid-period' the band is left with only a limited pool of tracks from which to draw.

There is also the issue of Metallica not performing these songs as well as they once did. The obvious comparison to *Through the Never* is 1993's *Live Shit: Binge & Purge* triple CD. On the more recent offering the musicality is present and correct, but the fury is long gone. No two songs better highlight this disparity than the respective versions of 'Creeping Death' and 'Battery'. On *Through the Never* the tracks are accomplished and invigorating, and it would be wrong to suggest that this is a band that has lost touch with the qualities that made it unique in the first place. But on *Live Shit* . . ., the two songs are explosive in their violence. A generation on, the sound of James Hetfield heralding the arrival of Kirk Hammett's guitar solo with the words, 'You ought to know by now, motherfucker' is the sound of a man who fronts a band that intends to be nothing if not utterly dominant. Similarly the speed at which 'Battery' is dispatched is staggering, while twenty years later it is merely impressive.

It is unreasonable to expect that the feral quality heard on *Live Shit*'s . . . most forceful moments would be recreated with the same kind of restless hunger two decades on. But what is reasonable is to question their authors' complete reliance on this part of their career, at the expense of other periods. Similarly, one is not without cause in wondering if it might have been at all possible for Metallica to have written more songs in the intervening years.

What can be said for sure is that there will probably be no more than twenty new songs over two albums before James Hetfield, Lars Ulrich, Kirk Hammett and Robert Trujillo decide to call it a night. As yet there is no sign of a successor to *Death Magnetic*, and at this pace by the time the quartet have completed the album after next they will be in their sixties.

The group are already some distance into their autumn years, and as such seem to occupy much of their time embarked on one jolly after another. One moment they are in Antarctica playing 'Master of Puppets' while wearing fingerless gloves and woolly hats, the next onstage at the Harlem Apollo, or else playing 'Enter Sandman' at Yankee Stadium in honour of retiring relief pitcher Mariano Rivera. It would be churlish to criticise the time Metallica dedicate to such escapades, because as ever even at their most playful this is a band who accomplish things untried by others. The problem is that not much else is accomplished.

The latest and perhaps most striking example of Metallica not so much thinking outside of the box as kicking the box to smithereens came in the announcement in May that the band would headline England's most famous and best-loved music festival, Glastonbury. Traditionally home to acts such as Coldplay and Radiohead, not to mention legends of the standing of the Rolling Stones, Paul Simon and Neil Diamond, Glastonbury may well be the festival of choice for the liberal elite – and as such draws a measure of predictable derision – but the varied nature of each summer's bill suggests that this is the country's most open-minded musical gathering. In adding their name to the top of Saturday night's bill Metallica committed themselves to appearing for far less money than usual. But in earning 'just' £300,000 for this shift, the band is able to do something its members always enjoy doing – something different.

'To be honest with you we didn't sit around and have a big conversation when the call came,' revealed Ulrich, speaking to BBC Radio 1 DJ Zane Lowe. 'In Metallica we have a saying . . . "no-brainer". Headlining Glastonbury is a no-brainer. We didn't need to sit around thinking about the pros and cons.

'It's great [that] thirty-two years into our career we're still able to knock down doors,' he added, and not just that but 'doors we didn't think were open to us'.

Predictably the reaction to the announcement was mixed. Just as predictably the most hostile noises were made from those who consider themselves Metallica fans. Most prominent among these was Dom Lawson, the former *Kerrang!* journalist, now writing for the *Guardian* newspaper.

Under the headline 'Another half-baked vanity project', Lawson writes how 'unfortunately from the perspective of someone who grew up listening to Metallica and can clearly remember when they weren't just the biggest band in metal but also the most important, Metallica headlining Glastonbury is just the latest in a series of excruciatingly misjudged manoeuvres by a band that seems to have completely forgotten why they started making music in the first place . . . So yeah, Metallica at Glastonbury. Whoopee-fucking-doo.'

On the afternoon of Saturday June 28, 2014, seven hours ahead of their headline appearance on Glastonbury's Pyramid Stage, Metallica's official event T-shirt went on sale at the festival's merchandise stalls. The front of the 'Glastallica' shirt bore the words 'Peace, Love & Metal', and featured the band's familiar 'Scary Guy' mascot sporting green wellington boots and a peace pendant. But it was the back of the garment which truly caught the eye. As they had done with the Damage Inc. tour programme in 1986, and with the artwork for their 'Whiskey in the Jar' single twelve years later, Metallica chose to mark their inaugural appearance at Worthy Farm by reprinting some of the negative feedback they had received, gently mocking those who had poured scorn upon their decision to headline the event. Among these notices, in bold black type, was Dom Lawson's sneering *Guardian* quote: 'Metallica at Glastonbury: Whoopee-fucking-doo.'

Not for the first time, Lars Ulrich was having the last laugh.

✝

It has been six years since Metallica's last litter of stand-alone songs crashed into the ears of strangers. The odds of a new album appearing before 2015 are so long that even the most committed gambler would decline to make the bet. Where once stood music overwhelming in both its power and its creative inquisitiveness, now the only things that can be heard are the sound of a clock ticking on and of water being trod. For thirty years Metallica have been a universal sonic opiate of such resonance that the band is now able to coast on petrol fumes in lieu of new music.

The question, however, is, how long will this remain the case?

The fact that Metallica's public today regards the band with less ferocity than in the past is hardly a surprise. More than this, it is inevitable. But the fact that so little is being done to address this matter is alarming. It is five years since the San Franciscans last performed indoors in the UK in support of a new album. Instead, each summer the musicians embark on whistle-stop money-grabbing excursions to the festivals in Europe and busy themselves with increasingly preposterous ideas with which to dress these commitments. Eight years ago the decision to honour the twentieth anniversary of *Master of Puppets* by performing the album in its entirety was as well conceived as it was executed. Five years later the band was back on the same stages, this time playing 'The Black Album'; this they did twenty-one years after its release – hardly a landmark anniversary – and reversing its running order, thus avoiding the awkward truth that the collection tails off badly in the final two songs. More ludicrous still was the quartet's decision to allow fan club members to vote for the tracks they'd like to hear on the European festival circuit two years later. Once utterly certain of themselves, the move speaks of a band who are now slavishly saying, 'Tell us what you want, and we'll give it to you.'

That is, of course, unless it's a new album.

The notion that Metallica not only understand that their best days are now behind them but are also at peace with this dismal state of affairs is galling. What this line of thought comes down to, essentially, is that this is a band no longer worthy of your time. For Metallica's core adherents this position is utterly depressing. The more optimistic among this number live in hope that it will prove not to be case; the least demanding appear content to subsist on the increasingly chicken-in-a-basket fare bestowed on them each summer in the fields of Europe. But the number of people in that camp is falling.

For Metallica to have triumphed over the numerous obstacles that once obstructed their path – obstacles both external and internal – only to become, at least in the present tense, a creative irrelevance would be a tragic end to what is an otherwise truly inspiring story.

Yet despite mounting evidence to the contrary, it would be unwise to write the band off before they have done so themselves. For while it may be true that the time Metallica have spent *not* recording the successor to *Death Magnetic* will exceed the period in which they released their first four albums – albums that many fans believe to be their best – if James Hetfield, Lars Ulrich, Kirk Hammett and Robert Trujillo can plot a course that leads them to once more becoming the band they *are* rather than *were*, there may just be life in the old gods yet.

Even if this does not come to pass, even if it all ended tomorrow, Metallica now stand at the logical conclusion of everything they have striven towards in the past thirty-three years.

After an association that had endured for almost three decades and which had earned both parties millions upon millions of dollars, following the release of *Lulu* Metallica's contract with the Elektra Records owned Vertigo label came to an end. For the first time since Johnny Zazula was forced to found his own record label, Megaforce, because not a single record label in America wanted to sign the band, Metallica were without a home.

This, though, is where the similarities end. Whereas twenty-nine years earlier no label wanted to sign Metallica, this time it was the band that didn't want to sign to a label. Instead they wanted to create their own. And this, of course, is exactly what they did.

Metallica made their own home.

Launched into public view with the release of the soundtrack to *Metallica Through the Never*, Blackened Recordings represents an extraordinary achievement on the part of Hetfield, Ulrich, Hammett and Trujillo. This new label is not only the imprint on which all future Metallica albums and long-form videos will be released, but it is also home to every piece of music and footage the group have recorded since releasing *Kill 'Em All* in 1983. In severing their ties with Vertigo the band took ownership of the master tapes that previously had belonged to the Warner Group, the label's parent company in the US.

It is usually the case that no matter how successful a band may be, it is their record company that owns copyright on the recordings of songs and albums released while the act is under contract. This may be one of the great injustices of modern business – not least because it is the artist that pays for the costs of recording this music – but it is one to which all but a vanishingly small number of artists adhere. Those who have bucked the trend can be counted on the digits of a hand that is recovering from an industrial injury. U2, Radiohead, Sex Pistols and Foo Fighters.

And, now, Metallica. The announcement of this change of status was made explicit in a public statement by the band themselves. But despite this, while Radiohead were hailed as ground-breaking visionaries for their decision to strike out for independence, Metallica's move received far less comment than did the announcement that they would be appearing at Glastonbury. But in taking their own music under their own wing, Metallica are now sole trustees of the riffs they wrote, the songs they recorded and the albums they released. The few people that did offer comment on this *coup d'état* concluded that the band's motivation was money, as if this were ever really the point.

Once again, Metallica stated their case in plain and simple language.

'It's always been about control for us as a band,' said Ulrich. 'Forming Blackened Recordings is the ultimate in independence, giving us one hundred per cent control . . .'

Once the band that claimed they had nowhere else to roam, this is a group that has no mountain left to climb. From this vantage point, the view is surely magnificent. The first metal band to combine high entertainment with good art, they can lay claim to having transformed the genre they so defiantly represent more than any other band. With violent opposition they arrested heavy metal's slide towards vacuity and turned the tide on the movement's drift towards a sound that was little more than pop music amplified by Marshall. The effect of their life's work is to have made the genre harder, faster, heavier and better than it was at their point of entry. So total is their influence and dominance of their parish that it is fair to comment that every good metal band that followed in their wake came together because of Metallica.

Just as Hetfield, Ulrich, Hammett and Trujillo own their own music and record label, they also own the world they represent. Thirty-three years after a front man too shy to speak and a drummer who couldn't play first found themselves in each other's company, in all senses of the term Metallica are finally at the point of destiny.

Accountable to no one but themselves, they are an island.

The game's over. Metallica won.

ACKNOWLEDGEMENTS

In May 2012 the authors of this book were in San Francisco. Having agreed terms with Faber and Faber in the UK and Da Capo in the US for a two-volume biography of Metallica, we decided that the best thing to do would be to decamp to the city that more any other gave the band a home as well as an identity. This expedition was undertaken in the name of research. That and the odd drink or two.

On a stroll towards the address that was once the location of The Stone club on Battery Street – a thoroughfare that would provide the title for 'Battery', one of the band's most enduring songs – a thought groaned into life.

'Do you reckon that at the end of these two books we'll be sick of Metallica?' one author asked the other.

This enquiry was considered by the other man.

'Hmmm,' he said, before answering in a tone of quiet sadness: 'Yeah, probably.'

This was a tricky proposition. More than any other band, Metallica had provided the soundtrack to our lives, both in teenage and adult form. Now into our forties, both of us hold the quartet close at hand – close at heart, actually – in a manner that while occasionally tragic (and certainly undignified) is nonetheless crucial. There is for both of us a part of our beings that will forever be comprised of 'Birth, School, Metallica, Death'.

The notion that in attempting to excavate all that can be known about the band we might cast this love into the fire seemed a perverse price to pay.

It is, then, with a stiff measure of relief and a chaser of joy that we can reveal that this has proven not to be the case. Whether at vertiginous peaks or in terrible troughs, the story of this most unlikely of unions is never less than compelling. The manner in which the group time and again seek out roads less travelled – from eleven-minute music videos in which they do not appear to inviting their own tribute band as a support act on tour – is (and there is no better description) just so damn 'cool'.

Then, of course, there is the music. That over the course of the past twenty-three years Metallica have put their name to songs that are below code is beyond doubt. But many of the compositions that have long been dismissed and forgotten (even, it seems, by the band themselves) are much, *much* better than most readers will recall them being. If nothing else, it is our pleasure to at least attempt to rebut the notion that the Nineties were the group's 'wilderness years'. Not only is this not the case in a creative sense – 1999's *S&M* set remains one of their finest releases – but neither is it true in a commercial sense either. In the US both *S&M* and its predecessor *Garage Inc.* sold more than five million copies each. This is twice the number attained by Justin Timberlake's *The 20/20 Experience*, the best-selling album in the US in 2013.

Most of all, though, the conclusion that both authors draw from the evidence presented in this book is this: no one can be sure what Metallica will do next.

✝

Into the Black differs from its predecessor (*Birth School Metallica Death* published in 2013) because it relies less on the eyes of others and more on the first-hand recollections of the authors themselves. By the Nineties we were no longer 'just' fans; we were fans with tape recorders, passports and bylines in national music magazines. From a first hesitant phone interview with James Hetfield and Lars Ulrich in 1992, we have dogged Metallica at every period covered in this book. From Dallas to Osaka, San Francisco to New York, Ghent to Warsaw – as well as at many other locations – if Lars Ulrich said it, we were there to try and make some kind of sense of it.

Yet despite this, *Into the Black* is a labour of love that could not exist without the help of an army of people who gave their time free of charge and for no other reason than generosity of spirit. A number of these did so in violation of Q Prime's wishes. That Metallica's management company – and perhaps even the band themselves – thought sufficiently highly of both this book and its predecessor as to view them as a threat is something the authors view as a compliment. Those who chose to obey the organisation's 'omertà' – under the implied threat of excommunication – did not derail this book's cause. But the contributions of people who did deign to speak with us have enhanced the narrative with a richness for which we are truly grateful.

Glasses, then, are raised in the direction of Wendy Ainslie, Sam Coare, Paul Curtis, Dave Everley, Jerry Ewing, Doug Goodman, Laurence Langley, Lisa Johnson, Freddie McCall, Mörat, Matt Mahurin, Dan Silver, Brian Slagel, Slash, Tony Smith, Kim Thayil and Jennyfer J. Walker.

Extra special thanks go to Phil Towle, Performance Enhancement Coach and reluctant movie star.

The authors are also indebted to the services of Scarlet Borg, whose fine eye for detail and relentless pursuit of picture quality can be seen in the photographs included in this book. By far the most stable and reliable part of our own little organisation, Scarlet is also a friend of the most precious kind, and for reasons other than the fact that we're both scared of her.

The authors are honoured to have a corner man of the experience and ability of Matthew Hamilton, our agent at Aitken Alexander Associates. Resisting the temptation to spend his working day gently banging his head against his desk,

Matthew provided expert release from the pressure we had placed ourselves under on more than one occasion. Similarly, thanks go to all the members of the AAA family. Five time zones east, our American agent Matthew Elblonk of DeFiore & Company also stood as an oasis of calm amid the world of chaos the authors had created.

It is with no pride but not enough shame that the authors are honour bound to reveal that in writing this book we have tested the patience of others to a quite extraordinary degree. With deadlines whistling by like a postman on a bike, people who by rights should have been consulting lawyers were somehow keeping the faith. On home shores few people better exemplify this triumph of hope over adversity than Angus Cargill, our editor at Faber and Faber. A fine man in the employ of a sensational publishing house, 'Big Gus' kept his head in the face of outrageous provocation and in doing so improved the quality of this book to a vast degree. At the same office, the authors are also indebted to Anna Pallai, Gemma Lovett, James Rose and the other members of Faber's 'Bloomsbury Set' who rallied to this cause.

On the continent to our left, Ben Schafer at Da Capo has once again proved himself to be a sympathetic ally as well as a fine editor. Sincere thanks also go to Lissa Warren, who worked tirelessly to make sure that readers in the US knew of the existence of our book from England.

We would also like to thank our European editors, Henrik Karlsson at Massolit in Sweden, Kristina Sarasti at LIKE in Finland, Julia Krug at Droemer Verlag in Germany and Jakub Kozlowski at In Rock/Vesper in Poland. Our sincere gratitude is also extended to Paula Turner at Palindrome as well as Sarah Barlow, our forensic proofreader. Sarah's keen eye for detail and redoubtable grasp of grammar means that our blushes are spared and no one need know that even today neither of us is entirely sure whether the surname 'Hammett' has one 't' or two.

On a personal note, Paul wishes to send love and gratitude to his beautiful, brilliant family Hiroko, Yuki and Tyler, who, more than anyone in his life, are exposed to the fall-out generated by the emotional highs and lows of this writing malarkey. Sincere thanks are also extended to the Brannigan and Kato families, dear partners-in-crime – known to Hiroko as 'your young friends' – Sammy Andrews, Nick Knowles, Chris, Jen and little Pixie Venus McCormack; my Derry sisters Aíne and Síle McDaid, Seamus and Yanaina, Natalie Nissim and Nathan Connolly; plus Alex, Scott and all at *TeamRock.com*; Sian, Dave, Fraser and all at *Classic Rock*; Merlin, Amit, Luke and all at *Metal Hammer*; Ben Mitchell, Matthew Tibbits, Andy Cairns, as well as my lifelong loves AC/DC and Arsenal Football Club.

Ian would like to thank the patience of my dear friends Wendy Ainslie, Paul Harries, Sean Hogan, Emily Rayner, Dan Silver and Giles Ward. I'm also grateful for my friends and colleagues at 'home' at *Kerrang!* for keeping my seat warm for a time that now exceeds the gestation period of an elephant. A printed shout also goes out to Chris Hunton, Dave Wilcox and Roger Williams, my eternally suffering Barnsley FC football pals who despite not knowing a thing about Metallica never failed to enquire how work on the book was proceeding (and who did not press the matter when I invariably replied that it was something about which I did not wish to speak). Similar thanks also go to Tim Sledmere. Most of all, I would like to thank the kindness and patience of my mother, Kathy, my sole remaining parent who provided her only child with comfort, cheer and support in what were by any measure hours and hours of need.

At the conclusion of this second volume, it seems strange to both authors to be leaving Metallica behind. We can only hope that our efforts are deemed worthy of the time of the band's most devoted constituents. That the authors count themselves among this body of men and women is undeniable – and, we hope, obvious – so much so that even this book's darkest moments cannot extinguish the light that shines from the band's name and music.

Like millions of others, we cannot kill the family Metallica has found in us.

SOURCES

All interviews conducted by Paul Brannigan and Ian Winwood, except where noted below.

introduction

'That's every year . . . ' David Fricke, 'Metallica are back in action with a festival and 3Dmovie', *Rolling Stone*, May 31, 2012

'We're doing what we can. . . ' David Fricke, 'Metallica are back in action with a festival and 3Dmovie', *Rolling Stone*, May 31, 2012

'I'm not sure what's going. . . ' David Fricke, 'Metallica are back in action with a festival and 3Dmovie', *Rolling Stone*, May 31, 2012

chapter 1

'It was very lonely being Metallica . . .' Sam Dunn and Scott McFayden, *Metal Evolution*, 'Thrash' 2011

'You've got an incredible album . . .' Adam Dubin, *A Year and a Half in the Life of Metallica*, 1992

'You think one day some fucker . . .' David Fricke, 'Metallica: From Metal to Main Street', *Rolling Stone*, November 14, 1991

'I can definitely understand people' Sam Dunn and Scott McFayden, *Metal Evolution*, 'Thrash', season 1, episode 6, 2011

'I know there were . . .' David Fricke, 'Metallica: From Metal to Main Street', *Rolling Stone*, November 14, 1991

'I used up all my hangovers . . . David Fricke, 'Don't Tread On Me: Metallica's James Hetfield', *Rolling Stone*, April 15, 1993

'They say a lot of . . .' David Fricke, 'Don't Tread On Me: Metallica's James Hetfield', *Rolling Stone*, April 15, 1993

'There are too many people . . .' David Fricke, 'Don't Tread On Me: Metallica's James Hetfield', *Rolling Stone*, April 15, 1993

'It really was a magical event,' Tom Doyle, Slash interview, *TeamRock.com* (Unpublished)

chapter 2

"You know, people are going to be . . ." Robert Hilburn, 'Rock's Dream Team: They Said the Guns N' Roses/Metallica Tour Could Never Happen, But the Bands Worked It Out Over Dinner at Le Dome', *Los Angeles Times*, August 9, 1992

'I had to get in there . . .' Slash with Anthony Bozza, *Slash: The Autobiography*, Harper, 2008

'Promoters were calling us all the time . . .' Robert Hilburn, 'Rock's Dream Team: They Said the Guns N' Roses/ Metallica Tour Could Never Happen, But the Bands Worked It Out Over Dinner at Le Dome', *Los Angeles Times*, August 9, 1992

'I've always wanted to play . . .' Steffan Chirazi, 'The Rise of an Egotist', *Kerrang!*, August 1991

'Every band in the world . . .' Mark Putterford, 'A Real Ugly Personal Experience', *Select*, August 1992

'I always find it amusing . . . drag each other down.' Robert Hilburn, 'Views From Inside Rock's Dream Team', *Los Angeles Times*, August 9, 1992

'I'm getting more and more confused . . .' Mark Putterford, 'A Real Ugly Personal Experience', *Select*, August 1992

'I'm sure he had his reasons . . .' Slash with Anthony Bozza, *Slash: The Autobiography*, Harper, 2008

'And that was when . . .' VH1, 'Behind the Music: Metallica', 1998

'Axl's down there with . . .' VH1, 'Behind the Music: Metallica', 1998

'We could hear the stampede overhead . . .' Slash with Anthony Bozza, *Slash: The Autobiography*, Harper, 2008

'I felt like an ass . . .' Slash with Anthony Bozza, *Slash: The Autobiography*, Harper, 2008

'We used to have these things . . .' Ben Mitchell, unpublished Kirk Hammett interview, 2007

'There's a lot of people . . .' Mörat, 'The Struggle Within', *Kerrang!*, September 1992

'I sit here and don't look . . .' Mörat, 'The Struggle Within', *Kerrang!*, September 1992

'Out of the four of us . . .' Mörat, 'The Struggle Within', *Kerrang!*, September 1992

'I can definitely sense that . . .' Mörat, 'The Struggle Within', *Kerrang!*, September 1992

'We didn't go out on purpose . . .' Mörat, 'The Struggle Within', *Kerrang!*, September 1992

'We said a lot of shit . . .' Johnny Black, 'Get in the Ring', *Classic Rock*, July 2012

'It was pretty difficult . . .' K. J. Doughton, *Metallica Unbound: The Unofficial Biography*, Warner Books, 1993

'It's very difficult for me . . .' Neil Perry, 'I Love This Shit', *Kerrang!*, April 1993

'Who knows what he's on . . .' Neil Perry, 'I Love This Shit', *Kerrang!*, April 1993

'It [the tour] was different . . .' K. J. Doughton, *Metallica Unbound: The Unofficial Biography*, Warner Books, 1993

'When you look out . . .' fax printed in *Live Shit: Binge And Purge*, 1993

chapter 3

'I'm not looking forward . . .' Steffan Chirazi, 'Stir Crazy',
    Kerrang!, July 1993

'It's easy, you go down to 16th . . .' Ben Mitchell, unpublished
    Kirk Hammett interview, 2007

'I was curious . . .' Ben Mitchell, unpublished Kirk Hammett
    interview, 2007

'It was not the drug for me . . .' Ben Mitchell, unpublished Kirk
    Hammett interview, 2007

'The reason it costs $89.95 . . .' Author unknown, 'A Discussion
    with James Hetfield and Lars Ulrich about *Live Shit: Binge
    and Purge*', origin unknown, reprinted online

'For the last 10 years . . .' David Fricke, 'Married To Metal: The
    Rolling Stone interview with Metallica's Lars Ulrich', *Rolling
    Stone*, May 18, 1995

'We went back and forth for . . .' David Fricke, 'Married To
    Metal: The Rolling Stone interview with Metallica's Lars
    Ulrich', *Rolling Stone*, May 18, 1995

'All this material had built . . .' Tom Beajour, 'Born Again',
    Guitar World, July 1996

'We're almost having fun . . .' Steffan Chirazi, 'D-Day Landing',
    Kerrang!, July 8, 1995

'The ride out was brutal . . .' Paul Elliott, 'White Hunter, Black
    Heart', *Kerrang!*, April 6, 1996

'I wanted the guitars back . . .' Tom Beajour, 'Born Again',
    Guitar World, July 1996

'When someone says "Metallica" they think . . .' Barney
    Hoskyns, 'The Alternative Metallica', *Mojo*, July 1996

'It's been give years since . . .' Dan Silver, 'We Were A Heavy
    Metal Band Seven Or Eight Years Ago', Dan Silver, *Metal
    Hammer*, July 1996

'A lot of people die . . .' David Fricke, 'Pretty Hate Machine',

Rolling Stone, summer 1996

'You know, when everyone's . . .' Steffan Chirazi, 'Come Out
And Play', *Kerrang!*, July 13, 1996

'I saw some guy . . .' David Fricke, 'Pretty Hate Machine',
Rolling Stone, summer 1996

chapter 4

'Wear a tie, don't wear a tie . . .' David Fricke, 'Don't Tread On
Me: Metallica's James Hetfield', *Rolling Stone*, April 15, 1993

'I've stopped trying to calculate anything . . . .' Dan Silver,
'Metallica', M*etal Hammer*, 1997

'I think [Woodstock 1999] was probably . . .' Steffan Chirazi, *So
What!*, volume 6, issue 4

'Any other band would say . . .' Steffan Chirazi, 'For Whom The
Phone Rings . . .' *So What!*, volume 6, issue 1

'With the orchestra you've got . . .' Steffan Chirazi, 'Roundtable'
So What!, volume 6, issue 4

chapter 5

'There's no chance that . . .' Brian Hiatt, 'RIAA Sues Napter,
Claiming "Music Piracy"', MTV.com, July 12, 1999

'There are certain things I do . . .' Ben Mitchell, unpublished
Jason Newsted interview, 2007

'You're going to talk to me . . .' Ben Mitchell, unpublished Jason
Newsted interview, 2007

'James and Lars started this . . .' Rob Tannenbaum, 'Playboy
Interview: Metallica', *Playboy*, April 2001

'I just can't get caught up . . .' Rob Tannenbaum, 'Playboy
Interview: Metallica', *Playboy*, April 2001

'We're getting really close . . .' Rob Tannenbaum, 'Playboy
Interview: Metallica', *Playboy*, April 2001

'Where would it end? . . .' Rob Tannenbaum, 'Playboy
    Interview: Metallica', *Playboy*, April 2001
'I've spoken with Jason . . .' Rob Tannenbaum, 'Playboy
    Interview: Metallica', *Playboy*, April 2001
'I just hope we can . . .' Rob Tannenbaum, 'Playboy Interview:
    Metallica', *Playboy*, April 2001

chapter 6

'As [the band] became more popular . . .' Ben Mitchell,
    unpublished Jason Newsted interview, 2007
'I said, "Who is this . . ..' Ben Mitchell, unpublished Jason
    Newsted interview, 2007
'We couldn't just hang out . . .' Ben Mitchell, unpublished Jason
    Newsted interview, 2007
'Excuse me, I respect . . .' Joe Berlinger, with Greg Milner,
    Metallica: This Monster Lives, Robson Books, 2005
'I know he's homophobic . . .' Rob Tannenbaum, 'Playboy
    Interview: Metallica', *Playboy*, April 2001
'I wasn't surprised that Jason . . .' Rob Tannenbaum, 'Playboy
    Interview: Metallica', *Playboy*, April 2001
'My wife finally told me . . ..' Ben Mitchell, unpublished James
    Hetfield interview, 2007
'My wife said "You're not . . .' Ben Mitchell, unpublished James
    Hetfield interview, 2007

chapter 7

'I think my calmness . . .' Ben Mitchell, unpublished James
    Hetfield interview, 2007
'No one ever does anything for me . . .' *Some Kind of Monster*,
    2004
'I do. There is . . .' Ben Mitchell, unpublished James Hetfield

interview, 2007

'We're both pretty passionate . . .' Ben Mitchell, unpublished
Lars Ulrich interview, 2007

chapter 8

'I didn't know if they . . ..' Mark Sinclair, 'Branding Metalllica',
CreativeReview.co.uk, September 18, 2008

'It was clear that all . . .' Mark Sinclair, 'Branding Metalllica',
CreativeReview.co.uk, September 18, 2008

'With branding there comes an . . .' Mark Sinclair, 'Branding
Metalllica', *CreativeReview.co.uk*, September 18, 2008

'The logo itself was a . . .' Mark Sinclair, 'Branding Metalllica',
CreativeReview.co.uk, September 18, 2008

'There's now this atmosphere . . .' Mark Sinclair, 'Branding
Metalllica', *CreativeReview.co.uk*, September 18, 2008

'After nearly three decades of . . .' K. J. Doughton, *So What!*,
volume 16, issue 2

chapter 9

'That's what Scott told me . . ..' Greg Prato, 'Megadeth's Dave
Mustaine talks New Riffs, Old Drama', *RollingStone.com*,
July 29, 2009

'That tour is not going . . .' WKLS Project 9-6-1 96.1 FM,
October 4, 2009

'We're a US export the way . . .' Neil Shah, 'Overweight in
Metal, This Band Tries to Play Tunes in Forex', *The Wall
Street Journal*, December 5, 2011

'He was not super-receptive . . .' Author unknown, *www.chud.
com*, July 8, 2004

'I had aspirations at one point . . .' Joel McIver, 'Megadeth',
Record Collector, September 2004

'As much as this would . . .' Dave Mustaine, *Mustaine: A Life in Metal*, Harper, 2011

'143 arena shows, 34 festivals . . .' Steffan Chirazi, 'The Last three Shows . . . The End of the Line . . .The Beginnning of Another . . .' *Metallica.com*, November 21, 2010

'I don't think it will turn . . .' Matt Diehl, 'The Big 4 Put Aside Their Differences for Spectacular Metal Show', *RollingStone.com*, April 25, 2011

chapter 10

'Lou likes being as spontaneous . . .' Keith Cameron, 'Anger Management', *Mojo*, October 2011

'There is no question that . . .' Keith Cameron, 'Anger Management', *Mojo*, October 2011

'It was insane . . .' Keith Cameron, 'Anger Management', *Mojo*, October 2011

'At some point there was talk . . .' Steffan Chirazi 'Lars Ulrich – Studio '99', *So What!*, volume 6, issue 5.

'We sat down [as a band] . . .' Steffan Chirazi, 'Metallica: Through The Never', *So What!*, volume 20, issue 3

''For now we're pretty sure . . .' Steffan Chirazi, 'Metallica: Through The Never', *So What!*, volume 20, issue 3

picture credits

BIBLIOGRAPHY

Berlinger, Joe, with Greg Milner *Metallica: This Monster Lives*, Robson Books, 2005

Doughton, K. J. *Metallica Unbound: The Unofficial Biography*, Warner Books, 1993

Halfin, Ross *The Ultimate Metallica*, Chronicle Books, 2010

McIver, Joel *Justice for All: The Truth about Metallica*, Omnibus, 2009

Mustaine, Dave *Mustaine: A Life in Metal*, Harper, 2011

Slash with Anthony Bozza, *Slash: The Autobiography*, Harper, 2008

Various, *Guitar World Presents Metallica*, Backbeat Books, 2010

Wall, Mick *Enter Night*, Orion, 2010

The following magazines have also been invaluable in researching *Into the Black*:
Classic Rock, Kerrang!, Metal Hammer, MoJo, NME, Q, Rolling Stone, So What! Sounds, Spin.

INDEX